THE FOUR PILLARS OF REAL ESTATE INVESTING

THE ESSENTIALS OF RISK/REWARD ANALYSIS

THE FOUR PILLARS OF REAL ESTATE INVESTING:

THE ESSENTIALS OF RISK/REWARD ANALYSIS

CROCKER H. LIU, PhD

JEANNE DARROW PECK

DEAN LARKIN

JOHN OHARENKO

The Real Estate Capital Institute®

Published by The Real Estate Capital Institute® January, 2023

ISBN: 978-1-7332872-2-7

Since internet content is fluid, any references to web sources and online information may not be current since the publication date. The author's views and opinions may not reflect others preparing this publication.

Word definitions are created by The Word Manufacturing Company, a wholly-owned subsidiary of The Real Estate Capital Institute®.

To complement your reading experience, please visit reci.com

DEDICATIONS

"Gratitude for the present moment and the fullness of life now is the true prosperity." -Eckhart Tolle.

We dedicate Four Pillars to all those people devoting their talents and energy to real estate investing to make the world a better place to live, work, and play, one property at a time. In particular, Dr. James A. Graaskamp influenced our careers by preaching to "do the right thing" in real estate and beyond.

The world is yours! Use it. Protect it. Respect it. Save it for future generations to enjoy.

Table of Contents

INTRODUCTION

"Knowing what to look for and how to organize the information offers the key to the success of any investment." – Michael J. Farrell.

The Four Pillars of Real Estate Investing: The Essentials of Risk/Reward Analysis is a handy reference guide for income-property investors. This guide discusses the key features uniquely characterizing real property as a distinct investment asset class focusing on land, labor, capital, and entrepreneurship. After that, *Four Pillars* presents how risk/reward principles apply to judging investment opportunities, including evaluating profitability, timing, funding, and civic responsibilities. Four separate "pillars," spelling R-E-C-I, illustrate these realty investment principles as follows:

Risk/Reward– Definition: The first pillar, *Risk/Reward*, covers formulating the proper real estate investment structure and balancing profitability with risks. Investors need to be aware of a wide range of risks, including universal, direct ownership, and other known and unknown. After understanding and accepting such risks, investors review potential rewards, including tangible and intangible benefits, based on different investment strategies (core, core plus, value add opportunity).

Evaluation – Risk/Reward Underwriting: Having selected an appropriate risk/reward investment strategy, the next step in the process focuses on finding fitting project opportunities. The second pillar, *Evaluation*, delves into reviewing projects using the 5 P's of Underwriting: People, Place, Project, Performance, and Pros/Cons. Recommended financial tools allow opportunities to be evaluated and compared based on return-on-investment benchmarks tied to Static and Dynamic Analysis (e.g., simple tests, Front Door/Backdoor, Net Present Value, Internal Rate of Return).

Cycles – Timing Risk/Reward Decisions: Based on the third pillar, cycles, crucial decisions involve gauging market cycles for implementing the investment within the risk/reward parameters. Given the cyclical nature of the real estate industry, wrong timing shatters well-conceived ventures. As a result, understanding emerging patterns within liberal, conservative and neutral cycles creates additional opportunities to restructure or abort pending projects. Maintaining solvency remains the best risk/reward management tool for carrying salvageable assets through unforeseen cycles based on acceptable financial loss tolerances.

Investing – Risk/Reward Capital: Lastly, finding capital to trigger an investment proves one of the most rewarding steps in the analysis process. At this stage, the investment opportunity converts to a "real deal," in contrast to a financial exercise. The search for funding includes qualifying equity, debt, and hybrid combinations matching investors' profitability [risk/reward] goals. The selection process covers funding capacity and compatibility with the ownership team (e.g., LLC, REIT), lenders, JV partners, guarantors, and other capital contributors. In addition to funding the venture, discussions include creating a solvency plan to provide sufficient liquidity to cover unforeseen risks (e.g., cycle shift).

Four Pillars concludes by glancing into future investment trends for formulating risk/reward strategies, including technology, inflation, and the national housing shortage. Closing thoughts cover the investor's total responsibility to embrace Environmental Social Governance ("ESG") principles as an integral part of the ownership strategy. Final recommendations focus on promoting a real estate atmosphere based on health (the property and environment), happiness (employees, users, and the community), and success (ownership) for the benefit of a better world, one property at a time!

CHAPTER 1: REAL ESTATE INVESTING BASICS

"Under all is land" - Adam Smith – Land, Labor, and Capital

Land, labor, and capital, orchestrated by entrepreneurship, form the basis for real estate investing. These components breakdown as follows:

LAND

Everything in real estate starts with the land. Land represents "a portion of the earth's solid surface distinguishable by boundaries or ownership."[1] Land represents the site's position relative to the earth and can include mineral, water, and air rights. Land serves as "the grounds" for investing in real estate ventures. Land comes first. No land, no location. No land, no deal. No land, no buildings or improvements.

Illustration: In America, land resources remain plentiful. The United States has about seven percent of the earth's landmass or nearly 3.5 million square miles. Cities cover over three percent of the land but account for over 60 percent of approximately 330 million people. Commercial real estate accounts for nearly 53 billion ft.^{2} within these urban areas, and residential dwelling units add another 138 billion ft.^{2} of inventory. On an individual level, about 525 ft.^{2} of space exists per person, demonstrating the enormity of the US real estate industry.[2]

Observation: Despite the abundance of land, no real estate investment exists without converting the land and its resources into a productive venture with the idea of generating an income stream.

Labor combined with capital and entrepreneurship applied to land creates the transformation into a potentially profitable venture.

LABOR

Merriam-Webster defines *labor* as "(1): the services performed by workers for wages as distinguished from those rendered by entrepreneurs for profits; (2): human activity that provides the goods or services in an economy."[3]

As a primary component of any economic activity, labor represents the "human side" of investments. Real estate ownership depends upon labor for nearly every facet, including development, management, operations, and maintenance. Without labor, real estate subsists as a raw, undeveloped commodity.

Labor force participation serves as one of the most important macroeconomic indicators, offering investors decision-making insights into potential realty opportunities. Some notable statistics on the US labor market include the following: (1) The economy employs nearly 160 million people; (2) The service sector carries over 70% of the workforce in the private industry, mainly in transportation and trade; (3) Self-employed and related personnel account for about thirty percent of the jobs; (4) Millennials form the largest age group, representing about a third of the workforce; (5) Earnings of young adults continue increasing for the college-educated, as the education-wage gap becomes the widest in decades; (6) Seniors (defined as 65 years or older) remain employed longer than in previous decades.

A general estimate of the total number of workers employed in the real estate industry, directly or indirectly, equates to about seventy-five million people. This estimate excludes labor indirectly involved in the various subsectors such as warehouse workers, retail salespeople, the lodging industry, and other "brick-and-mortar" space users. The impact on labor is clear – real estate plays a substantial role in the American workforce, potentially accounting for nearly half of all jobs in some shape or form.

Illustration: The real estate sector represents a small fraction of the workforce. Nearly two and a half million people, or less than 1.5% of the labor market, directly work as third-party professionals in renting, selling, buying, leasing, and other property-related services.[4] Occupational groups related to real estate, including architecture, engineering, building maintenance, and construction, account for an additional 10% of the workforce.[5]

Observation: No official labor statistics factor in the entrepreneurial do-it-yourself real estate industry, as it's challenging to track. An estimated 70% of nearly 80 million American homeowners prefer to tackle home improvement projects themselves.[6] Therefore, the labor workforce involved in the owner-occupied residential market adds over 55 million people, assuming one member per household takes on this labor role.

After land and labor, capital ranks as the next crucial ingredient in the real estate investment process, as no project exists without funding.

CAPITAL

Capital is defined as: "(1) a stock and value of accumulated goods, especially at a specified time and in contrast to income received during a specified period of time; (2) accumulated goods devoted to the production of other goods; and (3) accumulated possessions calculated to bring in income."[7]

If land represents the earth and labor, its inhabitants, then capital symbolizes the planet's motion. In real estate investment terms, capital makes the world go around. Capital facilitates the land purchase and pays for the labor to construct the improvements.

How much capital globally spins in circulation? Estimates vary according to researchers, but combined statistics offer insight into the size and scale of wealth, including real estate as a segregated asset class. The world's wealth computes to more than $360 trillion.[8] A further breakdown shows that the combined global property value equates to nearly $220 trillion (over 60% of wealth), including commercial and residential property along with forestry and agricultural land.[9]

Illustration: The United States accounts for one-third of the world's wealth, with real estate representing about 80% (under $100 trillion) of the domestic total, including private, corporate, and public holdings. On an individual basis, the average value of real estate per person in America represents just over $300,000.

Observation: Statistics confirm that real estate wealth is the most significant component of the United States economy. However, the nation's combined wealth (including real estate) is disproportionally skewed. The top ten percent of households control seventy percent, while the bottom half controls about two percent.[10]

ENTREPRENEURSHIP

An entrepreneur identifies as "one who organizes, manages, and assumes the risks of a business or enterprise."[11] The entrepreneur fills the role of coach, director, commander, and every other position of leadership responsibility coordinating the business enterprise that provides goods and services.

As the final ingredient of any business venture, entrepreneurship demands skillfully assembling and crafting land, labor, and capital into a successful investment opportunity. The best outcome occurs after discovering and implementing the most innovative methods of combining land, labor, and capital resources. When the market value generated by the new combination of resources exceeds the individual cost, the entrepreneur makes a profit.[12]

In finding an optimal combination for success, the entrepreneur often capitalizes on change rather than rigidly following existing norms. The most successful entrepreneurs eagerly incorporate new ideas, fresh talent, and technology in the face of uncertainty. Properly mitigating the uncertainty leads to new opportunities, and real estate is no exception.

Real estate entrepreneurs share a passion for opportunities ("land"), assembling talent ("labor"), and raising funds ("capital"). Beyond this passion, entrepreneurs come in all shapes and sizes. No single element links these entrepreneurs other than the drive to succeed within the real estate industry. However, some common details emerge, including autonomy, monetary reward, and recognition.

By definition, entrepreneurs are independent risk-takers seeking autonomy. Their successes are self-driven; their failures are self-inflicted. Entrepreneurs in all forms value freedom from conventional norms. Countless hours of hard work drive autonomy. It's not about the work hours. Autonomy focuses on self-fulfillment – a priceless reward. Entrepreneurs freely choose work schedules, priorities, and where and how to work independently.

To achieve a profitable result, realty entrepreneurs define their mission statement with autonomy, including property type, location, investment format, and ownership horizon. A strong sense of purpose, persistence and extreme focus are the hallmarks of reaching stated goals and objectives. These entrepreneurs maintain flexibility depending on changing market conditions, supply and demand factors, and other variables. However, the commitment to achieving the mission statement remains steadfast.

Illustration: Entrepreneurs of different industries share these elements to varying degrees. But real estate ventures also add socioeconomic factors to the land-labor-capital formula. *Premisist* serves as an expanded definition of realty entrepreneurship by introducing the concept of a "steward of the premises." Such an entrepreneur focuses on providing socially responsible ownership and investment services.[13] The *premisist* idea strikes a balance that recognizes the best interests of investors but within the limits of properly serving users (tenants), the community, and the environment – the central theme of real estate ownership.

Observation: The vastness of the real estate market, backed by appropriate resources and a strong labor pool, assures the entrepreneur will find ample investment opportunities. For instance, real estate transaction volume has remained relatively healthy since 2015. Despite the pandemic, commercial real estate transaction volume was forecast to reach 478 billion US dollars, down from 500 billion US dollars in 2019.[14]

Real estate entrepreneurship's ultimate success [or failure] starts with appropriately assessing risk and rewards for developing an investment strategy. The next chapter covers risk and reward principles for selecting qualified investment opportunities.

CHAPTER 2: RISK/REWARD – DEFINITION

"It's largely about risk." – Sam Zell

The first step of considering any investment opportunity requires investors to explore financial rewards measured against perceived risks. If the potential rewards outweigh the risks, the venture appears of interest. Otherwise, investors judge the risk/reward scenario as out of balance, requiring repricing, or rejecting the opportunity.

Based on this logical decision-making sequence, *Understanding Risk/Reward* translates to the first pillar of the *Four Pillars* investment strategy, as this chapter covers.

Merriam-Webster defines risk as "the chance that an investment (such as a stock or commodity) will lose value." Reward means "something that is given in return for good or evil done or received or that is offered or given for some service or attainment."[15] Such definitions reinforce the basic financial instinct of gravitating towards maximum rewards with minimum risks, translating to "acceptable" investment returns.

The definition of risk applied to real estate promulgated by Dr. James Graaskamp is "The degree of error between assumptions and realizations is what is termed risk, and in an enterprise economy, most parties are attempting to shift a disproportionate share of the risk to others while retaining a larger share of the benefits. Unlike many mass production industries, each real estate project is unique. The development process is so much a creature of the political process that society has a new opportunity with each major project to negotiate, debate, and reconsider the basic issues of an enterprise economy, i.e., who pays, who benefits, who risks, and who has the standing to participate in the decision process."[16]

How to determine "acceptable" investment returns? Risk stands out as the ultimate differentiator. According to the legendary investor Sam Zell, "Always make sure you're getting paid for the risk you take, and never risk what you cannot afford to lose. Keep it simple. A scenario that takes four steps instead of one means there are three additional opportunities to fail. Taking risks provides the only way to consistently achieve above-average returns — in life and in investments."

RISKS

Embracing risk, rather than fearing it, pave paths toward rewards. Identified risks pose minimum harm if adequately addressed. Hidden risks bring unexpected outcomes, typically with adverse results. Furthermore, the risk is about consequences[17] investors must be prepared to accept or mitigate.

Risks include universal, ownership, location, property type, asset, liquidity, operating, research, and unknown variables, discussed as follows:

UNIVERSAL RISKS

Universal risks surface as threats beyond the control of the investor. Such dangers emerge as immediate and unpredictable under rapidly changing economic conditions. Or, the risks may offer predictability, but no timely solutions, such as aging infrastructure. These risks include:

THE WORLD

Global events rarely impacted local real estate decisions in the past. The information age and international economic interdependence traverse political boundaries, posing potent risks. Domestic and overseas events such as climate change, softening economies, the nuclear arms race, war, and raw materials shortages impact the US economy, potentially trickling down to the property performance level. Rising sea levels along the domestic coastline, for instance, ranks as a serious concern, prompting major real estate organizations and institutional investment advisors to explore the effects and future of climate change and where investment might be affected. For example, Houston, Virginia Beach, New Orleans, and Miami rank among the world's cities that could disappear by 2100.[18][19]

CAPITAL MARKETS

Credit availability and costs always create risks for investors, as these elements drive property pricing. For example, in June of 2022, the Fed raised interest rates by 75 basis points, the most significant increase since 1994. Property sales plummeted by 16% over the year after 13 consecutive months of gains.[20] Predicting these results seems impossible. Other examples impacting the capital markets include the Russian invasion of Ukraine and the COVID epidemic. Investors often consider economic changes strategic risks, but such capital market events produce inconsistent results given their unpredictability.

POPULATION SHIFTS

Changes within various population segments, as well as locational preferences, drive demographic risks. Aging Baby Boomer needs and continued migration to the Sunbelt states stand out among the most notable changes. A noteworthy statistic states that older people expect to outnumber children for the first time in US history.[21] Furthermore, as the chart below shows, plentiful employment opportunities and relatively affordable housing continue to drive population growth in the Sun Belt. The region's largest states, including Texas, Florida, Arizona, North Carolina, and Georgia, led the nation to nominal population gains in 2020.[22] As a result, states losing population suffer more significant risks, including job losses and declining tax revenues.

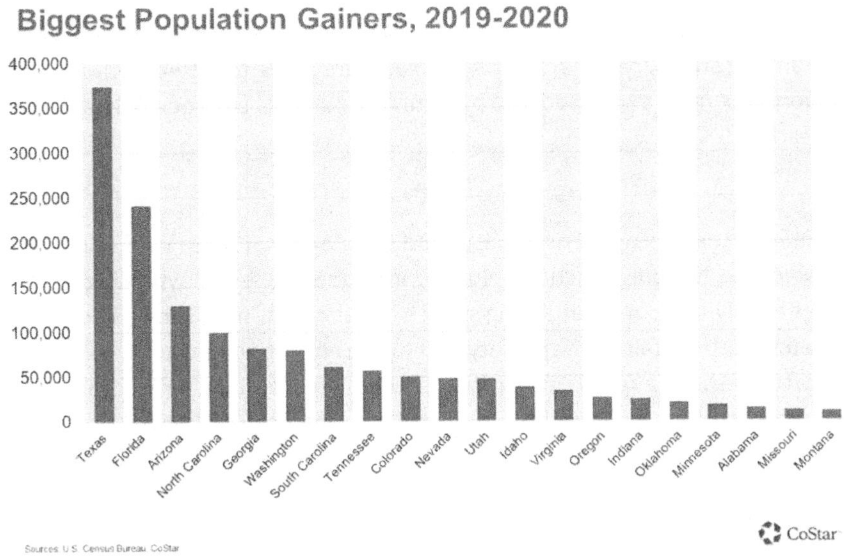

PUBLIC HEALTH CRISES

The worst outbreaks in the US history list include smallpox, yellow fever, cholera, scarlet fever, typhoid, H1N1 flu, Diphtheria, polio, H2N2, measles, cryptosporidium, whooping cough, HIV and AIDS, and most recently, COVID-19. Public health crises present reoccurring risks relying on medical science for cures. The good news is that most outbreaks mentioned are rare and, in some cases, preventable. Also, the CDC publishes the Current Outbreak List.[23]

LOCAL ISSUES

Real estate is a local business with many variables beyond investor control. These include a lack of affordable housing, labor shortages, crime, poverty, poor infrastructure, misallocated resources, ineffective governance, and supply-demand imbalances. However, local realty tax policies rank one of the most critical issues.

Universal risks extend beyond investors' control, targeting investment areas with favorable local policies. Property taxes account for nearly three-quarters of local tax collections, a significant revenue source for funding K-to-12 education, police and fire departments, parks, etc. [24] Property taxes greatly vary among states, regions, and local areas. The range for effective real-estate property tax rates expressed as a percent of value falls between 0.3% (Hawaii) to nearly 2.5% (New Jersey).[25]

Countless other universal risks exist. And since many of these risks appear unavoidable, the only practical solutions include completely bypassing specific issues or relying on market timing strategies for capturing pricing corrections. Such methods certainly offer safety, but at the cost of numerous missed opportunities. As a result, investors spend time researching direct real estate ownership risks, but not at the expense of ignoring universal risks.

Investors seek direct ownership control beyond universal risks, which features the risks discussed below.

DIRECT OWNERSHIP RISKS

The real estate industry offers investors countless opportunities to directly own and operate all types of properties. Approximately 15% of Americans invest in real estate outside their primary residence. Direct ownership shifts all decision-making responsibilities to the investor, requiring more qualifications and expertise. These risks include location, property type, obsolescence, liquidity, operations, research, and known/unknown.

LOCATION

The physical location is the base element of any real property investment. Investors tolerate many errors, but choosing an inappropriate site ranks as a paramount issue. Site selection depends upon the understanding of the surrounding area, accessibility, and a host of other factors that may be too costly to overcome by a single investor—given enough capital, time, and creativity, formerly unsuitable sites in emerging neighborhoods witness [re]development. Ultimately, locational choices involve too many variables to specify "right" or "wrong" sites, so site research is a potent risk mitigant.

Numerous reliable research sources provide site data about location desirability and pricing differentials between different areas for various commercial property types. A couple of examples include the NCREIF Index and CBRE Research. The NCREIF index, a benchmark frequently used by institutional investors, shows national investment allocations for income properties by regions broken down as follows: West (34%), East (29%), South (22%), and Midwest (15%). For instance, the urban versus suburban property pricing range for Class A retail projects shows a 50% variance between these location classes per the chart below.[26]

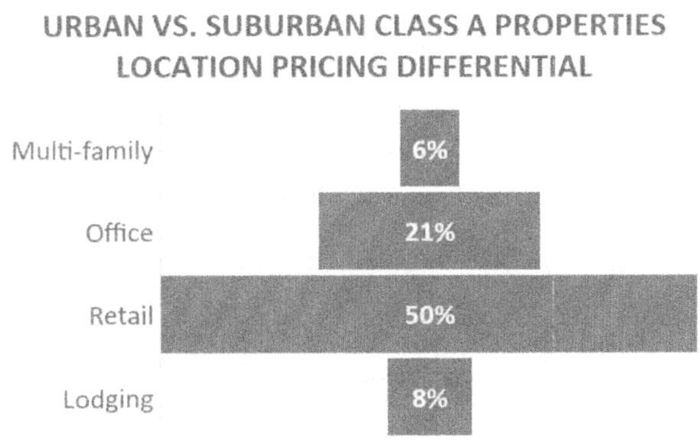

Upon understanding locational dynamics, the investor needs to analyze the risks associated with property types.

PROPERTY TYPE

Ranked in order of popularity, the common types of assets attracting investment capital include single-family residences, multifamily, industrial, retail, office, and lodging assets, further described as follows:

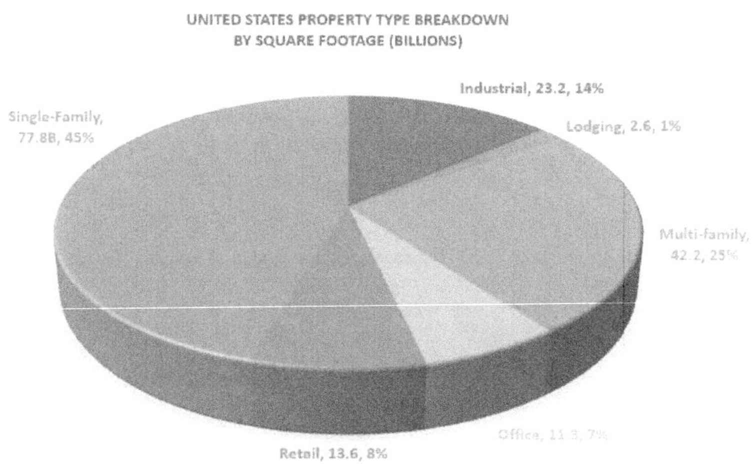

Single-Family

The Great Recession of 2008 created a demand vacuum after housing prices plunged nationally. Buyers avoided this sector, especially in areas further away from employment centers. However, Millennials continue exploring homeownership as family needs change and income levels improve within this demographic group. As with other property sectors, new construction opportunities follow talent, increasing the demand for development in denser urban areas. Post-WWII "Bedroom" communities remain "asleep" regarding values, posing more ownership risk, as today's buyers desire less automobile-centric, smaller, more efficient, and technically connected housing near public transportation. However, the most recent pandemic created a resurgence in suburban housing demand that counters this long-term trend. Regardless of urban or suburban housing, limited affordability and high construction costs plague this sector, creating massive supply shortages. Another emerging trend in US housing, built-to-rent houses, now accounts for over 6% of new homes constructed annually. This residential rental format should double over the next three years.[27]

Multifamily

Investors flock to multifamily properties. Why? Apartments rank as the most affordable housing option for most residents in the United States, accounting for over a third of the population. Apartments offer rental space as cheaper alternatives to homeownership in many high-cost markets. The rising demand for more carefree housing options, and luxury lifestyle choices, create even more development prospects for constructing highly-amenitized communities. Student housing and senior living complexes also offer multifamily opportunities, with these segments requiring more specialized management. Risk concerns within this sector include rent control and ongoing property tax hikes.

Industrial

Compared to most other property types, industrial space benefits from technological advances. E-commerce growth fuels "last mile" logistics demand, creating a tighter supply chain. Industrial users require flexible space close to consumers. Risks focus on maintaining the right blend of more significant distribution hubs to serve smaller, local facilities. Highly specialized subsectors include cold storage, data centers, high-cube distribution, manufacturing, and consumer-driven self-storage facilities (now ranked as a distinct property type). Rising construction costs and the lack of affordable sites near population centers surface as substantial risks for new construction ventures within this sector.

Retail

The US ranks as the most over-retailed country globally due to the massive building sprees of the 1990s and early 2000s. With over 25 $ft.^2$ per person, this country offers more than six times the retail space of Europe or Japan. In the face of consumers' rapidly accelerating use of e-commerce, the retail industry flushes out weaker merchants while consolidating and converting obsolete brick-and-mortar facilities to alternative uses. Well-located physical stores remain relevant, but larger department stores continue to decline, replaced by internet fulfillment centers. More entertainment, dining, recreational, health-fitness, and experiential uses help improve the outlook for this sector.

Office

Talent continues gravitating towards dense urban districts. People seek to live, work, and play in the same areas, shunning long commutes. Successful office space follows the talent, offering more private workspace and larger communal areas for idea exchanges. Informal settings, as well as "smart" flexible space, attract users. Service amenities, including health, fitness, daycare, and pet facilities, help attract tenants to these complexes. Specialized usages within this sector, namely medical offices, offer selective investment opportunities resulting from the growing demand for outpatient facilities. A significant risk of office properties is repurposing older buildings in urban and suburban areas further from employment nodes. Another threat to office space demand is remote work and work-at-home trends accelerated by the COVID crisis. A survey conducted during the pandemic noted that nearly half of the employees polled desired to work remotely three days a week or more. [28]

Lodging

Since the Great Recession, the hospitality industry witnessed tremendous expansion in the US and globally. Hotels directly respond to consumer and business travel movements more than any other sector of commercial real estate. The hotel sector relies upon intensive management, in some cases from owner operators who also control the entity responsible for day to day management. Most hotels are "flagged" and utilize a brand or chain that actively participates in facility design, upgrades, and other operational decisions as well as providing sophisticated reservation systems that adjust room rates instantly. Such brands offer customer loyalty programs, strongly impacting occupancy. Managers associated with brands or third party managers serving a variety of owner/investors, focus on current lodging trends such as room experience, authenticity, service value and staffing. Cybersecurity and home-sharing services threaten traditional lodging. For example, the largest space-sharing service (Airbnb) offers more accommodations than the world's top five hotel brands combined.[29] However, the most substantial risks remain those always faced by hotel investors: changing travel conditions driven by outside forces (e.g., pandemic, sluggish economy.)[30]

OBSOLESCENCE

Functional obsolescence adds the additional element of physical-asset uncertainty risk to any real estate venture. America's real estate stock continues to age. Commercial properties average over fifty years old. The residential market inventory is barely newer, with about half of the housing constructed before 1980. Furthermore, the American Society of Civil Engineers estimates that by 2025 a total investment of nearly five trillion dollars must be injected to improve the nation's infrastructure.[31] The apparent risk lies in understanding the physical condition and budgeting for repairs and maintenance. Even as properties meet acceptable physical standards, technology and user needs change.

LIQUIDITY

Liquidity represents "the quality of being capable of exchange or interchange."[32] For assets, liquidity inversely relates to yield. More liquid assets typically have low yields; low liquidity demands higher yields. Cash on hand, the ultimate example of instant liquidity, offers no gain but no risk. Naturally, real estate investors expect higher returns than those earned by liquid assets.

Numerous variables affect real estate liquidity risk, including transaction size, location, project economics, and market timing. The expectation for the lack of liquidity demands higher profitability. In some instances, real estate investments generate 5% to 7% higher returns over longer timelines of 10 to 25 years than public equities. Investing in real estate requires strategic thinking, usually expressed in months or years, not tactical financial maneuvering described in seconds, minutes, hours, or days.[33]

OPERATIONS

Direct investing requires property management, irrespective of project type or deal size. Low risk exists with passive investments such as triple-net leased projects or vacant landholdings. Alternatively, higher risk surfaces with labor-intensive assets, including full-service lodging, healthcare facilities, and apartment buildings. More tenant-user services demand more significant management expertise. Ownership must navigate many operating issues such as property maintenance, rent collections, leasing, tenant relations, and legal compliance issues. Investors ill-equipped to handle operations shift risk to third-party managers, with more than 280,000 firms available in the United States. Operational risks still loom, even with hired organizations. Property managers need supervision, as ownership bears ultimate responsibility for asset performance.[34]

RESEARCH

In real estate investing, research data often lack real-time accuracy. Investors and appraisers rely upon collecting commercial property market data for sales and leases, usually dated three months or longer ("Comp Lag Error"). Also, random differences exist between comparable transaction data and the researched project ("Comp Sample Error"). As a result, relying upon historical data poses substantial risks, especially during market volatility. Valuation data varies, in some cases, by as much as ten percent versus actual sales prices.[35]

Numerous research sources and tools exist for measuring local, regional, and national realty markets. Ultimately, property-level research responsibility remains with buyers. Such independent research demands more investor competence for understanding risk, especially for generating forward-looking valuation forecasts – the territory of entrepreneurs and visionaries.

KNOWN/UNKNOWN

Investors quantify as many risks as possible and rewards for measuring financial outcomes based on the abovementioned risks. However, some risks and rewards elude definability. Investors refer to these risks as "known and unknown."

Investors view unknown risks as any undetermined ownership perils. Such risks remain impossible to predict or quantify. The fears lie in not knowing what risks face investors. The unknown unknowns pose the most concern[36]. On the other hand, investors measure different types of known risks. The table below illustrates the particulars of known and unknown risks:[37]

Known Knowns *Risk is known both abstractly (in correspondence to events which do or may happen) and as a concrete risk exposure whose portents or impacts can be described using available evidence.*	**Unknown Knowns** *Risk is less well known abstractly, but individual or organisational experience of it nonetheless necessitates its management.*
Known Unknowns *It is understood that a particular type or category of risk deserves attention, yet there is lack of convincing evidence for its presence as a concrete risk exposure for the organisation at a particular time.*	**Unknown Unknowns** *Possible risks which have not been imagined/conceptualised and evidence for whose relevance within some specific organisational context might exist embryonically as scattered information, but not as coherent risk knowledge.*

By reviewing the combination of known and unknown risks, investors can easily be discouraged and overwhelmed from pursuing real estate ventures. Yet without taking risks, rewards are non-existent. Real estate investments offer significant potential for rewards, as discussed in the next section.

REWARDS

Investing in income-property ventures offers numerous rewards. These rewards break down into tangible and intangible formats, further discussed as follows:

TANGIBLE

Tangible rewards focus on quantifiable factors, namely profitability. Real estate investing offers cash flow, diversification, inflation protection, and income tax savings backed by a hard asset.

Hard Asset Reward

Real property represents the most classical definition of a hard asset, offering visible improvements on an immovable site. Investors benefit from having physical proof of the asset, over and above any financial documents. Other hard assets include oil, natural gas, gold, silver, farmland, and natural-colored diamonds. In general, commodities and hard assets negatively correlate to stocks and bonds.[38]

Cash Flow Reward

Most investors choose real estate to collect rental income over the ownership period. Mortgage markets provide substantial capital to this industry as proof of the demand for realty cash flow and appreciation potential. Mortgages represent investments similar to bonds, offering defined cash flow streams to investors. Mortgage-related funds represent about a quarter of the $40 trillion US bond market.[39]

Diversification Reward

In addition to stocks, bonds, and other financial assets, real estate provides investors with the opportunity for diversified holdings. Over a third of Americans surveyed view real estate as a preferred investment instead of stocks and bonds.[40] This asset class lies between stock and bonds in the risk/reward profile, carrying more risk than bonds, but returns tend to be more stable than stocks.[41]

Inflation Protection Reward

Investors view real estate as inflation protection. Commercial property income performance typically correlates to inflation, as evidenced during the 1970s and early 1980s. The connection is imperfect as other factors influence values, including interest rates and secular forces (e.g., demographics, e-commerce).

In the short run, rising construction costs hamper the creation of new supply. Realty prices often converge to replacement costs directly linked to inflation in the long run. And as inflation escalates, more investors flock to this sector. For example, home prices increased year-over-year by nearly 20% in June 2021, the most considerable rise on record.[42]

Income Tax Savings Reward

Few investors avoid paying income taxes (e.g., pension funds, nonprofits). Otherwise, real estate ranks among the top tax shelters for American investors, retirement accounts, employment benefits, and business ownership. If enough income tax savings exist, the investor shifts into a lower tax bracket, saving even more.

Several tax-saving incentives emerge from owning income properties. Investors claiming federal tax returns deductions adjust income by subtracting mortgage interest, property taxes, insurance, and other operating expenses.

For the homeowner, the mortgage interest and real estate tax deductions rank as the nation's most extensive housing subsidy programs. This tax break provides homeowners subsidies totaling over one hundred billion in recent years, more than double the entire budget for the Federal Department of Housing and Urban Development.[43]

Federal income tax benefits include annual depreciation, capital gains tax rates upon sale, and tax-free exchanges. Properties with physical improvements qualify for depreciation ranging up to 40 years. Upon sale, short-term capital gains rates apply for investment properties owned a year or less, ranging from 10% to 37%, depending on various income tax brackets. In contrast, long-term capital gains (held over one year) enjoy lower taxes, reaching from zero to 20%.[44] As an alternative to an outright sale, a tax-free exchange (1031X) allows investors to replace the property of equal or greater value to the asset sold if done within a six-month timeline. Lastly, opportunity zones, tax credit deals, and other specific programs targeting underserved communities round out the broad spectrum of investor tax benefits. These programs include bypassing capital gains, reducing construction costs, and receiving subsidies for developing projects within these areas.

Passive income also plays into tax savings. According to the Internal Revenue Service, passive income represents monies earned from rental or business activity, whereby the investors don't materially participate in operations. Passive income benefits from a more favorable tax treatment today than in the past, when this income was limited to offsets with passive losses. With the introduction of the Tax Cuts and Jobs Act (2018), businesses earning qualified business income (QBI), including rental income, can receive a deduction of up to 20% of taxable income. This pass-through deduction only qualifies for profitable ventures; not all income types qualify for this deduction, which is currently available until 2025.[45]

INTANGIBLE

Intangible realty ownership rewards abstract target factors, including pride of ownership, recognition, and civic responsibility.

Pride of Ownership Reward

The bragging rights of saying, "I own that," rank as one of the most potent rewards of real estate investing. This asset class offers life-long opportunities for self-promotion or a branding legacy. Examples of ownership pride focus on property naming rights (e.g., Rockefeller Center, Salesforce Tower). Furthermore, investors often monetize such rights.

Recognition Reward

Closely related to the pride of ownership, ownership recognition serves as an additional reward for investors. As tangible edifices, properties offer visual proof of investment success. Major lodging industry operators typically use recognition as a branding tool for attracting travelers (e.g., Marriott, Hilton). In addition, branding allows recognition of pricing tiers for differentiating consumer spending levels by quality rankings.

Civic Responsibility Reward

Civic responsibility directly ties into Environmental, Social, and Governance ("ESG"), a crucial topic for investors today. Investors target specific realty ventures with goodwill as the primary objective rather than profitability. While environmental sustainability remains topical in the industry, the long-overdue spotlight on social performance in ESG is finally having its moment.[46] More positive changes lie ahead as industry leaders redirect resources to the needy and underserved segments of society (e.g., Terwilliger Center for Innovation in Shelter).

Understanding risks and rewards require blending as much information as possible to make rewarding investment decisions. And regardless of the various risks mentioned, real estate investments offer abundant rewards. How will owners share in the rewards from such industry growth? An answer lies in understanding how to quantify risk and reward.

RISK/REWARD QUANTIFIED

Measurable risks and rewards help determine project feasibility. Risk and reward strategies focus on maintaining solvency (principal repayment) in pursuit of financial gain (profit).

In order of importance, principal repayment supersedes any profits. Commonly known as the return "*OF* "principal, this financial concept forms the basis for all risk/reward modeling. On the other hand, profit, the return "*ON*" principal, represents the ultimate goal of any business venture. The greater the risk of principal repayment, the higher the profit expectation.

Principal and profit interlace with risk/reward modeling to identify vital yield benchmarks. Since losing value (e.g., principal) defines risk, describing the "safest" investment serves as the minimum profit baseline. Any yield gains above this benchmark represent profits; losses, or negative yields, sink below the baseline. The Real Estate Capital RateStack[47] illustrates this risk/reward concept as follows:

THE REAL ESTATE CAPITAL RATESTACK

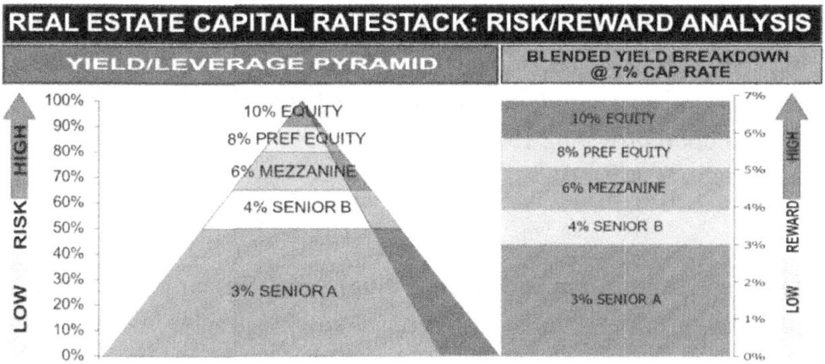

The Yield/Leverage Pyramid displayed side-by-side with The Blended Yield Breakdown chart illustrates the positive relationship between risk and reward. The pyramid shows that all parties' total capital contributed represents 100% of every real estate project. Each layer of money within the pyramid shows the various sources of capital contributions. The pyramid base indicates the "safest" funding component, offering the most negligible yield. The adjacent graph compares the various yields in leverage and risk, resulting in a combined return for the entire investment. Color-coded zones separate the different degrees of risk for each layer of capital. Green shows "safe"; grey indicates "moderate," and red warns of "high" risks. In order of risk/reward ranking, each of these layers breaks down as follows:

Senior Debt (A- and B-piece) Green Zone - First Mortgage Position: For decades, lenders underwrote senior-level debt at a level of 75% loan-to-value ("LTV") for most commercial properties. Today, higher overall prices result from investors accepting lower returns. Since lenders require minimum debt coverage ratios, 65% LTV represents the current benchmark. The above charts illustrate that the senior lenders' annual return in the "green zone" shows a 3.92% blended yield. The Senior A funding provides a 50% LTV exposure yielding 3%; Senior B receives 4% for the additional 15% loan amount, totaling 65% LTV.

Subordinated Debt (Mezzanine) Grey Zone: "Mezzanine" funds, otherwise referred to as loans secured by ownership interests rather than recorded property liens, remain legally subordinate to all senior debt. Typically, these funds share the same term as the senior loan ("co-terminus"). Subordinated debt usually falls above the 65% range, filling in the gap to as much as 90% of the capital stack. In the example, the subordinate lender's annual "grey zone" yields 6% based upon providing 15% additional funds above the senior debt for the combined debt of 80% LTV.

Equity (Preferred Equity, Cash Equivalent Value) Red Zone: Entrepreneurial capital with the appropriate risk profile signifies the first monies invested in the venture. At the top of the pyramid, "pure" equity and other investor funds directly benefit from any net profits (or losses). Net profits occur in order of lien priority after repaying: (1) senior debt, (2) subordinated debt, and (3) any quasi-equity sources such as preferred equity (further discussed in other sections of this book). The example shows "red zone" capital contributions from preferred equity and "pure" investor funds totaling 20% of project cost and formulated to generate a combined equity yield of 9%.

In summary, these charts illustrate the weighted average annual yield derived from the various funding sources equates to 6.85%, rounded to 7%. This yield ignores any reversionary event, such as a sale. The example illustrates that debt sources accept returns ranging from 3% to 6% for longer-term permanent loans (10 years +/-). Meanwhile, the equity capital sources target between 8% to 10%, plus reversionary upside. The downside risk of the equity investment extends to property values dipping below 80% of the project value. Any additional value losses harm subordinate and senior debt positions, respectively.

After quantifying risk, the investor must determine if the potential rewards further warrant investing based upon the capital stack risk positions. The answer lies in identifying and executing the appropriate risk/reward strategies that meet ownership profit goals.

RISK/REWARD STRATEGIES

Various terms exist for describing real estate risk/reward strategies, including the "Class A-B-C" rating system, or more simply, "high, medium, and low" risk/reward. These descriptions often seem too broad, lacking clarity regarding the types of risks/rewards. Starting earlier this century, real estate investors adopted the following income-property risk terminology: "Core," "Core-Plus," "Value-Add," and "Opportunistic."[48] In order of low-to-high risk undertaking, these categories are illustrated in the following chart using the same risk zone color-coding scheme mentioned in the Real Estate Capital RateStack.

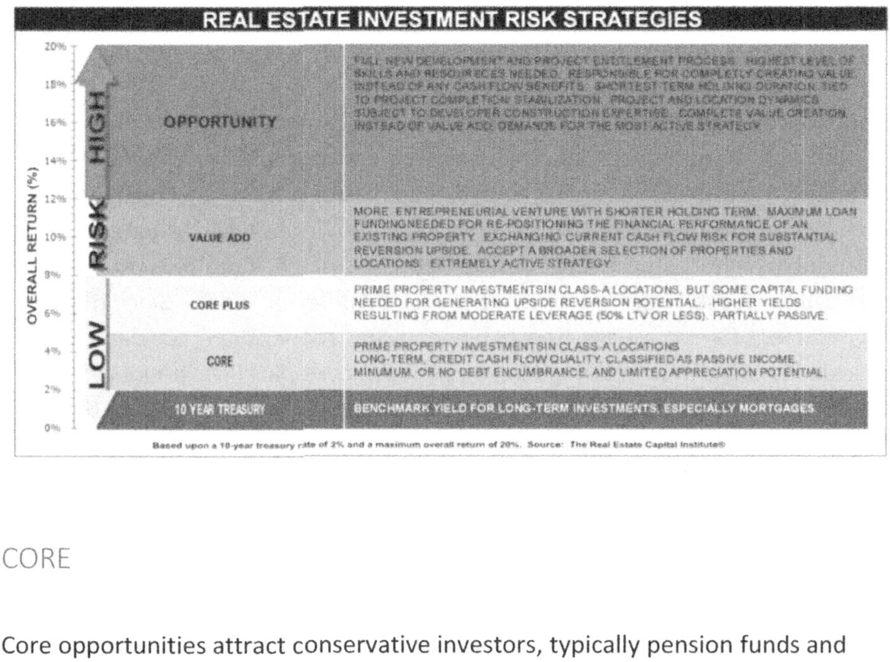

CORE

Core opportunities attract conservative investors, typically pension funds and wealth-preservation money managers. Investing in core properties consists of avoiding risk. This strategy parallels investing in AAA-rated corporate bonds. Only the best properties within the targeted industry sector qualify. Also, such assets typically feature all-cash contributions, eliminating any third-party debt default risk. If introducing any leverage, very low loan-to-value ratios of fifty percent or less suffice. Core investment holding periods tend to be longer, ten years or more. Another desirable core property characteristic demands minimal capital improvements, especially during the early years of the holding period. Property appreciation remains secondary to financial safety, prioritizing current cash flow rather than the reversionary upside. Core-investment examples include newer, credit-tenant properties backed by longer-term leases, "trophy" office buildings in central areas of major cities, and institutional-grade apartment buildings. Currently, such investments provide paltry overall yields within the lower-to-mid-single-digit range. Core yields reach 200 to 400 basis points over comparable-term treasuries, generating a perceived risk rating of "A+."

CORE-PLUS

Conservative investors seeking more reward and corresponding risk gravitate towards core-plus deals. Investment strategies similar to core opportunities apply, but more tolerance exists toward generating yield via minimal renovations, upgrades, and tenant releasing plans. Such investors team up with developers and owners to execute this funding strategy, which requires more "hands-on" operations. In most cases, twenty percent or less of the capital structure consists of funds allocated for improving project performance. Adding debt usually falls within this strategy. However, while leverage produces higher returns, debt repayment risks surface. Core-plus transactions equate to conservative income stocks, mainly preferred stock. Since this investment format usually creates higher values sooner than core deals, more flexibility exists in structuring holding periods. Core-plus investments offer overall leveraged yields in the mid-to-higher-single-digit range, translating to another 200 to 400 basis point premium above core returns. Core-plus opportunities are rated as "A-" or "B+," translating to lower-quality investment-grade corporate bonds, say A to BBB.

VALUE-ADD

Value-add investing adds even more operational risk in exchange for extra yield. Such ventures mirror "growth" opportunities in the stock market. Given the higher return requirements, shorter holding periods emerge, typically three to five years. Seasoned owners, developers, and others involved with "flipping" properties search for opportunities in the value-add investment sector. The current cash flow in value-add situations typically needs restructuring, and reversion expectations gain importance as the shorter investment horizon dictates creating more moving parts during the projected holding period.

Partially vacant structures, functionally obsolescent buildings, and properties in emerging locations fall within this risk/reward category. The capital structure reflects significant additional investment needs over and above the initial purchase price. Compared to core-type ventures, value-add opportunities offer more risk-balancing by sacrificing cash flow certainty in exchange for improved financial performance with value upside in the foreseeable future. Unlike most core-type ventures, value-add projects feature mortgage leverage, seeking maximum debt for yield enhancement, usually 65% or more. Such projects delve into double-digit yield territory by targeting returns in the lower to mid-teens. Value-add properties rank as "B" to "C" risk profiles.

OPPORTUNITY

The name says it all – "opportunity." On the opposite spectrum of "core," opportunity investments involve higher risks in pursuit of handsome rewards. Current cash flow seldom drives investment decisions, as capital moves to new construction or substantial redevelopment. Opportunity deals reflect the "venture capital" appetite familiar to stock investors. Experienced and highly entrepreneurial developers team up with investors to create such ventures. This investment format focuses on "manufacturing" real estate cash flow and value. Unlike value-add or core deals, developers generate demand for a project instead of fine-tuning existing tenant needs. To reflect project completion and performance uncertainty, attracting additional capital includes taking on higher leverage burdened with more expensive pricing (e.g., higher borrowing cost). In cases of extremely high risk, most debt funding sources avoid such ventures, requiring equity instead. High risk includes raw land holdings, adaptive reuse, and selecting unproven locations. Development ventures attract the highest yields, typically 15% or more, over a holding period of three years or less.

These risk/reward strategies serve as general guidelines, not concrete benchmarks. Investors often straddle between these strategies for achieving risk/reward diversification. Furthermore, the lines often blur. For instance, the overall yield of 8% ranks as a core investment for an entrepreneurial owner. At the same time, conservative institutional investors consider such a yield to reflect too much risk, reclassifying the venture as a value-add. For example, an investor purchases an unentitled site for development (an opportunity strategy). Due to an unsuccessful zoning battle, the investor settles for operating the site as a surface parking lot (a core strategy). Or Lady Luck strikes when a value-add property quickly becomes a core asset, in the case of a tenant-credit upgrade, resulting from a corporate merger or acquisition.

RISK/REWARD FLOW

Showing how the risk/reward relationship flows in real estate involves segregating various risks and rewards from macro to micro levels. The table below summarizes the risks discussed, including universal, direct ownership, quantified (type of investment), strategies (level of risk), and the specific investment risk/reward.

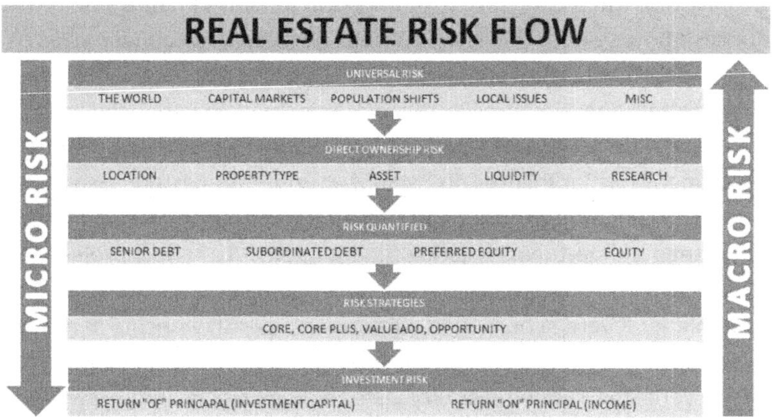

As the Real Estate Risk Flow chart illustrates, every investor categorizes this risk/reward sequence in evaluating an opportunity. Regardless of global and capital market risks, investors choose realty ventures based on location, property type, physical condition, and capital constraints.

Illustration: The following chart illustrates the real estate risk flow based on investing in a $65 million, newly constructed tech research lab in Boston's Wharf District.

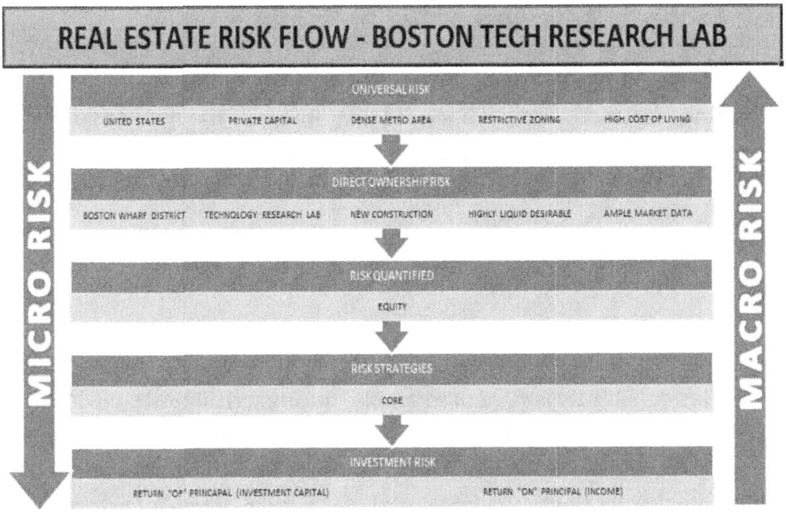

As the chart shows, the universal risk lies with investing in the United States with private capital in a dense metropolitan area (Boston) controlled by a highly restrictive development environment with a high cost of living. However, the area attracts strong research talent, given the surrounding universities and other public and private investments.

Observation: The direct ownership risk flow involves selecting a project located in Boston's Wharf District within a technology research park. Substantial market data identifies this property type as a highly liquid and desirable asset. The investor chooses an equity position for a core investment after quantifying risk. Finally, the investment risk/reward delineates a reasonably safe return of principal, given the other factors mentioned, but at a relatively low yield.

Risk/reward flows illustrate the methodology of approaching the analysis, yet many nuances exist.

RISK/REWARD NUANCES

Compression, variance, and payback are just of few of the nuances of risk/reward analysis discussed below.

COMPRESSION

Pricing cycles constantly vary. For example, during a rising-rate environment, a broad pricing compression [decline] occurs in nearly all real estate risk/reward segments, particularly in outright (direct) ownership. The combination of a capital surplus, and readily available market research, allow investors to generate more informed and quicker decisions. As a result, fewer profit opportunities surface from pricing discrepancies that traditionally result from market knowledge inefficiencies. Often, investors seek real estate as an additional profit opportunity due to increased pricing transparency.

VARIANCE

Value-add and opportunity investments present high degrees of variance from expected outcomes. These fluctuations prove that multiple risk/reward scenarios exist. Proper investment analysis, featuring a more comprehensive range of scenarios, helps identify more uncertainty. Sophisticated investors also assign probabilities to the scenarios to expand the decision-making process.

PAYBACK

Realistic risk/reward modeling always includes worst-case scenarios. Even with unprofitable ventures, investors still attempt to recoup principal. This "safety first" concept embodies metrics based on the payback (of principal) using two popular formulas: (1) The weighted average maturity ("WAM") and the (2) Capitalization Rate ("Cap Rate"). WAM calculates the required period (in years) for repaying the investment from cumulative cash flow. This method demonstrates that lower cash flows translate to extended repayment periods, reducing overall investment returns (e.g., IRR, NPV). Numerous investors use minimum payback periods in evaluating deals. This formula reduces the cap rate into a whole number, further divided into one hundred. For example, if the cap rate on investment equals 8%, the formula indicates the return of principal from net operating income in 12.5 years (100/8 = 12.5). The payback period calculation fluctuates depending on net operating income ("NOI") or cap-rate market value changes. For comparison, select public real estate companies factor in payback periods of fewer than four years[49].

AVOIDING RISK?

Risk mitigation includes some levels of risk/reward sharing. Sharing risk includes distributing profits via fixed payments, contingent rewards, or a combination. On the other hand, fixed payments account for insurance coverage and various financial hedges against operational losses. Contingent rewards cover any profit-sharing, including partnership promote structures and equity participation.

In conclusion, risk/reward management is an art and a science. Intuition and experience play essential roles in managing risk/reward dynamics. Mispriced risk/reward equals opportunity lost or taking more risk for less reward. Quantifying potential risks/rewards and segregating these elements removes uncertainty but rarely guarantees success. However, understanding potential risk/reward relationships and formulating proper strategies increases the chances of success. Ultimately, real estate investment is an exercise in risk/reward management.

Understanding key risk/reward principles lead to the next step of quantifying and evaluating risk at the real estate project level. The following section, Evaluation, represents the second of the *Four Pillars*.

CHAPTER 3: EVALUATION – RISK/REWARD UNDERWRITING

"Before anything else, preparation is the key to success." - Alexander Graham Bell

Real estate capital underwriting measures principal repayment risk and profit return over the expected investment horizon based on the investor's risk/reward profile. Mathematical modeling quantifies principal recapture and profitability using this underwriting. As engineers measure the physical strengths of building structures, investors measure the financial tolerances to determine stress levels under various economic scenarios.

The second of the *Four Pillars*, *Evaluation*, follows a systematic approach to sizing a project's risk/reward profile. The analysis reviews essential real estate ownership variables affecting profitability, known as "The Five P's of Underwriting. "After that, "Static" and "Dynamic" financial profitability formulas provide investment feasibility benchmarks for decision-making discussed below.

THE FIVE P's OF UNDERWRITING

For-profit property investment analysis, including existing or potential ventures (e.g., to-be-built, land acquisitions), uses most or all of the following components for underwriting a real estate transaction: Sponsorship, Collateral, Income, Expenses, Net Operating Income, Before Tax Cash Flow and After-Tax Cash Flow. These components translate to a more easy-to-remember format, referred to as The Five P's of Underwriting: People, Place, Project, Performance, and Pros/Cons, are discussed in order of review priority, including a sample illustration and observations for each:

1. PEOPLE

"People" underwriting refers to all items relating to sponsorship and other personnel responsible for the project, including investors, hired staff, lenders, third-party vendors, and local government officials.

Real estate offers universal appeal to investors. According to a leading consumer finance company survey, nearly a third of the respondents chose real estate over stocks, bonds, savings accounts, precious metals, and other investments when considering assets for longer-term holds of ten years or more. By age group, Millennials maintain the highest interest levels (36%), followed by Generation X (31%), baby boomers (30%), and the Silent Generation (23%). Approximately one-third of the respondents desire the real estate sector as a preferred investment, representing all income levels.[50]

Professional real estate investors include anyone purchasing an asset. Definitions of professional investors fall into two categories: active (full-time) or passive (part-time) participation. The Internal Revenue Service provides some definitive guidelines regarding investors: "More than half of the personal services you performed in all trades or businesses during the tax year were performed in real property trades or businesses in which you materially participated. [And,] You performed more than 750 hours of services during the tax year in real property trades or businesses in which you materially participated."[51]

The degree of background and qualifications for professional realty investing also varies. Investors originate from different areas of expertise, from working in the building trades to college graduates. Few owners possess all the talents and experience necessary to successfully perform within the industry's wide range of investment and operational expertise. However, hiring adequately trained and experienced professionals addresses any talent deficiencies.

Real estate talent comes from various sources: technical trade schools, universities, private schools, and industry trade groups. These organizations offer multiple resources for training, current industry news, and career advancement. A partial list of real estate trade groups includes The Appraisal Institute®, the Building Owners and Managers Association International®, the International Council of Shopping Centers®, the Mortgage Bankers Association® of America, NAIOP® Commercial Real Estate Development Association, the National Association of Homebuilders®, National Association of Real Estate Investment Trusts®, the National Association of Realtors®, the National Multi-Housing Council®, The Property Management Association, The Real Estate

Roundtable and The Urban Land Institute®. Furthermore, many of these organizations offer specific accreditations, providing additional comfort for varying degrees of expertise.

Depending on investment size and scope, these professionals include administrative, bookkeeping, accounting, leasing, construction, legal, insurance, and property operations personnel. Whether owner-controlled or third-party, such professionals need skillsets and licensing/compliance requirements matching the type, size, physical condition, number of tenants, and investment factors. For instance, property operations effectively need one maintenance professional to handle a single-family property. Operating more active investments such as apartments requires between one to two people per 100 units, and a hundred-room hotel needs ten to fifteen people. A high-turnover restaurant demands one employee per 100 $ft.^2$; a grocery store has about 940 $ft.^2$ per employee, and a warehouse needs one employee per about 2000 $ft.^2$. Lastly, passive deals such as absolute net-lease properties shift tenants' operating responsibilities. Naturally, these personnel counts dramatically depending upon age, tenancy, etc. [52] With everchanging technology, these ratios remain fluid.

The ultimate success of a real estate venture hinges on the ownership teaming up with the necessary talent to take the investment through the planned holding period. An illustration, followed by an observation shown below, provides a sample of how the *people* variable relates to the 5 P's concept.

Illustration: Helen Hoosier, of Bloomington, Indiana, is a middle-aged wealthy investor with limited ownership experience who enjoys owning real estate but avoids operational risk. This investor purchases a new, smaller shopping center with a limited number of tenants. As a result, she outsources all realty services, including management, repairs, and maintenance. Since the center is within ten minutes of the investor's home, regular property drive-by inspections occur to check on management success.

Observation: People underwriting discussions include understanding the personalities of key players in decision-making. Qualified professionals don't necessarily work well with ownership if character chemistry fails to materialize. Personal recommendations in a relationship serve as the best sources for clearing these personnel hurdles.[53]

When the ownership forms a real estate team, the second step of the 5 P's involves selecting a *place* (location) for targeting investments.

2. PLACE

Underwriting discussions regarding *place* include macro and micro elements of a site since property location remains fixed. The goal of place research focuses on the overall economic viability of the immediate area, the surrounding community, the metropolitan area, and maybe even the country. Such research gauges the short and long-term outlook for the continued prosperity of the location.

National information sources work best for macroeconomic research, especially for comparisons between various locations. Federal agencies form the best starting point, including the US Bureau of Labor Statistics, the Federal Reserve, the Treasury, the Census Bureau, the Department of Commerce, the Council of Economic Advisors, and Data.gov. Next, industry trade groups provide much data on specific property types. Lastly, independent research organizations offer paid and free data subscription services, including Real Capital Analytics, REIS, Zillow, CoStar, Esri GIS, Reonomy, and LandVision, among many others. Often, these services offer a host of data above and beyond locational information, including demographics, supply and demand statistics, and sales and leasing comparables.[54]

Microeconomic data collection follows, should the macroeconomic research prove a worthwhile location. This data collection focuses on checking for immediate issues and negative or positive trends. No proper substitute exists for "boots on the ground" homework. State and local government agencies, chambers of commerce, realty brokerage offices, law enforcement agencies, news media outlets, community groups, and neighborhood organizations provide the best local intelligence.

After completing broader macro and micro research, investigations of the actual site take precedence. The study focuses on physical site issues, including topography, environmental contamination, earthquake zone, drainage, flooding, soil stability, access to utilities, etc. Other facets include shape, ingress/egress, and municipal restrictions. For instance, questions include: Does the site shape and topography pose any issues for future development? Do ingress and egress provide sufficient access to the surrounding area? Are municipal ordinances too restrictive? Professionals handle specific areas of concern by hiring appraisers, lawyers, traffic consultants, property tax advisors, civil engineers, and others.

Once built, real estate remains fixed to the site. Locational dependency, mainly the economic health of the surrounding area, drives user demand. After that, demand generators of tenants, site characteristics that can enhance or inhibit a given location (transportation access), and regulatory actions such as zoning, which can either restrict future supply (moratorium) or increase it (rezone more land from agriculture to residential or commercial use). At best, the goal is to create a locational monopoly.

An investor gathers a sense of how well the local economy performs by using a research service such as the Bloomberg New York City Metro Index (BNYCM: IND), which tracks publicly traded local stocks, as shown below.[55]

Illustration: Roosevelt Field mall in Garden City, NY, is a 2.2 million square foot mall that ranks among the largest malls in the country. This mall is one of the few large shopping venues in the metro New York area, having substantial value given zoning constraints. The size draws customers from nearly all of Nassau County, given the strategic location in the heart of Long Island's Nassau County at the intersection of Old Country Road and Meadowbrook Parkway. Meadowbrook Parkway connects the mall to the Long Island Expressway, Northern and Southern Parkways, and other major routes. Since the mall lies within an affluent suburb of New York City (annual household income is $113,525), the site connects to the economic vitality of New York City and its long-term financial outlook.

Observation: Another location research tool, Location and the Economics of Agglomeration, or Use Clusterings, centers on examining the surrounding area. Most land uses tend to cluster, particularly in regions encountering high vehicular and foot traffic. Clustering related and complementary land uses attracts more consumers due to one-stop activities comparison shopping, which results in higher profits. At the same time, this clustering is evident for retail properties (e.g., automobile rows, restaurant rows), offices, and industrial properties cluster along major transportation corridors. Economies of scale, face-to-face contact, and business linkages drive these locational decisions. The example below illustrates a site in Houston representing office and industrial buildings in the 400,000 square foot range.

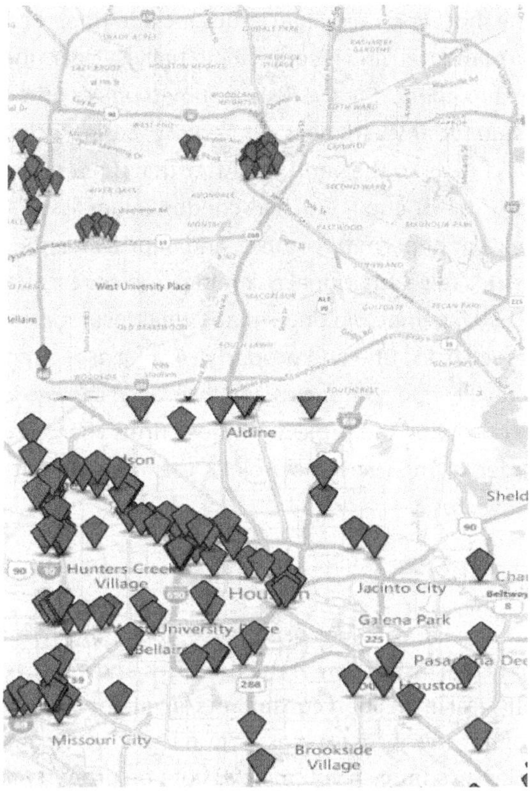

Upon researching the locational dynamics, inspecting the on-site improvements take precedence. The following section covers improvements, otherwise referred to in the 5 P's discussion as the *project.*

3. PROJECT

The "Project" represents the third "P" of the Five P's of Underwriting. This element examines legal issues governing the project, followed by addressing the physical suitability for the intended use of the investment, further discussed below.

Legal suitability focuses on governmental and other regulatory compliance issues relating to site improvements, including buildings and permitted uses on the premises. The most common legal issues include title, regulatory restrictions, environmental, and insurance. Initially, a clear title to the property shows full ownership rights. Clear title is assumed unless otherwise noted and priced/risk-adjusted for any variances. Otherwise, curing a clouded title adds additional risks and costs to the venture. After that, understanding any zoning and other regulatory restrictions, such as condominium association rules, determines the extent of permittable uses and improvements. On-site environmental issues raise additional risk mitigation concerns and potential legal liabilities. Lastly, ownership determines what insurance options offer protection from such risks, title and property ranking as the most important coverages. As a result, title companies and insurance carriers are excellent resources for prequalifying the project. If these firms charge very high premiums for underwriting a specific project, their assessment should be a risk indicator to the investor.

Should legal and compliance issues prove acceptable, the investment warrants an appropriate physical inspection of the premises and improvements. Trade organizations, physical inspection consultants/engineers, and other experts offer extensive options for property inspection services. Financial institutions and rating agencies also publish voluminous data on property inspections as part of their financial due diligence. For example, a property consulting firm generates a checklist, as shown below.[56]

Document	Date Received	Comment
D. Building Maintenance History		
1. Age of the Building		
2. Owner's Name and Telephone Number		
3. Building Manager's Name and Telephone and Fax Numbers		
4. Building Superintendent's Name and Telephone Number		
5. Names and Telephone Numbers of Service Firms		
a. Facade Repairs/Restoration		
b. Roofing		
c. Plumbing		
d. Water Tower		
e. Heating		
f. Boiler Water Treatment		
g. Air Conditioning		
h. Cooling Tower		
i. Electrical		
j. Elevators		
k. Sprinkler/Standpipe System		
l. Swimming Pool		
m. Life/Safety Alarm System		

In addition to simply providing an inventory of property components, an assessment of use, quality, condition, and functional obsolescence provides helpful underwriting information. An investor must know how much to budget for replacement reserves during the projected ownership period. For example, major building components of a typical building feature a lifespan of ten to thirty years, including roof, wood decking, paint, shutters, windows, and driveway. Brick, veneer, stucco, doors, and the foundation frequently last over fifty years. Interior components, including appliances, boilers, plumbing, and electrical systems, survive from three years to several decades. Craftsmanship and materials dramatically impact the lifespan of property improvements.[57]

Illustration: Gopher ElectroMotor Technologies Corporation of Minneapolis, Minnesota, distributes electrical components for motorized urban scooters.

Given the firm's recent growth, Gopher wants to decide whether to replace the existing facility with more significant new improvements or purchase an older, more functionally-obsolete facility nearby. After researching and comparing the two options, Gopher decides to buy an existing facility, priced at about 80% of new construction costs. Gopher fears unknown construction risks, including downtime, learning that building costs continue escalating more than 5.5% per year.[58]

Observation: Regardless of the physical condition and quality of the improvements, functional obsolescence haunts real estate more than any other investment asset class. In particular, technological advancements require redesigning buildings and replacing major property systems to accommodate "smart" technologies requiring less energy. Furthermore, basic construction techniques have remained nearly the same since the middle ages.[59] Radical changes in building materials, usage, efficiency, and assembly methods portend even more disruptive technology influences in the foreseeable future. Project planning should anticipate climate change, among other emerging development concerns. Fortunately, LEED certification, stricter tenant space demands, and legislative actions help accelerate such changes by establishing qualification standards.

Upon understanding the people, place, and project variables, investors examine a venture's financial *performance* as the next logical step in the 5 P's process.

4. PERFORMANCE

The fourth "P" of the 5 P's of Underwriting – Performance – focuses on investment economics to determine financial feasibility.

Purchasing a real estate asset translates to buying a set of assumptions about future cash flow streams, not too different from buying stocks and bonds. Essentially, the investor acquires a bundle of lease contracts, analogous to bundling other securities to form a portfolio. For instance, imagine purchasing a regional mall with over fifty tenants. Each tenant represents a cash flow enterprise with unique characteristics, including public or private ownership, a credit rating, financial performance, and lease term. In this example, the investor is like a closed-end fund manager (mall ownership) overseeing a diversified pool of assets (mall improvements) featuring varying risk profiles with different maturities and cash flow streams (leases).

Staying with the mall example, investors need to focus on important cash flow characteristics such as aggregation, credit quality, and correlation, further discussed as follows:

Agglomeration: Malls encompass major tenants supplemented with ancillary tenants – the critical principle of agglomeration. The major tenants, especially the anchor tenant, draw other tenants to the property. The higher the drawing power of the anchor, the lower the rent, combined with a longer lease term. Due to the strong customer draw power to the anchor, smaller tenants prefer to agglomerate, or cluster, in those parts of the center, creating a more holistic shopping experience.

Credit quality: The rents per square foot are higher for riskier tenants and vice versa for credit tenants. Owners usually categorize publicly-traded retail tenants with shorter-term leases (e.g., five years or less) as "high risk" if the credit rating is lower than "BBB."[60] The credit quality of cash flows constantly changes due to technological disruptions, changing consumer tastes, and a myriad of other factors hardly under the control of real estate investors.

Correlation: A cluster of tenants, even with solid credit backing, seldom suggests applying a stronger credit rating to the total project cash flow. For instance, assume two anchor tenants in different retail sectors occupy the mall and pay the same rents. The anchor tenant selling large-ticket home goods enjoys strong sales during a booming economic cycle. In contrast, the other anchor performs less impressively but steadily as a lower-credit clothing discount retailer. Both anchor tenants offer different hedge positions, even at equal rent payments – forming a more balanced cash flow correlation. In addition, a mall owner will target a wide variety of smaller tenants to increase diversification.

After considering the overall cash flow characteristics, the financial performance analysis moves to a more granular level. The main ingredients at this level of detail include thoroughly reviewing income and expenses to generate an accurate net operating income estimate ("NOI").

Net Operating Income

Net operating income ("NOI") defines as "The actual or anticipated rental income remaining, after all operating expenses are deducted from effective gross income, but before debt service and capital expenditures are deducted."[61] The NOI's foundation rests upon historical financial statements for existing, stabilized cash flows. The NOI relies on projected income and expenses for new construction, unproven, and stabilizing income streams, commonly referred to as proformas.

Most cash flow analysis centers on the NOI. This annual calculation, unique to each property, identifies the income stream, irrespective of the capital structure. The NOI determines the project's ability to cover additional payments, mainly replacement reserves (not classified as capital contributions) and debt service. A positive NOI leaves room for such charges; a breakeven or negative NOI indicates unsatisfactory financial performance for that period. As a result, NOI evaluations often span multiple years by applying averages and discounted cash flow analysis.

NOI computations classified as stabilized cash flow streams exclude extraordinary expenditures such as capital improvements or one-time payments. Examples of capital expenditures include tenant improvements, leasing commissions, and roof replacement. Extraordinary items include any special real estate tax assessments or refunds. Besides, NOI excludes any cash flows unique to the ownership structure, such as depreciation benefits and income tax payments. The cash flow at the property level (NOI) is allocated to various claim holders in the order of payment priority, with debt service carrying the first lien position, preferred equity, regular equity, or any other negotiated formula. Net operating income cash flows break down as follows:

Income

Income analysis based on regular annual cash inflows includes tenant rent roll, miscellaneous income, and vacancy assumptions supplemented by income growth projections. However, some realty ventures ignore income, such as land banking, instead relying on the reversion for principal recapture and profits.

Commercial real estate income starts with totaling all the Potential Gross Income ("GPI"), whether actual or realizable cash flow streams. Realizable cash flow is the potential cash flow the owner receives if the property performs at full occupancy, achieving maximum income. On the other hand, Gross Operating Income ("GOI") only accounts for actual income. Any type of revenue subject to income taxes applies to generating gross income, including regular rental payments, parking fees, laundry income, common area maintenance (CAM) charges, vending machines, service charges, internet usage fees, and facility membership dues. Also, percentage rents and other contingent performance income add to revenues, such as retail-tenants gross sales percentages relating to the specific property. However, income totals exclude various penalties, such as interest income from security deposits.

Leases and any other forms of contractual rent obligations secure income payments. Depending on the property type, lease formats vary by the extent of expenses the owners cover. For instance, absolute gross leases, also known as full-service gross, require the owner to pay for all space expenses, mainly pro-rated utilities, real estate taxes, maintenance, and insurance. Older apartment buildings with centrally controlled utilities commonly share this format. Modified gross rents provide cost-sharing arrangements, such as paying for base-year expenses. At the same time, tenants share any cost increases common to commercial properties, including retail, office, and incubator industrial assets. Absolute net leases shift the entire expense burden to the tenants, which is quite popular with more significant credit-tenant ventures. In some instances, especially with smaller apartment properties, tenants remain on a month-to-month basis absent of any leases.

The income growth assumptions link to market conditions, inflation, or any other agreed-upon formula for multiple-year NOI projections. Conservative growth assumptions lag the inflation rate, while more aggressive rates result from the tight supply, creating higher rent expectations. Absent any inflation index, ordinary annual growth rates range fall within two to five percent, as witnessed in much of the past decade. As an extreme example, in 1980, this index approached 13 percent.[62]

Beyond growth rates, income optimization strategies vary, depending upon applicable supply and demand factors directly affecting the investment. When supply outstrips demand, income reduction usually provides the most straightforward method for preserving cash flows, including lease concessions consisting of free rent, below-market rent, and more generous build-outs and tenant improvement ("TI") allowances. As demand overtakes supply, justifiable rent increases take effect. Given the real estate supply-demand lag time, whereby demand changes occur much faster than supply availability, income strategies seldom prove easy to execute.

In addition to any positive cash flows generated, negative adjustments to gross income mainly focus on vacancy and loss factors. Vacancy often rests with understanding the current rent roll and applicable market conditions. Vacancy calculations result from the greater of (i) actual or (ii) market vacancy unless the creditworthiness of tenants dictates less reliance on market vacancy. Submarket vacancy applies to those instances lacking market vacancy (e.g., fully occupied properties.) In addition to vacancy, a loss factor also applies to uncollectable rents. For example, if the loss factor climbs above one percent, management capabilities draw concern. Typical vacancy factors hover below five percent; weaker markets approach 7% or more. Office, retail, and lodging properties typically underwrite to higher vacancy levels, often starting in the mid-teen-percent range. Furthermore, a detailed analysis of the vacancy factor ties to understanding the tenant retention-rollover probabilities, new competitive supply, and rent pricing. Unrecovered common area maintenance costs ("CAM") for vacant [retail and commercial] space increase vacancy losses, as well.

Gross income adjusted for the vacancy and non-applicable income (e.g., interest income from lease deposits) is known as Effective Gross Income

("EGI"). This income calculation forms the basis for the expense ratio, default point (adding back vacancy), and select cash flow-participation calculations. However, these indices ignore fluid or non-existent EGI resulting from value-creation situations, applicable only when reaching cash flow stabilization. In particular, most land transactions fall into this category, including assemblage, entitlement, rezoning, site improvements, and vacating existing properties for demolition.

Upon aggregating all the income items, making vacancy/loss adjustments, and subtracting all applicable ordinary operating expenses, insurance, and property taxes, the results generate the net operating income (NOI). NOI is analogous to earnings before interest, income taxes, depreciation, and amortization (EBITDA) for regular corporations.

Pivotal decisions when analyzing income potential include tenant-credit quality, anchor impact, and lease term, as illustrated by the following example:

Illustration: Cardinal Stanford Capital Partners of Palo Alto is an investment bank accounting for nearly half of the Spartan Space Office Tower in Los Angeles. The lease period of this anchor tenant features a fourteen-year remaining term. This tenant's rental income remains below market based on a six-year-old lease. As a result, the income represents breakeven cash flow for this tenant after adjusting expenses. Despite the unfavorable income situation for the anchor space, the tenant's prestige attracts other desirable prospects to the premises at higher rates, thereby helping to mitigate the negative effect of the existing cash flow.

Observation: When estimating NOI in a stabilized projection, establishing a reasonable vacancy allowance creates more realistic assumptions. A "normal" market vacancy (e.g., five percent) covers overall conditions. Accounting for existing tenant lease rollover constitutes an extra vacancy adjustment, which differs year to year depending on lease terms. Typical adjustments assume two-thirds of the tenants stay, and the remaining one-third vacate the premises. Also, any tenant expense reimbursements count as lost income due to vacancy.

After computing vacancy losses, addressing expenses follows.

Expenses

Expense analysis covers ordinary annual cash outlays for operations, including insurance, utilities, ongoing repairs and maintenance, management fees, and property taxes. Other than absolute net lease investments, whereby the tenants bear full responsibility for any costs, expense adjustments apply to cash flow calculations for all projects.

Owners attempt to shift expense risks to tenants, where applicable. Most new commercial leases include partial or full expense pass-throughs. The trend continues towards passing more expenses to tenants for apartments as well. For example, the Ratio Utility Billing System ("RUBS") method involves allocating utility costs among residents.[63]

Typical expense ratios, expressed as a percent of the effective gross income, range from zero (absolute net) to 50% or more for older properties with limited pass-throughs. Operating expense ratios ("OER") vary by property type. Most apartment properties' typical expense ratios range from 35% to 45%.[64] Self-storage properties carry about one-third of the income load,[65] and office buildings often reach fifty percent.[66]

After completing income and expense calculations, the resulting NOI is the crucial benchmark for numerous investment underwriting tests. These tests establish critical decisions on modeling the capital funding structure, including debt, equity, and hybrid funding formats.

The type of cash flow behavior dictates growth and other income and expense underwriting variables. The behavior typically reflects local market norms. Such norms usually include equal growth rates applied to income and expenses. More conservative assumptions require expenses to grow at higher annual rates than income. Nevertheless, current income and expense historical performance (typically the trailing three years) drives most underwriting analysis, assuming properties demonstrate consistent operating histories.

Illustration: Fresh Cornhusker Motel Group of Lincoln, Nebraska, suffered a severe occupancy drop from 80% to 50% due to travel restrictions relating to a pandemic. Cornhusker and nearby competitors reduced room rates, but occupancy remained unchanged as tourism suffered. The ownership understood that income growth remains challenging for maintaining NOI growth. As a result, Cornhusker aggressively implemented an expense reduction program to improve profitability and minimize losses. The firm reduced the on-site health club's operating hours, focused on peak usage times, installed new energy-saving equipment, and negotiated lower property taxes. These actions resulted in substantial expense reductions while minimally impacting guest services. This illustration demonstrates cash flow underwriting during unusual market conditions, focusing on defensive financial strategies.

Observation: NOI and cash flow projections vary among investors, lenders, appraisers, assessors, brokers, and other real estate practitioners. Each professional tends to arrive at a different value estimate based on specific needs. Such professionals usually agree about calculating actual income and ordinary expenses such as utilities, insurance, real estate taxes, and management fees. However, debate occurs about substituting estimates instead of existing income and expenses. Since estimates introduce more significant uncertainty for projections, such NOI calculations demand additional scrutiny. Furthermore, the practice of adding extraordinary expenses, such as reserves or various cap-ex items, leads to skewed [lower] values. Capital "expenses" ultimately receive credit during project recapitalizations, usually refinancing or selling the asset.

After generating the net operating income, the pre-tax cash flow is the subsequent computation for measuring annual financial performance.

Pre-Tax Cash flow

Pre-tax cash flow ("PTCF") or before-tax cash flow ("BTCF"), or cash flow after debt service ("CFADS") focuses on the annual cash flow available for distribution to equity holders after debt service payment to debt holders. PTCF ignores capital expenditures, such as tenant improvements and renovation costs incurred during the year. As the term implies, PTCF disregards depreciation and other noncash (e.g., amortized principal loan reduction) items relating to income tax calculations.

$$PTCF = Net\ Operating\ Income - Debt\ Service$$

PTCF measures return-on-equity on an annual basis before any tax consequences. Absent any debt, PTCF otherwise equates to the capitalization rate for appraised values using the Income Approach. If the investment includes debt encumbrance, the PTCF reflects the NOI adjusted for debt service, showing the leveraged yield. This calculation appears in the discounted cash flow projections and other forecasting methods requiring year-to-year performance measures on a pre-tax basis.

Illustration: A&M Secure Storage Solutions operates a 200-unit self-storage facility in Houston. The A&M storage facility generates $850,000 NOI. Longhorn Metropolitan Casualty & Life, a regional life insurance company from Austin, Texas, funded a $9 million first mortgage. The annual debt service is $631,357, based on a five percent rate with a 25-year amortization schedule. The PTCF equates to $218,643.

Observation: PTCF focuses on the sensitivity of cash flow to debt service. If a project cash flow stream represents steady and predictable growth, PTCF mirrors this pattern, assuming fixed-rate debt service payments. However, erratic PTCF patterns indicate mismatched net operating income behavior vs. consistent debt service payments. The mismatch suggests various issues such as variable-rate debt fluctuations, a poorly-managed NOI, or a combination of both. Furthermore, using PTCF to analyze development projects and value-creation ventures lacking stabilized cash flow offers limited validity. In these cases, investors expect most of the profits to be at the sale of the property, not from annual operations.

In summary, PTCF represents an essential financial calculation for measuring the relationship of cash flow to debt payments. PTCF ideally suits non-profit organizations and other entities not subject to federal taxation. Even so, investments should be economically justified using PTCF since tax policy changes regularly occur. Most real estate investors pay federal taxes, which necessitates focusing on after-tax consequences, as illustrated by after-tax cash flow.

After-Tax Cash Flow

After-Tax Cash flow ("ATCF"), or Cash flow After Taxes ("CFAT"), is the next logical step of adjusting pre-tax cash flow for any income tax payments [or savings]. This cash flow computation accounts for debt service interest payments, depreciation, amortization, and other income tax liabilities, including state and federal obligations. And assuming the initial capital contribution remains unchanged and an amortizing fixed-rate loan encumbers the project, income tax benefits decrease over time due to principal accumulation and reduced depreciation allowances.

ATCF represents a highly-customized calculation and does not apply to all investors. The cash flow results vary depending on individual tax brackets, operating entities, and geographic origin of the venture and project, among other factors for generating different after-tax results. Also, non-taxable investors such as pension funds (PTCF equals ATCF) and some nonprofits bypass taxes altogether.

ATCF requires the following inputs for calculation: net operating income, debt service payment, loan amortization breakdown of principal and interest, cost recovery for improvements and personal property, amortization of loan points, and leasing commissions to generate the taxable income. Next, real estate taxable income gets multiplied by the applicable marginal tax rate to arrive at tax liability [savings]. Then, from NOI, the annual debt service is subtracted to equal the cash flow before taxes (CFBT). Finally, the cash flow after taxes (CFAT) is calculated from the CFBT, less the tax liability (savings) plus investment tax credit. ATCF breaks down as follows:

$$ATCF$$

$$\begin{gathered}
Net\ Operating\ Income \\
-\ Debt\ Service \\
= \\
Pre{\sim}Tax\ Cash\ Flow \\
-\ Depreciation \\
-\ Amortized\ loan\ cost \\
+\ Principal\ Recapture \\
= \\
Taxable\ Cash\ Flow \\
X \\
Investor\ Income\ Tax\ Rate \\
= \\
Income\ Tax\ Payment\ (or, +\ savings) \\
+\ Pretax\ Cash\ Flow \\
=
\end{gathered}$$

Illustration: Betty Buckeye of Columbus, Ohio, purchased the Highflyers Office Tower in Dayton for $45 million based on a net operating income of $3,630,000. Buckeye stays in the 30% tax bracket and depreciates the property at $923,077 per year based on an 80% building allocation and a 39-year straight-line depreciation schedule. She obtained $29,250,000 from Ohio State Mutual Assurance Life at a 4% rate, using a 25-year amortization schedule. As a result, the after-tax cash flow calculates to $850,419, as shown below.

FLYING YANKEES TOWER, 150,000 Ft.² OFFICE BUILDING, DAYTON OHIO		
Gross Potential Income @ $40 PSF (Gross) for 150,000 square feet	$	6,000,000
Purchase Price	$	45,000,000
Equity (Downpayment) at 35%	$	15,750,000
Total Project Cost (Original Price Plus Improvements)	$	45,000,000
First Mortgage	$	29,250,000
Monthly Mortgage Payment, 4% rate, 25-year Amortization	$	154,392.28
Total Interest Paid on Loan Over 12 months	$	1,157,344
Total Principal Reduction Over 12 months	$	695,364
Land Value (Original Purchase Price Appraisal)	$	9,000,000
Annual Depreciation Allowance, 80% of Purchase Price For 39 Years	$	923,077
Investor Income Tax Bracket		30%
INCOME AND EXPENSES		
Gross Income	$	6,000,000
Vacancy at 10%	$	(600,000)
Effective Gross Income	$	5,400,000
Expenses @ 45%	$	(2,430,000)
Net Operating Income	**$**	**2,970,000**
PRE-TAX CASH FLOW		
Net Operating Income	$	2,970,000
Annual Debt Service	$	(1,852,707)
Pre-Tax Cash Flow	**$**	**1,117,293**
AFTER-TAX CASH FLOW		
Pre-tax Cash Flow	$	1,117,293
Principal Payment Recapture	$	695,364
Annual Depreciation Allowance	$	(923,077)
Taxable Cash Flow	$	889,579
Income Tax Payment (Savings) Multiplied by Investor Tax Rate @ 30%	$	266,874

Pre-tax Cash Flow	$	1,117,293
Income Tax Payment (Savings) Multiplied by Investor Tax Rate @ 30%	$	(266,874)
After-Tax Cash Flow	**$**	**850,419**

Observation: The debt structure dramatically impacts ATCF. Profit objectives usually focus on income tax, leverage, and lower pricing. However, investors also hone in on the holding period. Market conditions change, demanding flexibility, sometimes even at the cost of sacrificing favorable income tax and yield objectives—the loan terms matter, including amortization, number of years, prepayment structure, and assumption provisions. For example, an attractive loan with stringent prepayment provisions locks the owner into a more restrictive hold strategy. Should the owner receive an unsolicited, captivating "all-cash" offer before loan maturity, a costly prepayment penalty interferes with the sale profitability -- especially during the earlier years of the holding period.

In summary, ATCF represents the income tax liabilities and savings of the annual cash flows. However, the most critical taxable event of the investment is usually the sale, known as the reversion.

Reversion

The reversion represents a lump-sum cash benefit that an investor receives or expects to receive upon the sale of an investment. This financial event is the ultimate or theoretical sale of a building after several years of holding the property. The reversionary value is thus the expected value of the building at that time.[67]

The reversion concludes the investment, resulting in either a profitable or unprofitable outcome at the end of the venture. Reversion analysis focuses on the exit strategy, mainly sale price and closing costs, shown in greater detail as follows:

INCOME PROPERTY REVERSION
SALES PRICE (INCOME)
Gross Sales Proceeds
Prepaid Expenses & Credits
Other
Gross Sales Proceeds
-
CLOSING COSTS (EXPENSES)
Loan Balance Payoff
Prepayment Penalties
Transfer Taxes & Fees
Legal, Title fees
Broker Sales Commissions
Other
Gross Sales Expenses
=
NET SALES PROFIT (LOSS)

The Income Property Reversion chart illustrates the essential elements of the reversion based on sales proceeds adjusted for closing costs. Sales proceeds include the gross price, prepaid expenses, and credits (real estate taxes, insurance). Additional proceeds account for agreed-upon contractual credits such as seller premiums and other items representing the sale profits. Lastly, sale expenses include the loan payoff, penalties, legal and title closing costs, transfer fees, and additional costs (e.g., participating loan payments, deferred equity, and interest premiums), resulting in a pre-tax net profit (loss). Income tax adjustments determine the taxable amount net of depreciation and ordinary-income or capital gain taxes [savings] to generate the after-tax profit [loss].

While reversion mathematics follows a logical flow, determining the resulting exit strategy remains challenging. Ownership optimally balances the decision to trigger a reversion with market timing, cash flow performance, and value at the time of sale. Market timing covers investment sales environment conditions, targeting the property type, size, interest rates, and other factors supporting the project's level of demand and liquidity. Cash flow performance emphasizes the investment lifecycle point, reflecting the level of financial profitability relative to similar competing properties. Naturally, well-performing properties generate premium values, reinforcing the buy-low-sell-high investment philosophy for timing the sale. Another factor to consider for properties encumbered by debt deals with the timing of any prepayment penalties.

Besides project economics, a capital improvement program is critical in deciding the reversion strategy. This discussion covers the physical condition of the property, functional obsolescence, and rent roll characteristics relating to turnover. Even if cash flow performance indicates outstanding yields, the longer-term outlook occasionally portends an earlier exit strategy. For instance, office properties with shorter-term leases typically require more tenant improvement and leasing commission reserves, indicating higher tenant retention and turnover costs vs. apartment properties. Requiring more capital expenditures than initially budgeted for the remaining holding period triggers the decision to sell the project sooner than planned.

Independent of project economics and capital improvements issues, ownership goals and objectives (particularly investor timeline preferences and income tax strategies) control reversion strategies. For instance, developers maintain shorter-term holding strategies linked to stabilizing and selling projects upon completion, usually between three months and three years. Such realty strategies often represent ordinary income tax planning, depending on the frequency and length of the development timeline. Conversely, many property owners acquire properties for asset appreciation, say five years or more. These longer-term strategies target capital gain income tax rates instead of higher ordinary income rates.

Modeling an ownership strategy for reversion draws similarities to designing military equipment based on the type of mission and resources. For instance, an aircraft carrier sails long distances, typically deployed for six months. This mission demonstrates steadiness and predictability. More importantly, the naval exercise helps maintain long-term peace in the region through the strategical show of force. Conversely, the tank covers a smaller, local radius deployed on specific missions close to the operating base. Tanks secure tactical targets, immediately returning to the military base. Institutional realty investors owning and operating longer-term strategic assets such as regional malls act like aircraft carriers. In contrast, local mom-and-pop investors acquiring properties in the community resemble tank platoons.[68]

Illustration: The SJMA Industrial Venture in Terrapin Park, Maryland, sold for $18 million. The owner netted $6,202,000 after paying all closing costs.

Adjustments to the sale price include credit for prepaid property taxes and installation of overhead cranes before closing. In addition to the loan payoff and prepayment penalties, the owner paid for brokerage commissions, attorney and title closing costs, transfer taxes, and a special assessment levied by the municipality. The chart below illustrates the reversion calculation.

INCOME PROPERTY REVERSION - SJMA INDUSTRIAL VENTURE	
SALES PRICE (INCOME)	**SALES PRICE (INCOME)**
Gross Sales Proceeds	$18,000,000
Prepaid Property Taxes	$180,000
Other - Overhead Cranes	$235,000
Gross Sales Proceeds	$18,415,000
-	-
CLOSING COSTS (EXPENSES)	**CLOSING COSTS (EXPENSES)**
Loan Balance Payoff	$11,450,000
Prepayment Fee @2% of Loan	$229,000
Transfer Taxes & Fees	$180,000
Legal, Title fees	$50,000
Broker Commission @1.5%	$270,000
Special Assessements Due	$34,000
Gross Sales Expenses	$12,213,000
=	=
NET SALES PROFIT (LOSS)	**$6,202,000**

Observation: Reversion yields include regular readjustments based on changing profitability expectations at any given time during the holding period. However, the shorter the holding period, the tighter the exit cap rate since the risk cushion reflects a narrower maturity risk element.

Upon reviewing the project's economic performance, the 4th P, the last step, requires determining the advantages and disadvantages of the investment. The 5th P, *pros/cons*, ties together the merits of the venture based on the preceding 4 Ps: people, place, project, and performance elements.

5. PROS/CONS

The Five P's closes with the final "P," known as "Pros/Cons." This process involves defining and quantifying all the positive (reward) and negative (risk) investment attributes. After that, depending upon the risk management strategy chosen, the decision is made whether or not the venture merits further investment consideration. The chart below provides examples of pros and cons based upon universal elements.

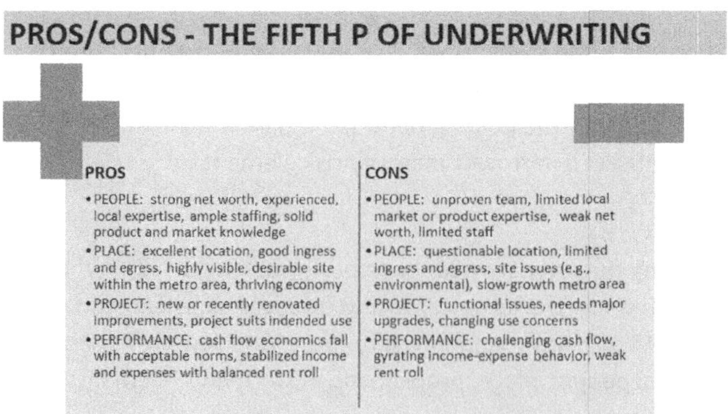

The chart presents a minimal list of pros and cons. In addition, other examples include many more details, specifically about the sponsorship, property type, location, etc. In addition, the flow of thinking to formulate meaningful pros and cons resembles the chart below.

THE FIVE "P"s of UNDERWRITING

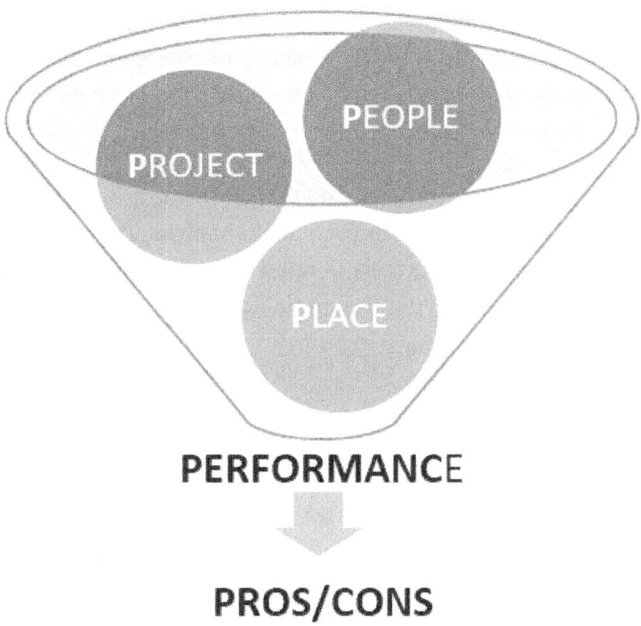

Illustration: Pepperdine Medical Investor Fund III, LLC identifies an attractive medical office property on the MariaCare Hospital campus in Redondo Beach, California. The project's location, physical condition, and financial performance demonstrate a potentially successful investment opportunity. However, Pepperdine appears insufficiently capitalized to carry the venture through significant hardships. Rather than bypassing this opportunity, Pepperdine's senior management team recommends raising more funds by adding extra investors to fortify the financial strength of the venture.

Observation: Pros/Cons discussions directly tie into due diligence and all other components of investment research. Ownership communications with all relevant players demand critical attention during the investigation process. If any research reveals significant issues, the transaction process requires reevaluation. "Go" vs. "No Go" should be reviewed step by step since an early bail-out beats wastefully expending precious time and resources.

In summary, most owners formally or casually use the 5 P's of real estate elements for underwriting an investment. Accurately underwriting the Five "P"s – people, place, project, performance, and pros/cons – requires understanding and quantifying risks from these different perspectives.

Since each investment features unique 5P risk/reward characteristics, the underwriting analysis differs with each deal. Applying the correct underwriting analysis leads to a more accurately defined risk/reward profile, improving the chances of financial success per the discussion below.

UNDERWRITING ANALYSIS

The underwriting analysis examines the merits and financial strength of the real estate investment based on the 5 P's research. Measuring investment profitability forms the basis for underwriting.

Investors gauge profitability using numerous techniques. These techniques measure different profit targets using the rudimentary concept of "return on capital." As such, the return-on-Investment ("ROI") is a universal benchmark for gauging profitability. ROI identifies the percentage change in investment value within a specified holding period. ROI yields three profit outcomes - increase, decrease, or unchanged value.

ROI yields vary according to real estate investment profiles, including anticipated holding periods. Investors target ROI yields matching risk tolerance levels given the intuition that higher risk should generate higher expected returns. But yield calculations sometimes provide different results for the same investment, depending on the timeframe used to calculate the yield within the holding period. As a result, investors use static and dynamic underwriting to capture such differences, bringing more clarity to the investment decision.

Static underwriting uses a single measurement to analyze a specific point in time within the holding period. The narrow focus of the one-period static approach provides minimal ROI yield results, ignoring the "big picture" analysis of the entire ownership time cycle.

Dynamic underwriting combines the appropriate static analysis tools to formulate a complete picture of ROI potential. And as needed, the dynamic multiple-periods (years) format allows additional adjustments to the cash flow streams for the time value of money during the holding period.

The following chart summarizes how static and dynamics underwriting formats compare:

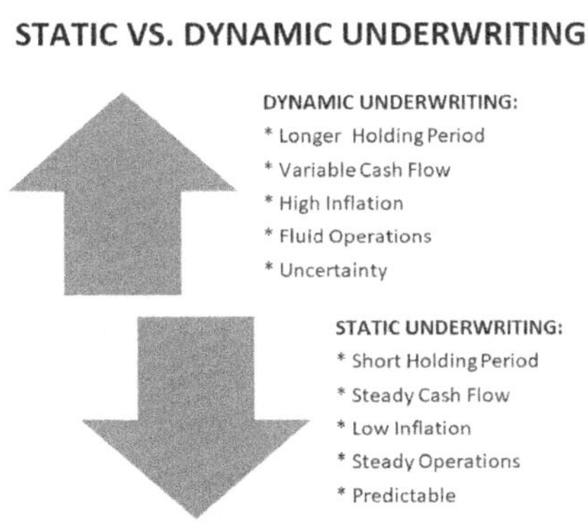

The chart stresses how dynamic underwriting applies to longer holding periods under conditions of cash flow uncertainty, including higher inflation, fluid operations, and fluctuating income. Conversely, static underwriting emphasizes cash flow analysis based on steady, predictable cash flows over one period. This single period can be trailing twelve months, the current year, or an annualized year-to-date metric.

The remainder of this chapter covers return-on-Investment, static, and dynamic underwriting analyses in greater detail.

RETURN ON INVESTMENT

Return on Investment ("ROI") represents "a measure of the value created by a real estate investment. It is the difference between the net gains from investing in the property less the net cost of investing in the property divided by the purchase price of the property. Usually, it is reported as a percentage." [69] Alternatively, ROI descriptions include the rate of return on capital, return on invested capital, investment return, and rate of return.[70] Used as a critical index for gauging profitability, the ROI calculates as follows:

$$ROI = \frac{Net\ Profit}{Net\ Investment} = \frac{Gain\ on\ Investment - Cost\ of\ Investment}{Cost\ of\ Investment}$$

The simplicity of ROI reflects the most basic investment principle - the return "on" capital. This ratio applies to the most complicated real estate ventures, ranging from discounting cash flows with assigned statistical probabilities to simple property "flips." Even as new underwriting techniques emerge, the building blocks remain the same – the profitability yield comparison of cash in vs. cash out of a venture to determine its profitability.

Despite this simplicity, ROI reigns as the "Master Equation of Real Estate," the essential profit measurement of any income-property calculation. The following illustration summarizes the significance of this ratio.

RETURN ON INVESTMENT: THE MASTER EQUATION OF REAL ESTATE

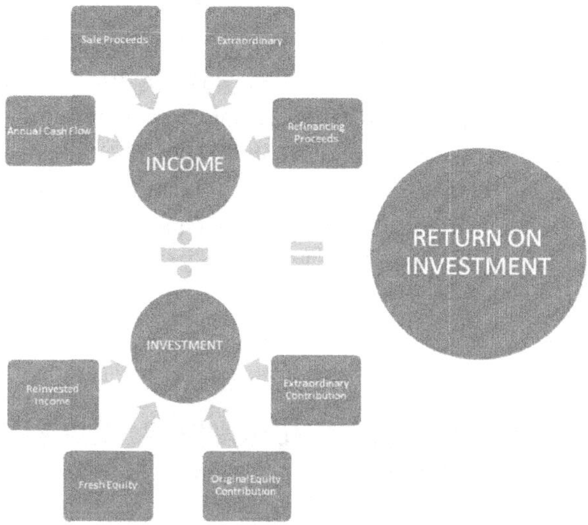

This diagram shows the most common forms of real estate income, such as annual cash flow, sales and refinancing proceeds, and any "catch-all" extraordinary items (e.g., special tax rebates) that ultimately generate profits. Realty investments include the original equity contribution, subsequent "fresh (new) equity" infusions, income reinvested into the venture, and any extraordinary capital calls.

ROI is related to indices using income/investment ratios in various forms. These indices include the capitalization rate, return-on-cost, the mortgage constant, debt yield, and cash-on-cash yield. Additional underwriting formulas help generate an ROI calculation, including the break-even point, debt service coverage ratio, loan-to-cost, loan-to-value, pre-tax cash flow, after-tax cash flow, payback period, and the net present value and internal rate of return.

These numerous indices represent different ROI yields to various investors involved in a real estate venture, namely lenders and investors. For instance, if a mortgage encumbers the real estate project, the lender resorts to various ROI benchmarks for the loan underwriting. The mortgage constant, including periodic principal repayment, represents the lender's cash-on-cash return if amortized. The loan "cap rate" provides a maximum debt ceiling defined as the Net Operating Income (NOI) divided by the Loan Amount. The break-even occupancy ratio, the default point, translates to the lender's return on cost (ROC). The breakeven occupancy results from computing total operating expenses added to the entire debt service. This numerator is divided by the potential rental income, defined as the income arising from full occupancy. And finally, both borrowers and lenders share NPV/IRR and payback periods for measuring the long-term metrics of investment contributions, particularly with projections based on variable cash flows. The chart below compares debt and equity sources usage and respective ROI indices, followed by a sample illustration.

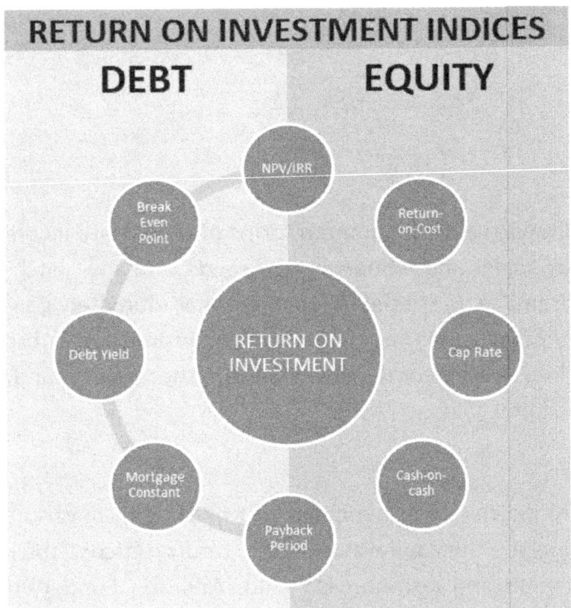

Illustration: Twenty-five years ago, Blue Devil Outdoor Recreational Property Corporation purchased an 18-hole golf course for $25 million in Duke, North Carolina. BD invested an additional $12 million in upgrading the club facilities and grounds. Blue Devil sold the golf course to a wealthy overseas investor for $52 million. As a result, BD achieved an ROI of 40.5% ($52,000,000-$37,000,000=$15,000,000/$37,000,000)

Observation: ROI helps define relative real estate performance, especially comparing various property types. However, depending on the stated income and investment capital, ROI yield distortion exists. For example, adding unrealized equity appreciation – namely, rising values and principal buildup from amortization – skews yearly yield. Dynamic underwriting quantifies this "latent" equity by applying discounted cash flow analysis, emphasizing the reversion and hence the equity gain (loss). NPV is a more comprehensive method to quantify ROI yield in such cases, as the present value of all the income streams is divided by the total capital investment.

This chapter discusses static and dynamic underwriting tools to measure ROI yields under various scenarios accurately.

STATIC UNDERWRITING

Due to simplicity, one-period static underwriting carries nicknames such as "calculator" and "back of the napkin" math. This underwriting technique forms the backbone of investment analysis by uncovering key ratios at exact points in time, measuring "static" risk and yield.

Static underwriting includes traditional investment calculations such as debt service coverages, loan-to-value ratios, and capitalization rates. Further analysis requires reviewing each ratio compared to standard and targeted benchmarks. Lastly, investors determine the relative importance of these statistics for generating appropriate investment conclusions.

Investors favor static underwriting for simplicity, consistency, and comparability. Ratios and percentages only require the basic math skills of addition, subtraction, division, and multiplication. Calculations generally remain consistent between measuring various types of investments, especially for gauging mortgage and other debt ratios. These calculations also compare to numerous published data sources.

Static underwriting consists of three popular formats: Simple Tests, Front Door/Back Door (aka, the Back of the Envelope Approach), and Debt Investment Cash flow Evaluation. A presentation of these follows.

SIMPLE TESTS

Simple tests cover fundamental real estate investment ratios and calculations for generating ROI yields to measure different elements of risk. These computations include capitalization rates, return-on-cost, loan-to-cost, loan-to-value, mortgage constant, debt service coverage ratio, debt yield, break-even point, pre-tax cash flow, after-tax cash flow, cash-on-cash, and payback period. Simple tests are further defined below, accompanied by descriptions, illustrations, and observations:

Capitalization Rate

The Capitalization Rate, or the total/overall cap rate, the going-in cap rate, or simply the cap rate, serves as one of the most popular ratios used to estimate property value. The cap rate refers to "The income rate of return for a total property that reflects the relationship between one year's net operating income expectancy and the total price or value. It's calculated by dividing the in-place net operating income by the sale price or value." [71]

$$Cap\ Rate = \frac{Net\ Operating\ Income}{Total\ \ Project\ Value}$$

The cap rate measures the initial all-cash investment return before obtaining any debt -- an unleveraged cash-on-cash return. The property sales price indicates the value at the acquisition if the purchase terms reflect an arms-length market transaction.

Industry professionals frequently use cap rates as primary calculations for measuring values. In appraisal, cap rates provide the foundation for one of the three methods of real estate valuation, the Income Approach.

Cap rates hovered between 4% and 8% for prime commercial properties during this century. Due to lower interest rates in recent years, property values often increased without necessarily improving cash flow performance. Such conditions create "cap rate compression," demonstrating that markets accept lower returns without benefiting from economic performance increases. The Capitalization Rate Sensitivity table illustrates cap rate compression by comparing increased values to cap rate equivalent yields as follows:

Cap Rate	CAPITALIZATION RATE SENSITIVITY Increasing Value ---> *Cap Rate Equivalent* *10%*	*9%*	*8%*	*7%*	*6%*	*5%*	*4%*	*3%*	*2%*	*1%*
10%	100%	11%	25%	43%	67%	100%	150%	233%	400%	900%
9%	-10%		13%	29%	50%	80%	125%	200%	350%	800%
8%	-20%	-11%	100%	14%	33%	60%	100%	167%	300%	700%
7%	-30%	-22%	-13%		17%	40%	75%	133%	250%	600%
6%	-40%	-33%	-25%	-14%	100%	20%	50%	100%	200%	500%
5%	-50%	-44%	-38%	-29%	-17%		25%	67%	150%	400%
4%	-60%	-56%	-50%	-43%	-33%	-20%	100%	33%	100%	300%
3%	-70%	-67%	-63%	-57%	-50%	-40%	-25%		50%	200%
2%	-80%	-78%	-75%	-71%	-67%	-60%	-50%	-33%	100%	100%
1%	-90%	-89%	-88%	-86%	-83%	-80%	-75%	-67%	-50%	

Key: Comparison of cap rate percentage value differences to other cap rates based on constant NOI.

Example: The same property previously valued at a 7% cap rate, currently appraises for 75% more value given a 4% cap rate equivalent. Alternatively, a property appraised at 5%, drops by 17%, if today's value reflects a 6% cap rate equivalent.

Comparing higher cap rates to lower cap rate equivalents shows the value adjustments when using the Income Approach based on the same net operating income. For example, if a shopping center previously sold for a 5% cap rate and dropped in value by about 30%, the change translates to a cap rate equivalent of about 7%. Or, if an investor purchases a property at a 6% cap rate, expecting a value increase of 20% from yield compression [price increase], the value needs to rise to a 5% cap rate.

Illustration: Scarlett Knights Extended Stay Lodging purchased a 300-room luxury hotel in downtown Rutgers, New Jersey, for $390,000 per room [key], or $117,000,000. At closing, the net operating income equated to $10,500,000, generating a 9% cap rate. However, Scarlett plans to renovate and reflag the hotel with a more prestigious brand, investing an additional $30 million, resulting in a total project cost of $147,000,000. This renovation will be completed within two years, with a target NOI of $12,200,000 and an expected reversion cap rate of 7%, or $174,300,000 ($581,000/key). The investor's "breakeven" cap rate is 8.3% (Target NOI/Total Project Cost), representing a 1.3% decrease in this ratio [vs. The reversion cap rate], indicating a profitable venture.

Observation: Cap rates rely entirely upon the accuracy of the net operating income to generate reliable results with the Income Approach. In some cases, investments such as vacant land may lack meaningful cash flow. As a result, appraisers and other experts use the Sales Comparison Approach (aka, Market Approach) and Cost Approaches as supplemental valuation methodologies. The Sales Comparison Approach focuses on similar property sales data for measuring value. The Cost Approach introduces the physical project costs to the valuation process: replacement cost, land value, new construction, and functional obsolescence concepts. The appraiser's challenge focuses on generating an accurate opinion of value that optimally blends these methodologies.

An investor's toolbox features several cash flow techniques backed by powerful computer modeling. Yet, the easy-to-calculate cap rate reigns as a significant investment analysis benchmark. However, like any toolbox, investors use other specialized indices, including those focusing on project cost, namely the return-on-cost ratio, a close cousin of the cap rate.

Return-on-Cost

A close cousin of the cap rate, return-on-Cost ("ROC") is a simple test that indicates the "wholesale" value of a real estate investment. The ratio considers the investment's total project cost, including capital expenditures (CapEx), divided by the net operating income. ROC ratio represents the break-even cap rate for ownership. The ROC climbs above the sale cap rate if the property sells at a profit. If sold at a loss, ROC drops below the cap rate. This ratio applies to acquiring an existing property, a ground-up development, or any other venture. In the case of new development, where the NOI remains unknown until project stabilization, the ROC is a calculated estimate. Upon stabilization, the ROC converts to an actual yield. An example of ROC is as follows:

$$ROC = \frac{Net\ Operating\ Income}{Total\ \ Project\ Cost}$$

The Return-on-Cost Sensitivity table compares profitability by measuring ROC against various cap rates.

RETURN-ON-COST SENSITIVITY															
Cap	Return-on-Cost (Percentage Profit/Loss Difference)														
Rate	10%	9.5%	9.0%	8.5%	8.0%	7.5%	7.0%	6.5%	6.0%	5.5%	5.0%	4.5%	4.0%	3.5%	3.0%
10.0%	100%	95%	90%	85%	80%	75%	70%	65%	60%	55%	50%	45%	40%	35%	30%
9.5%	105%	100%	95%	89%	84%	79%	74%	68%	63%	58%	53%	47%	42%	37%	32%
8.5%	118%	112%	106%	100%	94%	88%	82%	76%	71%	65%	59%	53%	47%	41%	35%
8.0%	125%	119%	113%	106%	100%	94%	88%	81%	75%	69%	63%	56%	50%	44%	38%
7.5%	133%	127%	120%	113%	107%	100%	93%	87%	80%	73%	67%	60%	53%	47%	40%
7.0%	143%	136%	129%	121%	114%	107%	100%	93%	86%	79%	71%	64%	57%	50%	43%
6.5%	154%	146%	138%	131%	123%	115%	108%	100%	92%	85%	77%	69%	62%	54%	46%
6.0%	167%	158%	150%	142%	133%	125%	117%	108%	100%	92%	83%	75%	67%	58%	50%
5.5%	182%	173%	164%	155%	145%	136%	127%	118%	109%	100%	91%	82%	73%	64%	55%
5.0%	200%	190%	180%	170%	160%	150%	140%	130%	120%	110%	100%	90%	80%	70%	60%
4.5%	222%	211%	200%	189%	178%	167%	156%	144%	133%	122%	111%	100%	89%	78%	67%
4.0%	250%	238%	225%	213%	200%	188%	175%	163%	150%	138%	125%	113%	100%	88%	75%
3.5%	286%	271%	257%	243%	229%	214%	200%	186%	171%	157%	143%	129%	114%	100%	86%
3.0%	333%	317%	300%	283%	267%	250%	233%	217%	200%	183%	167%	150%	133%	117%	100%

Key: Comparison of cap rates to return-on-cost ranges, 100%= break even, >100% as profitable, and <100% as loss.

Example: A project with a 6% ROC, shows an 18% profit if valued at 5.5%. Alternatively, a project yielding 5.5% ROC, reflects an 21% drop in value if currently appraised at 7%.

The table illustrates to intertwining relationship between ROC and the Income Approach to value. For example, a 6% ROC to target an 18% profit translates to a fifty-point-decreased cap rate (5.5%).

Illustration: Georgia State Regional Investors tried purchasing a ten-year-old core industrial building within Panther Logistics Distribution Park in Atlanta, Georgia. However, after an aggressive bidding war, the cap rate pricing dipped nearly three percent for this asset. Virtually no other similar quality assets exist within this highly desirable submarket. As a result, despite the timing, construction, and other development risks, Georgia State decided to pursue an alternative strategy of building a new warehouse building in the area based on an estimated 3.75% ROC.

Observation: Rising prices for various types of assets force investors to consider the new construction option. ROC gains relevance as a development benchmark since existing core-property pricing occasionally approaches or exceeds replacement costs.

In understanding project costs, obtaining third-party financing boosts yields; loan-to-cost ratios measure this phenomenon.

Loan-to-Cost

Loan-to-Cost ("LTC") represents a simple test ratio focusing on the loan amount compared to the total project cost. LTC measures a lender's risk exposure at the "wholesale" price level for stabilized assets and new construction or redevelopment ventures.

$$LTC = \frac{Loan\ Amount}{Project\ Cost}$$

Project costs carry different meanings. With existing stabilized projects, LTC and loan-to-value ratios generally reflect similar figures at the time of purchase, demonstrating that the purchase price and appraised property values closely match. Such a simple cost definition equates to the acquisition, not new construction.

LTC underwriting rarely works in a vacuum, often interchanging with LTV. For new construction, costs must justify values upon project completion/stabilization. If not, other indices dominate the analysis, namely loan-to-value. If the acquisition price dips below the lender's appraised value for existing projects, the LTC hovers below loan-to-value, presenting safer loan underwriting. Should the price climb above appraised value, the investor overpays, resulting in a LTC that exceeds the loan-to-value ratio, resulting in higher lending risk. Lenders choose the more conservative metric of the two underwriting benchmarks, with loans often quoted on the lower of LTC or LTV.

Typically, fundings occur within the fifty to seventy-five percent of the cost range for most projects. Higher leverage variations occur when justified by extraordinary conditions, such as more attractive LTVs, strong sponsorship, further credit enhancements, and additional profit participation.

In refinancing a stabilized property, LTC measures the equity appreciation based on the current appraised value vs. the total project cost basis aggregated during the investment holding period. If the appraised value dips below the project cost, the LTC represents a greater lending risk and vice versa. The Loan-to-Cost Sensitivity Analysis Based on the Exit Cap Rates table illustrates the LTC relationship between various reversionary cap rates affected by higher project costs.

LOAN-TO-COST SENSITIVITY BASED ON EXIT CAP RATES											
Exit	**» INCREASING COSTS** *(Return-on-Cost Valuation)* **»**										
Cap Rate	*10%*	*9.5%*	*9.0%*	*8.5%*	*8.0%*	*7.5%*	*7.0%*	*6.5%*	*6.0%*	*5.5%*	*5.0%*
10%	100%	105%	111%	118%	125%	133%	143%	154%	167%	182%	200%
9.5%	95%	100%	106%	112%	119%	127%	136%	146%	158%	173%	190%
9.0%	90%	95%	100%	106%	113%	120%	129%	138%	150%	164%	180%
8.5%	85%	89%	94%	100%	106%	113%	121%	131%	142%	155%	170%
8.0%	80%	84%	89%	94%	100%	107%	114%	123%	133%	145%	160%
7.5%	75%	79%	83%	88%	94%	100%	107%	115%	125%	136%	150%
7.0%	70%	74%	78%	82%	88%	93%	100%	108%	117%	127%	140%
6.5%	65%	68%	72%	76%	81%	87%	93%	100%	108%	118%	130%
6.0%	60%	63%	67%	71%	75%	80%	86%	92%	100%	109%	120%
5.5%	55%	58%	61%	65%	69%	73%	79%	85%	92%	100%	110%
5.0%	50%	53%	56%	59%	63%	67%	71%	77%	83%	91%	100%
4.5%	45%	47%	50%	53%	56%	60%	64%	69%	75%	82%	90%
4.0%	40%	42%	44%	47%	50%	53%	57%	62%	67%	73%	80%
3.5%	35%	37%	39%	41%	44%	47%	50%	54%	58%	64%	70%
3.0%	30%	32%	33%	35%	38%	40%	43%	46%	50%	55%	60%

Key: Assume 10% Mortgage Constant at 100% LTC for determining th lowest cost and highest leverage baseline. Compare exit cap rates to rising costs using ROI yields for generating declining LTC ratios.

Example: Project development at 6.5% return-on-cost generates a 85% loan-to-cost ratio based upon a 5.5% exit cap rate, requiring the investor to fund 15% equity. Or, 5% exit cap rate translates to a 91% LTC, if the project cost approximates a 5.5% ROC yield.

This table shows how lenders pay close attention to the LTC ratio. The chart indicates full funding (100% LTC) when the exit cap rate equals ROC pricing. ROC yields dipping below exit cap rates show project costs exceed values, indicating losses. Inversely, exit cap rates dropping below ROC yields support profitable sales transactions. However, lenders pay attention to the LTC ranges showing additional margins for equity, typically starting at twenty percent or more.

Illustration: Our Lady Holdings plans on developing a 200-unit apartment complex in South Bend, Indiana. The project construction costs are about $300,000 per unit, totaling $60 million. Our Lady requests an 80% LTC, or $48 million. The project value estimate computes $85 million upon completion and cash flow stabilization. USD Federal Savings Bank of San Diego feels secure with funding the loan to Our Lady since the loan-to-value will eventually lead to a conservative ratio of 56% LTC upon completion and stabilization.

Observation: LTC directly relates to the LTV ratio, as both indices measure justifiable funding levels. Sometimes, lenders inversely approach leverage underwriting by requiring minimum equity thresholds. In return, more competitive terms exist, such as favorable pricing, interest-only payments, and prepayment flexibility. Alternatively, "hard money" lenders dictate equity contribution terms for challenging ventures, demanding substantial equity, especially for unproven borrowers with limited track records and financial strength.

No discussion of lending ratios is complete without understanding the loan-to-value ratio.

Loan-to-Value

Loan-to-Value ("LTV") is a simple test that clearly defines the lender's risk profile, focusing on debt leverage as the critical underwriting benchmark. LTV measures risk exposure at the "retail" price level, based upon the appraised value or other agreed-upon value such as the purchase price, whichever is lower. The ratio is generated as follows:

$$LTV = \frac{Loan\ Amount}{Project\ Value}$$

Over several decades, lenders have traditionally underwritten permanent loans at 75% LTV or less. For example, over ninety percent of life insurance companies hold debt at LTVs of 71% or less.[72] Otherwise, higher LTV ratios signify funding sources are willing to assume more risk. An LTV ratio that approaches 100% implies a full or partial ownership position or the use of credit enhancements over and above the property collateral (e.g., personal guarantees, supplemental collateral).

Depending on interest rates and other factors, LTV underwriting metrics override other indices for structuring debt, namely DSCR (debt service coverage ratio or debt coverage ratio). The Loan-to-Value Sensitivity at 1.25 Debt Coverage Ratio demonstrates the values and mortgage rates LTV and DCR share familiar debt sizing territory.

LOAN-TO-VALUE SENSITIVITY at 1.25X DEBT COVERAGE RATIO										
Cap	Mortgage Rate (Interest-Only)									
Rate	10%	9.0%	8.0%	7.0%	6.0%	5.0%	4.0%	3.0%	2.0%	1.0%
10%	80%	89%	100%	114%	133%	160%	200%	267%	400%	800%
9%	72%	80%	90%	103%	120%	144%	180%	240%	360%	720%
8%	64%	71%	80%	91%	107%	128%	160%	213%	320%	640%
7%	56%	62%	70%	80%	93%	112%	140%	187%	280%	560%
6%	48%	53%	60%	69%	80%	96%	120%	160%	240%	480%
5%	40%	44%	50%	57%	67%	80%	100%	133%	200%	400%
4%	32%	36%	40%	46%	53%	64%	80%	107%	160%	320%
3%	24%	27%	30%	34%	40%	48%	60%	80%	120%	240%
2%	16%	18%	20%	23%	27%	32%	40%	53%	80%	160%
1%	8%	9%	10%	11%	13%	16%	20%	27%	40%	80%

Key: Assume static net operating income adjusted for 1.25X DSCR, divided by interest rate to generate maximum loan amount, then divided by value at cap rate.

Example: At a 9% interest-only mortgage applied with a 1.25X DSCR, a property valued at 8% cap rate yields a 71% LTV.

The table uses the long-standing industry benchmark of 1.25X DSCR for generating loan amounts based on a range of [interest-only] mortgage rates. The DSCR-based loan amounts translate to LTV calculations using different cap rates. For example, a 9%-mortgage restricted to a 1.25X DCR yields a 71% LTV based on an 8% cap rate.

Illustration: Ivy Cornell Properties of Ithaca, New York, purchased a fully occupied neighborhood shopping center for six million dollars, located within a block of the world-famous Niagara Falls. This older retail center includes established local souvenir shops and a convenience store, all secured by leases at significantly below-market rents with terms of five years or more. The purchase price reflects a ten percent cap rate. Furthermore, the land value of the center exceeds the purchase price by one million dollars, but in-place lease obligations prohibit redevelopment in the foreseeable future. At the same time, the National Park Service announced plans to renovate significant areas of the Falls over the next three years. This announcement dramatically impacts the center's short-term viability, given access restrictions. Due to positive deal dynamics, a local bank, Syracuse Orange Savings, funded the first mortgage of three million dollars, representing fifty percent of the purchase price. Although the bank had concerns about the cash flow risk resulting from the National Park announcement, the higher appraised land value created an additional risk mitigant, representing a more conservative 43% LTV.

Observation: LTV stands the test of time for judging debt leverage despite the popularity of other underwriting indices. As proof, the government-sponsored agencies (e.g., Freddie Mac) use LTV limits to set mortgage pricing, requiring mortgage insurance on loans above 80%.[73] Instead of selling assets, borrowers rely on higher LTVs to recover project equity by "cash-out" refinances. In these situations, the LTV ratios may exceed the borrowers' original equity – a significant concern for lenders. However, borrowers providing solid proof justifying value creation ("equity buildup") mitigate these concerns. If supported by project performance, the length of ownership holding period also addresses cash-out concerns; the longer the hold, the better the chance of cash out, as lenders observe more borrower time commitment to the investment.

In addition to measuring essential cost and value ratios, analyzing the cash flow quality provides further depth to the real estate investment underwriting process, as demonstrated by the debt service coverage ratio.

Mortgage Constant

The Mortgage Constant ("K"), or loan constant, is a simple multiplier applied to the loan amount to arrive at a level payment to retire the debt by payments of principal & interest over the specified term, usually 15, 20, 25, or 30 years. Said another way, the mortgage constant represents the annual payment of principal and interest stated as a yield. The difference between the mortgage constant and the interest rate represents the principal payment portion. With a standard amortizing loan, each subsequent payment proportionally includes additional principal buildup, resulting in less of an interest portion. The shorter the amortization schedule, the faster the principal repayment. The longer the amortization schedule, the less significant the principal repayment, as interest is a more substantial portion of the payment.

The first step for generating the mortgage constant necessitates computing the [monthly] debt service payments based upon a specified interest rate for a specific loan amount over a specified amortization period, shown below, but most often generated with a financial calculator or spreadsheet.[74]

$$A = P\frac{r(1+r)^n}{(1+r)^n - 1}$$

Where,

A = Amount to be paid per [monthly] period

P = Principal (loan amount)

r = interest rate per [monthly] period

n = total number of [monthly] payment periods; amortization period

After that, the monthly payment is multiplied by twelve to generate annual debt service, then divided by the loan amount to arrive at the mortgage constant.

$$Mortgage\ Constant\ "K" = \frac{Annual\ Debt\ Service}{Loan\ Amount}$$

Given the principal-repayment component, the mortgage constant requires a higher payment than an interest-only calculation at the same interest rate. In effect, the mortgage constant represents additional safety for lenders, as principal payments reduce the loan amount (outstanding loan balance) during the term. For borrowers, the higher payment acts as a “forced savings account,” helping build project equity, assuming property values stay the same or continue to rise while the loan exists. Regarding ROI indices, the mortgage constant calculation resembles the cap rate and return-on-cost calculations but replaces NOI with annual debt service and value/cost with the loan amount.

The mortgage constant equates to the lender's cap rate, otherwise known as the "mortgage cap rate."

Loans tied to an amortization schedule that allow full repayment over the amortization period are known as "self-amortizing" or "fully-amortizing" debt. The loan balance returns to zero at the end of the term. Loans seldom match the amortization timeline. The loan term is typically shorter than the amortization period due to the weighted average maturity of all tenant leases, frequently spanning ten years or less for commercial properties. These loans often retire sooner, either by refinancing or sale. By some estimates, the average life of a loan spans only three to five years.[75] Regardless of the term, lenders still use the mortgage constant as a loan underwriting tool for stress-testing the cash flow tolerance against various debt payment structures. The Mortgage Constant Sensitivity Table below illustrates how multiple rates and amortization influence loan balances.

MORTGAGE CONSTANT SENSITIVITY		
Mortgage%/	Loan Balance	
Amortization/K%	Year 5	Year 10
3%/20yrs/6.66%K	80%	57%
3%/30yrs/5.06%K	89%	76%
4%/20yrs/7.27%K	82%	60%
4%/30yrs/5.73%K	90%	79%
5%/20yrs/7.92%K	83%	62%
5%/30yrs/6.44%K	92%	81%

Key: Mortage Rate/Amortization[Years]/Constant

As the chart demonstrates, the lowest rate (3%) with the fastest amortization (20 years) indicates a loan paydown of 57% by the tenth year based on a mortgage constant of 6.66%. Conversely, the highest rate (5%) offers a lower mortgage payment but barely creates about a twenty percent loan pay-down during the same time. Also, the 30-year amortization schedule allows ten percent of the loan to be paid off over five years, illustrating how significant loan payback does not occur on shorter-term maturities.

The increasing-principal/decreasing-interest formula used for the mortgage constant presents cash flow yield issues relating to taxable income for the investor using debt. The faster loan paydown resulting from [shorter] amortization, the lower the income tax write-offs, diminishing net after-tax cash flow. The interest portion of debt service remains deductible in contrast to the non-deductible principal component.

Illustration: Big Blue Wolverine Credit Union of Ann Arbor, Michigan, funded a $3,000,000 first mortgage at an interest rate of 3.25% based on a 25-year amortization schedule, resulting in a monthly debt payment of $14,619. The annualized $175,434 debt service divided by the loan amount generates a 5.85% mortgage constant.

Observation: Deciding mortgage constants frequently involves negotiations between lenders and borrowers. Most borrowers targeting maximum cash flow insist on interest-only pricing. Conversely, lenders seeking more secure loans insist on some form of amortization. Shorter-term loans of five years or less for stabilized assets produce minimum principal paydown given a reduced loan maturity term risk. Development projects and other value-add ventures hope to create more investment value, so loan-amortization strategies rarely apply until project stabilization occurs. A compromise position is having interest-only (IO) payments for the years leading up to project stabilization, say 2-3 years. Subsequently, loan amortization (principal and interest payment) is required. Lastly, conservatively leveraged loans, typically 65% LTV or less, seldom need amortization as substantial equity exists. Another simple test, the debt service coverage ratio, also measures loan risk profiles.

Debt Service Coverage

In addition to measuring total cost and mortgage leverage ratios, exploring cash flow payment margins using the debt service coverage ratio ("DSCR") provides more loan underwriting clarity.

Along with the loan-to-value ratio, debt service coverage ("DCR," "DSCR") ranks as the most meaningful or critical static test for analyzing all types of projects encumbered with debt, hybrid debt, and preferred equity. The DCR measures the investment's ability to pay debt service by calculating how many times the income covers the debt service payment. Dividing the annual NOI by the total debt payment generates the ratio shown as follows:

$$DCR = \frac{Net\ Operating\ Income}{Debt\ Service}$$

DCR should reflect a percentage above 100% (or 1X), with acceptable levels of 120% (1.2X) or more for conventional properties and at least 130% (1.3X) for non-conventional assets. In some instances, DCRs as low as 100% are possible based on credit tenant income. The margin above 1.0 (e.g., the extra 30% coverage above a 100% DCR) represents a cash cushion or margin of safety, allowing for more income and expense volatility. This higher DCR requirement indicates a riskier loan; therefore, a higher cash cushion is necessary.

If proper cash flow enhancements exist, lenders will underwrite negative debt service coverage ratios (i.e., DCRs below break-even levels or less than 100%), such as interest-rate reserves and credit enhancements. Negative DCR typically applies to pre-stabilized projects (e.g., new construction) or contractual rent bumps justifying short-term payment deficits.

DCR addresses the issue of structuring additional layers of financing with various solutions. The extra funds include supplemental debt service payments to DCR calculations. Senior debt funding sources often apply the same coverage tests for combined debt vs. primary debt. Also, DCR is used dynamically for future funding of additional debt according to increased values and cash flow performance. Lastly, debt service secured through unrecorded liens backed by investor obligations (e.g., preferred equity payments) bypass the combined DCR tests with the permission of the primary funding source.

The type of mortgage payment, whether interest-only or inclusive of amortization, influences DCR tests. A loan features a higher DCR if payments are interest-only. However, even with an interest-only payment structure, lenders often apply DCR limits based on mortgage constants assuming amortization, adding the additional safety cushion to the underwriting equation. Furthermore, extending the amortization periods translates to lower mortgage constants that generate higher loans, while shortening amortization creates the opposite effect.

A complimentary ratio based on DCR, known as the Point of Insolvency, provides additional guidelines as discussed as follows:

$$\text{Point of Insolvency} = 1-(1/DCR) = BTCF/NOI$$

The point of insolvency indicates the percentage tolerance level of the NOI for reaching insolvency. The higher the DCR, the more significant the percentage decline in NOI the project can tolerate before loan default occurs. If the lender requires a DCR of 1.3X (or 130%), for example, then the point of insolvency equates to 0.23 (=1/(1/1.3)). In other words, NOI can decline by 23% before default (NOI<Debt Service) occurs.

Lenders require that debt service coverage typically be in the 1.2X to 1.5X range for conventional properties. DCRs for lodging and more special-purpose property underwriting reach as high as 2X coverage. These property types feature more risks due to the higher volatility of cash flows. DCRs below the 1.2X threshold usually include cash flow stabilization projects or development ventures. As an illustration, the Debt Service Coverage Ratio Sensitivity table compares different DSCR underwriting points based upon a 7% mortgage constant set at breakeven coverage (1X).

	DEBT SERVICE COVERAGE RATIO SENSITIVITY										
DSCR	Intrest Rate (Mortgage Constant) & DSCR vs. 7% Breakeven DSCR										
"X"	7%	6.5%	6.0%	5.5%	5.0%	4.5%	4.0%	3.5%	3.0%	2.5%	2.0%
1.00	1.00	1.08	1.17	1.27	1.40	1.56	1.75	2.00	2.33	2.80	3.50
1.05	1.05	1.13	1.23	1.34	1.47	1.63	1.84	2.10	2.45	2.94	3.68
1.10	1.10	1.18	1.28	1.40	1.54	1.71	1.93	2.20	2.57	3.08	3.85
1.15	1.15	1.24	1.34	1.46	1.61	1.79	2.01	2.30	2.68	3.22	4.03
1.20	1.20	1.29	1.40	1.53	**1.68**	1.87	2.10	2.40	2.80	3.36	4.20
1.25	1.25	1.35	1.46	1.59	1.75	1.94	2.19	2.50	2.92	3.50	4.38
1.30	1.30	1.40	1.52	1.65	1.82	2.02	2.28	2.60	3.03	3.64	4.55
1.35	1.35	1.45	1.58	1.72	1.89	2.10	2.36	2.70	3.15	3.78	4.73
1.40	1.40	1.51	1.63	1.78	1.96	2.18	2.45	2.80	3.27	3.92	4.90
1.45	1.45	1.56	1.69	1.85	2.03	2.26	2.54	2.90	3.38	4.06	5.08
1.50	1.50	1.62	1.75	1.91	2.10	2.33	2.63	3.00	3.50	4.20	5.25

Key: Debt Service Coverage Ratios compared to a 7% mortgage constant at break even (1.00 or 1X).

Example: Compared to a 7% mortgage constant ("K") at 1.20X debt service coverage ratio, 5%K supports a 1.68X coverage, based on the same cash flow.

The DSCR table shows lower rates produce higher coverage than debt with higher mortgage constants. However, the lower ranges also translate to shorter amortization schedules. For example, the table shows that the debt coverage improves from 1.2X to 1.68X when the mortgage constant drops from 7% to 5%, translating to forty percent more debt coverage or more borrower cash flow if maintaining the 1.2X.

Illustration: The Sun Devil Automotive Plaza of Tempe, Arizona, generates an NOI of $820,000, based on a single-tenant lease that expires in two years. This credit tenant recently agreed to extend the lease for an additional ten years for $880,000 annually. The ownership seeks a maximum loan amount based upon paying a four percent rate with a 30-year amortization schedule for a ten-year term (5.73%K). Applying a 1.25X DCR to the current income limits the maximum loan amount to $11,450,548. However, in two years, the supportable loan equates to $12,288,393 using the same rate and amortization. Should the lender initially agree to underwrite a higher loan amount, the DSCR drops to 1.16X, deemed an acceptable underwriting risk due to the pending contractual lease increase in two years.

Observation: The relevance of the debt service coverage ratio as an underwriting benchmark varies with mortgage rate cycles. DCR surpasses LTV as the most relevant static underwriting test during high-interest rate periods when values often decline. LTV governs loan proceeds during low-interest-rate cycles, as DCR levels automatically reach higher thresholds.

More recently, lenders introduced an alternative to DCR. Known as the Debt Yield, or Debt Yield Ratio ("DYR"), this simple test calculation draws more attention to the senior loan proceeds as the centerpiece of analysis.

Debt Yield

The Debt Yield Ratio ("DYR") is derived by dividing the NOI by the senior mortgage loan amount. In this context, DYR equates to the "lender's cap rate." In other words, in the event of foreclosure, this yield reflects the lender's "purchase price" based on the loan amount. DYR represents the lender's risk-adjusted mortgage constant underwritten to a 1.0X DSCR ratio for generating maximum loan proceeds. However, the [higher] debt yield pricing calculation differs from the [lower] mortgage constant used for actual debt service calculations.

The debt yield formula, as part of the ROI index family, is expressed as follows:

$$DY = \frac{Net\ Operating\ Income}{Senior\ Loan\ Amount}$$

The larger the debt yield, the lower the underwritten loan amount. This inverse relationship provides an additional benchmark for underwriting in a worst-case foreclosure scenario. For instance, if the property sold at a cap rate equal to or below the stated DYR, the lender successfully recovered the loan amount.

Debt funding sources favor the DYR as an additional leverage restriction. This test ignores debt coverage ratios, mortgage constants, LTV, LTC, and cap rate measurements. Instead, the DYR serves as a highly conservative yield for capitalizing the net operating income to reflect lower loan proceeds than other indices might allow. This formula bypasses any appraisal interpretations of value, as a single risk-adjusted rate determines the loan amount.

Minimum debt yield ratios used by lenders are typically in the higher single-digit-to-lower-teens range. However, like mortgage and cap rates, the debt yield moves with market changes, as lenders need to remain competitive.[76]

The Debt Yield Sensitivity table below illustrates how cap rates and LTV ratios influence DY underwriting. The DSCR chart demonstrates lower rates impact coverage than debt with higher mortgage constants. Lower coverages translate to shorter amortization schedules, not necessarily reflecting more risk associated with lower DSCRs.

DEBT YIELD SENSITIVITY

	Debt Yield to Cap Rate Conversion Based Upon LTV Ratio at 6% Rate/100% LTV Baseline										
LTV	6%	6.5%	7.0%	7.5%	8.0%	8.5%	9.0%	9.5%	10.0%	10.5%	11.0%
100%	6.00%	6.50%	7.00%	7.50%	8.00%	8.50%	9.00%	9.50%	10.00%	10.50%	11.00%
95%	5.70%	6.18%	6.65%	7.13%	7.60%	8.08%	8.55%	9.03%	9.50%	9.98%	10.45%
90%	5.40%	5.85%	6.30%	6.75%	7.20%	7.65%	8.10%	8.55%	9.00%	9.45%	9.90%
85%	5.10%	5.53%	5.95%	6.38%	6.80%	7.23%	7.65%	8.08%	8.50%	8.93%	9.35%
80%	4.80%	5.20%	5.60%	6.00%	6.40%	6.80%	7.20%	7.60%	8.00%	8.40%	8.80%
75%	4.50%	4.88%	5.25%	5.63%	6.00%	6.38%	6.75%	7.13%	7.50%	7.88%	8.25%
70%	4.20%	4.55%	4.90%	5.25%	5.60%	5.95%	6.30%	6.65%	7.00%	7.35%	7.70%
65%	3.90%	4.23%	4.55%	4.88%	5.20%	5.53%	5.85%	6.18%	6.50%	6.83%	7.15%
60%	3.60%	3.90%	4.20%	4.50%	4.80%	5.10%	5.40%	5.70%	6.00%	6.30%	6.60%
55%	3.30%	3.58%	3.85%	4.13%	4.40%	4.68%	4.95%	5.23%	5.50%	5.78%	6.05%
50%	3.00%	3.25%	3.50%	3.75%	4.00%	4.25%	4.50%	4.75%	5.00%	5.25%	5.50%

Key: Assume 6% Mortgage Constant at 100% LTV as the baseline, generating/comparing debt yields to cap rates at LTV different ranges.

Example: A 6% debt yield at 100% LTV equates to a 6% cap rate; a 6% DY=7.5% cap rate at 80% LTV; an 8% cap rate at 75% LTV; and, 10% cap rate at 60% LTV.

The Debt Yield (DY) table, for example, shows that a loan amount generated by a 6% DY translates to an equivalent of a loan underwritten to a 7.5% cap rate with an 80% LTV. Underwriting reassembles the project value using the DY as a "stressed mortgage constant."

Illustration: Tyger Apartments, a 25-year-old mid-rise multifamily complex in Princeton, New Jersey, recently appraised for $38,000,000. The project supports a $2,250,000 NOI, translating to a 5.92% cap rate. The Tulane Mortgage Fund of New Orleans offers a 5% interest-only rate using a 9.68% debt yield for underwriting older apartments in smaller markets. As a result, the maximum loan amount available is $23,200,000, indicating 61% LTV, along with a 1.94X DSCR.

Observation: Debt yields and cap rates share many similarities. The debt yields are initially higher than cap rates since the loan amount is less than the property's value. Lenders gain assurance of carrying the loan below appraised values, primarily if the mortgage rate spreads over comparable-term US Treasuries reach a comfortable range of 300 basis points or more. If the mortgage spreads between these two indices appear too wide, lenders are reluctant to accept higher valuations via lower cap rates. Should spreads narrow, borrowers take advantage of more competitive financing options, as lenders assume higher default risks based on yield compression.

The break-even point also works as another loan ratio used by lenders.

Break-Even Point

Another simple test alternative to the DCR and the DYR, the Break-Even Point, bypasses net operating income for testing static cash flows.

The break-even point ("BEP") is also known as the break-even ratio, default point, break-even occupancy ratio, breakpoint, minimum cash flow threshold, or zero cash flow. BEP refers to "The stage at which an investment produces an income that is just sufficient to cover recurring expenditures. For an investment in real property, the point at which gross income is equal to ordinary operating expenses, including debt service (the stage at which the following cash flow stream becomes positive).[77] Or more simply, BEP represents the occupancy percentage level necessary for the rental income to cover all annual expenses, including debt service. The break-even point cash flow calculates as follows:

$$BEP = \frac{Operating\ Costs + Debt\ Service}{Gross\ Income}$$

Unlike debt service coverage, BEP focuses on operating costs instead of net income, ultimately honing in on the occupancy level necessary to pay all the bills and keep the lights on. Favorable BEP ratios indicate lower break-even points, resulting in more substantial cash flow safety margins. Alternatively, higher ratios indicate weak income cushions and more risk. Acceptable occupancy break-even levels typically reach eighty percent, depending on property type and market conditions. Otherwise, many lenders require occupancy levels approaching ninety percent.

The BEP works most effectively for gauging occupancy levels of multi-tenant "granular rent roll" investments, namely apartments, lodging, self-storage, and select retail or industrial properties. Those assets relying upon fewer tenants or single-tenant lease profiles demonstrate too much binary risk for this ratio. Should one or two such tenants vacate the premises, the occupancy levels may dip below fifty percent or even zero (single-tenant).

BEP offers limited accuracy, as actual occupancy requirements fluctuate with rental rate adjustments, often varying above or below market averages (credit vs. local tenants). Also, investors typically exclude miscellaneous rents and other smaller income items from the occupancy calculations. Finally, some expenses will vary with occupancy levels, thereby affecting accuracy.

The Break-Even Point Sensitivity table below describes cash flow volatility at different BEPs and mortgage constants.

BREAK EVEN POINT SENSITIVITY											
Break Even Point Using Full Mortgage Constant Payment at 10% Baseline (Gross Income - Debt Service)											
BEP	10%	9.5%	9.0%	8.5%	8.0%	7.5%	7.0%	6.5%	6.0%	5.5%	5.0%
100%	100%	95%	90%	85%	80%	75%	70%	65%	60%	55%	50%
95%	95%	90%	86%	81%	76%	71%	67%	62%	57%	52%	48%
90%	90%	86%	81%	77%	72%	68%	63%	59%	54%	50%	45%
85%	85%	81%	77%	72%	68%	64%	60%	55%	51%	47%	43%
80%	80%	76%	72%	68%	64%	60%	56%	52%	48%	44%	40%
75%	75%	71%	68%	64%	60%	56%	53%	49%	45%	41%	38%
70%	70%	67%	63%	60%	56%	53%	49%	46%	42%	39%	35%
65%	65%	62%	59%	55%	52%	49%	46%	42%	39%	36%	33%
60%	60%	57%	54%	51%	48%	45%	42%	39%	36%	33%	30%
55%	55%	52%	50%	47%	44%	41%	39%	36%	33%	30%	28%
50%	50%	48%	45%	43%	40%	38%	35%	33%	30%	28%	25%

Key: Assume 10% Mortgage Constant at Breakeven with no expenses.

Example: Compared to a 10% Constant at a full (100%) break even point, a rate drop to an 8% Constant and 70% BEP requirement, allows the gross income to drop 44% -- reaching the break even point of 56%.

Lower rates and occupancy levels illustrate a range of cash flow stress tests using a 10% mortgage constant as a break-even point. For example, dropping the mortgage constant to 8% and adjusting to a 70% occupancy level allows the gross income to plummet by 44%, reaching a break-even point of 56%.

Illustration: Hoya Student Towne Center, a new multifamily development in Washington, DC, features 150 micro apartments averaging $1,700 per month, offering a gross potential income of $3,060,000. The annual operating expenses equate to $1,071,000. The property value is $39,800,000 using a five percent cap rate based upon $1,989,000 NOI. The project carries a first mortgage of $31,824,000 (80% LTV) at a four percent rate, interest-only, resulting in annual debt service payments of $1,113,840. As a result, the BEP calculates just over 71% occupancy at current rents since $2,184,840 equates to a break-even sum.

Observation: Break-even point tests work best by using sensitivity analysis. For instance, reducing replacement reserves and increasing rents generate lower occupancy break-even thresholds. Alternatively, more conservative income/expense assumptions burden the cash flow, resulting in higher BEP levels. Too many adjustments to expenses or debt service payments distort this index.

In addition to BEP, cash-on-cash ranks as a reliable realty investment ratio.

Cash-On-Cash

Cash-on-cash return ("COC") is a simple test representing an annual rate of return on the investor's equity contribution to a real estate venture. This financial ratio ranks extremely popular among investors, carrying many different names. Synonyms for cash-on-cash include the equity yield rate, equity cap rate, equity dividend rate, cash throw-off rate, pretax cap rate, and equity IRR.[78] The COC is as follows:

$$COC = \frac{Annual\ Cash\ Flow}{Equity\ Investment}$$

The COC shows the first year of cash flow divided by the downpayment upon acquisition. In the case of an all-cash purchase, COC equates to the cap rate and return-on-cost (assuming no additional equity contribution). Depending upon the depth of analysis, COC reflects positive [negative] yields on pre-tax and after-tax cash flows.

Illustration: Brigham Young Memorial Realty Fund recently purchased Cougar Coves apartments in Salt Lake City, Utah. The acquisition highlights include a $2,400,000 purchase price supported by a $168,000 stabilized NOI (7% cap rate), translating to $100,000 per unit cost. Young obtained a $1,800,000 (75% LTV) first mortgage at a 3.75% for a ten-year term, featuring a 30-year amortization schedule, requiring payments of $8,336 per month (5.56% K). As illustrated below, the first year of operations results in an 11.33% pre-tax COC return.

PURCHASE PRICE & LOAN TERMS		
Purchase Price	$	2,400,000
Less Downpayment (Equity)	$	(600,000)
Loan Amount	$	**1,800,000**
Multiplied by Mortgage Constant (3.75%, 30-year Amorization)		5.56%
Annual Debt Service	$	(100,033)

PRE-TAX CASH FLOW		
Net Operating Income	$	168,000
Less by Annual Debt Service Payment	$	(100,033)
Cash Flow	$	**67,967**

CASH-ON-CASH YIELD		
Pre-Tax Cash Flow	$	67,967
Divided by Equity Contribution	$	600,000
Cash Flow		**11.33%**

Observation: Cash-on-cash ignores asset appreciation, providing a quick snapshot of equity performance at a selected year within the holding period. If calculated annually, COC integrates with other indices for forming dynamic underwriting, namely net present value and IRR.

Investors still use other static ratios, including the payback period.

Payback Period

In addition to measuring yields as with COC, investors monitor financial performance relating to liquidity. The Payback Period reflects such underwriting, calculating the length of time necessary to recover the equity investment from projected cash flow.

The Payback Period ("PB") measures the years necessary for the investment to break even; the time needed to achieve full capital recovery. The payback formula calculates the cumulative equity requirements, divided by the expected annual cash flow stream, shown in years as follows:

$$PB = \frac{Cumulative\ Equity}{Annual\ Cash\ Flow}$$

Term and liquidity form the backbone of payback analysis: the shorter the payback period, the more profitable the venture. Development deals, "flip," value-add, and opportunity ventures garner shorter holding periods. Shorter holding periods with substantial value creation hardly fit annualized cash flow calculations, as the income fluctuates heavily, emphasizing the reversion. More extended payback periods reflect lower-yielding investments paid off more gradually. Core and core-plus investments usually involve longer-term payback strategies. Furthermore, payback periods lengthen or contract, depending upon debt terms, pre-tax or after-tax analysis, and other underwriting variables.

Investors view the payback period from two viewpoints, first, as a risk management tool. Different iterations measure the time required to recapture the equity contribution(s). Second, the payback period helps define the projected holding period.

The Payback Period Sensitivity chart shows the logarithmic relationship between capitalization rates and investment capital recovery.

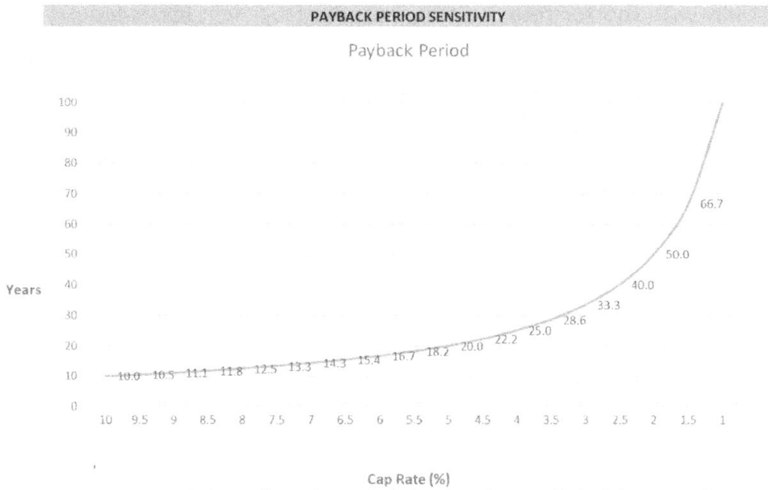

Key: Assume Cap Rate reflects unleverage annual return with average (flat) cash flows each year

Example: 5.5% cap rate investment fully repaid in 18.2 years.

Based on calculating average cash flows compared to the initial investment, the chart illustrates a payback range of ten to a hundred years displayed in order of decreasing cap rates. For example, a 5.5% cap rate investment requires 18.2 years (1÷5.5%) to recover the principal amount.

Illustration: The Columbia Lion Property Investment Syndicate purchased a single-tenant, net-lease property secured by a long-term lease in New York City. A drugstore tenant occupies the property with a remaining term of eight years and six months. After accounting for contractual rent increases, the rent averages $31,800 per month. The investor paid $7.2 million on an "all cash" basis reflecting a 4.5% capitalization rate. The expected payback on this retail property equates to 8.87 years ($7,200,000 / ($31,800 *12) = 8.87). The liquidity risk extends beyond the lease term (8.87 vs. 8.5 years). However, Columbian Lyon gains comfort with the prime location because the re-leasing risk extends slightly beyond the payback holding period.

Observation: The payback period, like other static underwriting tools, ignores discounted cash flow analysis, favoring predictable annual cash flow streams. During prolonged low-interest-rate cycles, PB demonstrates reliable results due to the minimal impact of discounting on the cost of money. "Flat" contractual cash flow streams (e.g., net lease ventures) comfortably fit this metric, especially with shorter-term holding periods. However, extended payback periods often mask more profitable deals as appreciation benefits are ignored. Regardless, PB serves as a leading benchmark for deciding an investment holding period, providing the additional term "cushion." The extra months, or years, potentially reflect better risk underwriting by allowing more time to recover cash invested.

Static ratios are most effective when combined with various simple tests. The following case study illustrates static underwriting on a specific project using the cap rate, return-on-cost, loan-to-cost, loan-to-value, mortgage constant, debt service coverage, debt yield, break-even point, and cash-on-cash ratios.

Simple Test Case Study

The Lui Garden Apartments, located in Honolulu, Hawaii, consists of a 120-unit multifamily facility, averaging $2000 per month. After purchasing the property for $23,500,000, the owner obtained a 75% loan, translating to a $5,875,000 down payment. Lui Crockett plans to spend an additional $1,200,000 on a renovation program expected to generate higher income. Rents are projected to increase from $1,594,461 to $1,750,000 over the next five years as the program is completed. Key transaction highlights are as follows.

LUI GARDEN APARTMENTS, HONOLULU, HAWAII - ASSUMPTIONS		
Monthly Rent	$	2,000
Appraised Value	$	26,575,000
Original Purchase Price	$	23,500,000
Equity (Downpayment)	$	5,875,000
Project Renovation/Capital Improvements Program Cost	$	1,200,000
Total Project Cost (Original price plus improvements)	$	24,700,000
First Mortgage	$	17,625,000
Monthly Mortgage Payment, 4% rate, 30-year amortization	$	84,144
Total Interest Paid on Loan over 12 months	$	699,351
Total Principal Reduction over 12 months	$	310,383
Land Value (Original Purchase Price Appraisal)	$	4,700,000
Annual Depreciation Allowance, 80% of Purchase Price for 27.5 Years	$	683,636
Investor Income Tax Bracket		30%

INCOME AND EXPENSES		
Gross Income	$	2,880,000
Vacancy at 5%	$	(144,000)
Effective Gross Income	$	2,736,000
Expenses	$	(1,141,539)
Net Operating Income	**$**	**1,594,461**
Projected Average Net Operating Income after Renovation, during 5-year hold	**$**	**1,760,000**

Each static underwriting measure rests on transaction economics, as discussed below.

CAPITALIZATION RATE (APPRAISED VALUE USING INCOME APPROACH)		
Net Operating Income	$	1,594,461
Divided by Appraised Value	$	26,575,000
Capitalization Rate		**6.00%**

RETURN-ON-COST		
Net Operating Income	$	1,594,461
Divided by Total Project Cost	$	24,700,000
Return-on-Cost		**6.46%**

LOAN-TO-VALUE		
Loan Amount (Original First Mortgage)	$	17,625,000
Divided by Value (Original Purchase Price)	$	23,500,000
Loan-to-Value		**75%**

MORTGAGE CONSTANT		
Annual Debt Service Payment	$	1,009,733
Divided by Loan Amount (Original Loan at Purchase)	$	17,625,000
Mortgage Constant		**5.73%**

Capitalization Rate: The capitalization rate based on existing income translates to 6%, within a reasonable price range for this type of asset that requires some value-add structuring, converting to an appraised value using the income approach of $26,575,000.

Return-on-Cost: The return on cost equates to 6.46% based on the original purchase price plus an additional $1,200,000 in renovation costs. Compared to a 6% capitalization rate evaluation, nearly a 50-basis point margin represents a "fair" return for entering any value-add deal such as this apartment complex.

Loan-to-value: The loan-to-value reflects the original loan amount of $17,625,000 divided by the actual purchase price of $23.5 million, yielding a 75% ratio. For underwriting purposes, LTV represents the lesser of (i) the purchase price or (ii) applied appraisal value upon completion of the renovation. After reaching the projected income, the project could be re-underwritten to acknowledge a higher value and costs associated with the renovation.

Mortgage Constant: The mortgage carries a 5.73% Mortgage Constant, based on determining the annual debt service payment, $1,009,733, divided by the original loan amount of $17.625 million. At the 4% rate, a 30-year amortization adds 1.73% to the interest rate (4% + 1.73% = 5.73%) to account for principal paydown as part of the overall payment structure. Interest-only payments could boost the cash flow, but this transaction has too many moving parts (i.e., risk) to merit an interest-only loan structure.

DEBT SERVICE COVERAGE		
Net Operating Income	$	1,594,461
Divided by Annual Debt Service Payment	$	1,009,733
Debt Coverage Ratio		**1.58**

DEBT YIELD		
Net Operating Income	$	1,594,461
Divided by Loan Amount (Original Loan at Purchase)	$	17,625,000
Debt Yield		**9.05%**

BREAK EVEN POINT		
Expenses	$	1,141,539
Annual Debt Service	$	1,009,733
Total Cash Flow Outlays	$	2,151,272
Divided by Gross Income	$	2,880,000
Break Even Point		**74.70%**

Debt Service Coverage: Debt service coverage of 1.58x reflects the number of times that the in-place net operating income of $1,594,461 can cover the annual debt service payment of $1,009,073 (1.58 = $1,594,461 ÷ $1,009,073). Since mortgage rates are reasonably favorable given the going-in cap rate (purchase price capitalization rate), the debt service coverage ratio is higher than the required minimum of 1.20x-1.25x. These metrics show that the loan-to-value restricts the loan more than debt service coverage.

Debt Yield: A Debt Yield of 9.05% represents the lender's perception of the property default capitalization rate, leaving a comfortable margin for the loan to be sold with an ample equity buffer for repayment. The debt yield hovers within 200 basis points of the capitalization rate, indicating aggressive underwriting associated with core investments.

Break-Even Point: The breakeven point illustrates that the property needs approximately 75% occupancy to achieve breakeven. Alternatively, the breakeven point indicates that the property can tolerate almost a 25% vacancy before cash flow fails to cover operating expenses and meet debt service payments. Also, the breakeven point represents a comfortable margin for the lender and borrower to manage the property in the softer leasing market.

PRE-TAX CASH FLOW		
Net Operating Income	$	1,594,461
Annual Debt Service	$	(1,009,733)
Pre-tax Cash Flow	**$**	**584,728**

AFTER-TAX CASH FLOW		
Pre-tax Cash Flow	$	584,728
Annual Depreciation Allowance	$	(683,636)
Taxable Cash Flow	$	(98,908)
Income Tax Payment (Savings) Multiplied by Investor Tax Rate @ 30%	$	(29,673)
Pre-tax Cash Flow	$	584,728
After-tax Cash Flow	**$**	**614,401**

RETURN ON INVESTMENT (PRE-TAX AND AFTER-TAX)		
Pre-tax Cash Flow	$	1,594,461
Divided by Equity	$	5,875,000
Pre-tax Return on Equity		**27.14%**
After-tax Cash Flow	$	614,401
Divided by Equity	$	5,875,000
After-tax Return on Equity		**10.46%**

PAYBACK PERIOD (PRE-TAX)		
Original Equity Investment	$	5,875,000
Renovation Upgrade Cost	$	1,200,000
Cumulative Equity Investment	**$**	**7,075,000**
Projected Average Net Operating Income after Renovation, during 5-year hold	$	1,760,000
Annual Debt Service	$	(1,009,733)
Projected Average Pre-Tax Cash Flow	**$**	**750,267**
Payback Period (Years)	**9.43**	

Pre-Tax Cash Flow: The pretax cash flow shows ample annual cash flow at more than 50% above debt service payments.

After-Tax Cash Flow: After-tax cash flow indicates that the borrower enjoys an additional $29,673 from tax benefits allowed from depreciation at the 30% tax rate.

Pre-Tax Return on Equity: The return on investment on a pretax basis yields 27%, which is a favorable cash-on-cash return on a leveraged basis.

Payback Period: A payback period of nearly nine and a half years indicates a stable asset falling within the popular long-term holding range of ten years or less.

In conclusion, the study of various static indicators relating to the acquisition and subsequent renovation provides reasonable investment and underwriting metrics. Independently, these indices offer acceptable measures of specific benchmarks. However, in combination, the indices provide a better understanding of the risk/reward characteristics of the project.

By combining these ratios using sensitivity analysis, investors open more "doors" to measuring a project's financial feasibility.

FRONT DOOR/BACK DOOR ANALYSIS "THE DOORS"

"The Doors" represent a more extensive use of sensitivity analysis using simple tests. These two static underwriting formats are referred to as "the Doors" and "DICE" (Debt Income Calculation Economics) and are described below.

"The Doors," known as Front Door/Back Door investment analysis, allow for testing project economics compared to targeted returns. The Back Door analysis views the investment based upon justified value. Alternatively, the Front Door approaches the investment according to the required income to produce the targeted investment yields. Interchanging both doors is used for screening investments with predictable income streams as follows:

Back Door

Back Door underwriting assumes a stabilized net operating income, which indicates the justified minimum loan, equity, and overall project values. The Back Door formula involves capitalizing an adjusted NOI as follows:

BACK DOOR ANALYSIS
DEBT
Net Operating Income
÷ Debt Service Coverage Ratio
Debt Service Payment Limit
÷ Mortgage Constant
Justified Mortgage Amount
+
EQUITY
Net Operating Income
- Debt Service
Pre-Tax Cash Flow
÷ Cash-on-cash (Minimum)
Justified Equity Amount
=
BACK DOOR PROJECT VALUE
Debt (Justified Mortgage Amount)
+ Equity (Justified Equity Amount)
Justified Project Value

The NOI, divided by the debt service coverage ratio, yields cash available to service debt. The mortgage constant capitalizes this number to compute the justified loan amount. However, the LTV ceilings also restrict loan amounts. In most cases, the computation generating the lowest loan amount prevails. The next step involves capitalizing the pre-tax tax cash by the cash-on-cash (return on equity) to arrive at the justified equity amount. After that, the calculation involves adding justified debt and equity amounts to generate the justified project value per the net operating income.

Illustration: The Chicago Maroon Phoenix Shopping center, containing 401,170 ft.², and located in Hyde Park, Illinois, generates a stabilized net operating income of $6,985,265. The owner expects to secure a permanent mortgage at a 4.5% interest rate for a ten-year term based on a 30-year amortization schedule (6.08%K). The lender, Southside City Life, requires a minimum DSCR of 1.3X. Maroon's partners also desire a 12% cash-on-cash return. As a result, the project's Back Door value equals nearly $102 million, as shown below, translating to a 6.85% cap rate.

BACK DOOR ANALYSIS	
DEBT - BORROWER REQUEST	
NOI	$ 6,985,265
÷ DSCR	1.30
Debt Service	$ 5,373,281
÷ Constant	6.08%
Loan	**$ 88,373,080**
EQUITY	
NOI	$ 6,985,265
- Debt Service	$ 5,373,281
Pre-Tax CF	$ 1,611,984
÷ C-O-C	12.00%
Equity	**$ 13,433,200**
BACK DOOR PROJECT VALUE	
Loan	$ 88,373,080
+ Equity	$ 13,433,200
Value	$101,806,280

Observation: The Back Door analysis provides financial modeling using mortgage debt, equity pricing, and leverage levels to arrive at yield-based values.[79] Such methodologies emphasize the importance of different risk components within the capital stack for assembling a total project value. In effect, the Back Door method tests how well an investor's yield requirements fit with lender requirements for pricing the venture. The model shows how debt pricing and leverage ratio variables can dramatically impact investor yields. The Front Door analysis offers an alternative approach to the Back Door for evaluating the investment.

Front Door

Front Door underwriting measures the required net operating income and effective gross rent necessary to support the purchase price of an existing building or the cost of a new building. Consequently, the Front Door measures the required NOI essential to support the requested loan amount. The loan amount is multiplied by the mortgage constant to determine the annual debt service payment. Then, the debt service payment is multiplied by the debt service coverage ratio to compute the necessary net operating income. The net operating income is divided by the appropriate cap rate to generate a project value and the corresponding LTV limit. Should the loan amount exceed the LTV limit, a reduction in loan proceeds becomes necessary.

The Front Door analysis ignores the actual or projected operating income and expenses. Instead, the analysis uses market-derived data to ascertain the justified income. In effect, the Front Door methodology rewards [and punishes] any property performance deviations from statistical market averages. The Front Door formula methodology works as illustrated below.

FRONT DOOR ANALYSIS

INCOME
Property Value
* Market Going-In Cap Rate
Required Net Operating Income
÷ Gross Leaseable Area
Required NOI per square foot
+ Operating Expenses psf
+ Real Estate Taxes psf
Effective Gross Rent psf
÷ Occupancy Rate (1-Vacancy Rate)
Potential Gross Rent psf
÷ (1 – Contract Rent Discount)
Required Asking Rent psf
Required NOI
÷ Lender Debt Coverage Ratio
Maximum Debt Service

Illustration: Golden Bear Advanced Technology Park, a 318,566 ft.^{2} office complex in Berkeley, California, carries an appraised value of $40,000,000. Golden Bear approaches Husky Assurance of Seattle, Washington, seeking a first mortgage. Husky requires a minimum DSCR of 1.68X and currently prices mortgages at 4.9% for ten years based upon a 30-year amortization schedule (6.37%K).

Recent market comparable sales data indicate that competing properties support a 7.1% cap rate based on a 73.4% occupancy rate with asking rents of $21.28/ft.^{2} and an additional 7.7% rent concession discounts. These properties typically reflect $8.43 PSF operating expenses and $1.84 PSF real estate taxes. As a result, the Front Door calculations show that a pre-tax cash flow of $1,149,524 is required to support the various value and operation assumptions. As a result, the Front Door analysis shows that an asking rent of $28.30/ft.^{2} is necessary to make the investment viable. Since the required asking rent significantly exceeds the asking rents ($21.28/ft.^{2}) justified in the market, Golden Bear's financing request fails to meet Husky's funding parameters, illustrated as follows:

FRONT DOOR ANALYSIS	
INCOME	
Property Value	$40,000,000
* Cap Rate	7.10%
NOI	$2,840,000
÷ GLA psf	318,566
NOI psf	$8.91
+ Oper Exp psf	$8.43
+ RealtyTaxes psf	$1.84
EGI psf	$19.18
÷ Occupancy %	73.40%
GI psf	$26.13
÷ Effectitve Rent	92.30%
Asking Rent psf	$28.30
Required NOI	$2,840,000
÷ DSCR	1.68
Debt Service	$1,690,476
NOI	$2,840,000
- Debt Service	$1,690,476
Pre-Tax Cash Flow	$1,149,524

Observation: Project costs weigh into the LTV and debt coverage discussions. In addition to underwriting yields, the return-on-cost metric provides another facet of analysis to the Door formulas. ROC calculations help justify project costs for new construction and substantial rehab project ventures. Generally, ROC yields should be at least 100 to 250 basis points higher than Front and

Back Door capitalization rates. For instance, the Golden Bear project should generate at least an 8% ROI to be reasonably profitable.

As with any ROI index, new construction and redevelopment return-on-cost yields may not necessarily warrant the investment in creating an incremental value increase. In other words, the spread between the ROC and the Front Door and Back Door cap rates would be too narrow to justify either new construction or renovation.

Understanding each door leads to asking which "entrance" to use for real estate underwriting, as both present strengths and weaknesses.

Which Door Entrance?

Choosing the correct "entrance," the Front Door or the Back Door, involves clearly understanding the investment objectives. The best strategy requires checking entrances and using the door most suitable for reaching the profitability goals. Regardless, the results of Front and Back Door analyses are restricted by underwriting limits, defaulting to the lower: (a) loan-to-value or (b) debt service coverage ratio.

The Doors offer an excellent underwriting methodology for measuring investment thresholds but fall short of addressing variables outside project economics, namely investor/sponsorship considerations. DICE analysis fills this static analysis void per the discussion below.

DEBT INCOME CALCULATION ECONOMICS ("DICE")

Debt Income Calculation Economics, or "DICE," is a static analysis tool incorporating numerous ROI ratios. Front Door/Back Door elements add sponsorship underwriting to the investment analysis process, focusing on debt. In most commercial realty transactions, debt constitutes the largest component of the capital stack. Furthermore, DICE integrates the 5 P's (People, Place, Project, Performance, Pros/Cons) into the investment underwriting.

With DICE, successful funding outcomes are possible despite weak project economics, financially challenged sponsorship, etc. For example, an underqualified borrower backed by non-cash-flowing collateral (e.g., vacant land) still might result in an attractive financing opportunity at a specific funding level.

The DICE model offers six successive levels of loan analysis, from the basic tests (Level I) to the most rigorous metrics (Level VI). Each level progression shows below.

DEBT INCOME CALCULATION ECONOMICS "DICE" - LEVEL ANALYSIS

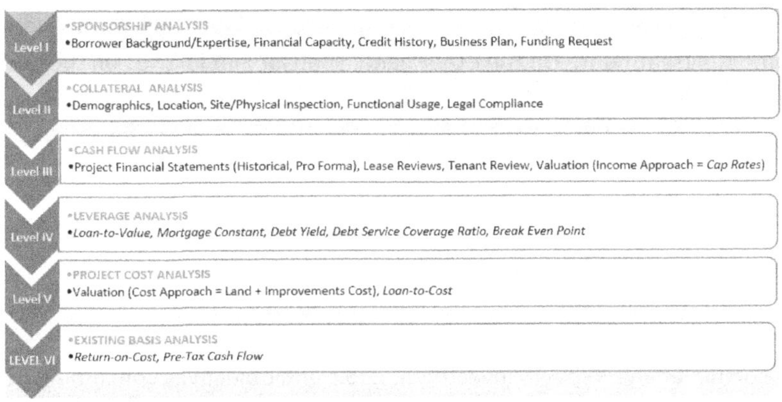

The DICE levels included six types of analysis of loan underwriting: sponsorship, collateral, cash flow, leverage, project cost, and existing basis. Sponsorship analysis covers borrower issues such as financial capacity and experience. After that, the collateral analysis explores physical improvements and locational characteristics. Next, cash flow analysis delves into project economics. Leverage analysis follows, revealing a project's ability to support the debt service and principal repayment. Finally, project cost and basis analysis consider how much additional loan underwriting cushion exists beyond the venture's financial performance benchmarks. Each of these levels is outlined as follows:

Level I. Sponsorship Analysis

Sponsorship character forms the starting point of any loan funding discussions using DICE Level I. This level mirrors the "people" of the 5 P's.

Real estate professionals frequently use the terms ownership and sponsorship interchangeably. Ownership typically refers to the legal entity formed to purchase a property. Ownership entities include limited liability corporations ("LLC"), partnerships, sole proprietorships, and corporations. Investors take on various active or passive roles depending on the entity format. Furthermore, each entity carries different financial rewards, legal duties, liabilities, and income-tax treatment. On the other hand, sponsorship focuses on the individuals directly controlling the ownership. These individuals create an ownership format depending on the preferences of the investors.

Sponsorship analysis forms a baseline for investment decisions. This mandatory step determines how to judge the project as ownership collateral, not a stand-alone investment (e.g., Back Door/Front Door). Also, the sponsorship analysis covers investment goals and objectives concerning the requested capital structure.

No two sponsors are identical in real estate or real life.[80] Honesty is one of the essential elements of the sponsorship's relationship with lenders. So, full disclosure remains critical for discussing any relevant issues. The experience level of the sponsorship also requires scrutiny. Other sponsorship topics, including bankruptcy, lawsuits, and impaired credit history discussions, deserve special attention.

In particular, financial statements offer insights into sponsorship loan guaranty and repayment capacity. As a rule of thumb, commercial real estate lenders generally target liquidity reserves of six months to a year of carrying debt service payments. Acceptable net worth targets range from 1X to 2X of the loan amount.

Lenders accept lower net worth and liquidity if the requested loan amount meets a more conservative leverage threshold. As a result, unproven borrowers with limited track records can qualify by providing additional collateral. Conversely, extremely wealthy sponsorship rarely offers detailed financial information. Instead, lenders rely on references furnished by ownership accountants and other financial institutions.

While financial capacity aids in determining loan repayment capacity, many borrowers avoid signing personal guarantees. Seasoned developers, institutional owners, wealthy families, and professional real estate owners, among others, use non-recourse debt as part of an investment strategy. Non-recourse debt promotes the concept of a lender not having recourse against any borrower's assets (i.e., the right to pursue recovery via personal assets) other than those given explicitly as collateral.[81] Life companies and securitized mortgage lenders originate the largest share of non-recourse debt. However, most banks, thrifts, and credit unions require some recourse (guarantee.)

The following illustration demonstrates how sponsorship plays a crucial role above and beyond project economics.

Illustration: Boulder Buffalo Investors, a privately-owned partnership, seeks limited partners to invest in a portfolio of older, value-add multifamily properties in Denver. These limited partners share ownership risk but are restricted from participating in operational decisions. Instead, the partners rely on Earwig, the general and managing partner, as the key figure in the sponsorship.

Boulder successfully renovated and operated over 10,000 units during a career spanning more than twenty decades. Earwig owns and controls most of the company, with other employees carrying minority ownership rights. Also, Earwig heavily advertises his professional expertise on Boulder's company website. The promotional materials and investment offerings state that "Earwig contributes his value-add experience to Boulder."

However, within six months, Earwig secretly plans to sell his entire holding ownership interests to an undisclosed buyer. He never discusses such intentions with anyone, except for two of Boulder's ten employees. These principals are also veteran operators but lack any proven independent track record.

Is Earwig behaving like a "principal without principles?" Does Earwig act like a premisist[82], keeping the fiduciary interests of Boulder's investment partners in mind? The answer remains elusive without knowing all the facts about the intended sale of ownership interest. That said, the lack of transparency poses an ethical dilemma.

Observation: Extensive project due diligence often reveals limitations on sponsorship's ability to control a project. Even if sponsorship receives high marks, specific legal restrictions surface regarding property operations; for example, co-tenancy provisions occasionally encumber retail properties, hampering sponsorship's leasing rights by limiting the tenants allowed to occupy the center. Alternatively, locally mandated affordability requirements within [larger] multifamily units impact sponsorship's abilities to raise rents to fair market levels.

Ultimately, sponsorship analysis determines what direction to steer the DICE loan underwriting. If the sponsorship proves too challenging, the other merits of the investment might override such fears, especially with higher quality collateral. DICE Level II discussions cover this analysis in more detail.

Level II. Collateral Analysis

Beyond sponsorship analysis (DICE Level I), reviewing real estate collateral is the next step for checking loan funding feasibility. Collateral Analysis, or DICE Level II, covers the relevant variables related to the project's geography, improvements, and other physical attributes. The lender's analysis includes reviewing demographic data and trends, specific site issues, and property improvements. This level represents the lender's consolidated underwriting analysis for two of the 5 P's, "place" and "project."

In addition to any existing physical collateral and location concerns, Level II Collateral Analysis includes an investigation of any other restrictions, expansion rights, development options, and items affecting the legal and usage rights of the improvements on-site, both positive and negative. For new construction, this level emphasizes the suitability of a project for the site.

Level II relies on the Cost Approach of appraisal valuation as the minimum base value indicator. In other words, the project cost establishes what an investor pays to construct the improvements, regardless of justifiable value indices based on project economics.

After that, data from competing properties are collected using the Sales Comparison Approach to ascertain support for rent levels and project economics (e.g., Front Door). Lastly, Level II concludes with a project's justified market value compared to total costs. If the Sales Comparison Approach value is equal to or higher than the cost, the project deserves further consideration, moving to the next level of analysis. Otherwise, the project is infeasible because costs are higher than the justified value based on market conditions.

Illustration: Commodores Vanderbilt Consolidated Development Company, Ltd. plans to construct a 250,000 $ft.^2$ spec warehouse in an opportunity zone of Nashville. Researching competing properties in the area show no facilities exist within a two-mile radius. The site offers a good 10-minute commute downtown. Furthermore, industrial zones closer to downtown witnessed residential and office redevelopment, leaving displaced warehouse users with limited options for finding space to serve "last-mile" distribution channels. The project supports a $120/ft.^{2} cost, translating to approximately $30 million. Market rents average $7.50 PSF. As a result, the justified net operating income computes to $1,875,000. The return-on-cost yield equates to 6.25% ($1,875,000/$30,000,000). Newer spec industrial properties sell for an average of about $136 PSF, demonstrating a value estimate of just over $34 million, translating to a $4,000,000 potential profit margin using the Sales Comparison Approach in contrast to the Cost Approach. Therefore, the project is financeable.

Observation: DICE Level II analysis helps determine project financeability. However, loan duration also plays into the equation when exploring pricing. Should the longer-term prospects of the collateral and location prove worthwhile, more liberal pricing, loan amounts, and longer terms could be available.

Assuming Level II analysis qualifies, the next step in the DICE investment decision involves understanding project cash flow.

Level III. Cash Flow Analysis

DICE Level III evaluates project performance for existing asset financing opportunities and offers testing of pro forma assumptions for new-construction ventures.

Upon filtering through the first two DICE analyses of sponsorship and collateral, lenders examine how actual [or projected] cash flow streams match the loan funding request. In other words, Back Door thinking dominates Level III research. Project economics dominates this analysis. Loan guarantee discussions occur at this level as more financial weight transfers to the project vs. sponsorship. As such, Level III adds to the project's "performance" thresholds in the underwriting analysis using the 5 P's.

Level III requires an in-depth analysis of income and expenses to determine the capacity of the net operating income for servicing debt. An accurately underwritten NOI involves reviewing the quality and duration of the existing cash flow stream, followed by comparing historical and future performance projections. Level III also covers income tax considerations, reintroducing sponsorship discussions.

Trailing income and expense history for existing properties (typically three years) is a reliable measure of cash flow stability based on proven performance. Some assets, such as self-storage facilities, require more extended stabilization periods. Specialty property types, such as lodging, demand additional scrutiny, as daily changes and other travel behavior patterns closely linked with the local economy can quickly impact the amount of daily income. Conversely, contractual rent rolls featuring longer-term leases with credit tenants require less scrutiny since such income flows have higher quality and durability. Lastly, historical occupancy and turnover rates data help model future cash flows.

Underwriting a variable-income project requires establishing a cash flow cushion. Overage rents and other less predictable income streams generally account for a high percentage of cash flow for retail properties, for example. At the same time, higher breakeven points and debt service coverages are required as higher safety margins.

Proforma income and expense statements represent the final step of the analysis, blending historical information with the most recent financial performance for forecasting the future. Other than contractual cash flow streams, market data and planned improvements for generating rental premiums form the mix of ingredients for this analysis. In decades past, utility costs, namely energy bills, wreaked havoc on expense growth projections. Real estate taxes and property insurance gain considerable attention as expenses remain challenging to control today. As for the future, income growth and expense savings heavily rely on “smart” building technology to manage utilities, security, space usage, etc. Another factor that requires consideration in the future is the impact of climate change on a property's operations. For example, consider the potential impact of rising water levels in Miami Beach.

Illustration: Northwestern Universe Townhomes of Evanston, Illinois, a 1980's vintage multifamily complex, historically operates at 95% occupancy, supported by steady net operating income growing at three percent annually. Northwestern is seeking to refinance this property based on its solid operational history. However, earlier this year, a new apartment property entered the market. This competitive situation created tenant retention problems, with fifty percent turnover within the Universe project. As a result, the ownership lowered rents by five percent to maintain occupancy, demonstrating that historical financial performance analysis is not necessarily applicable for cash flow projections. In discussions with lenders, this situation illustrates that reliance upon historical financial statements has limits.

Observation: Level III analysis often requires financial information that is not necessarily consistent. As discussed above, historical operating statements might not be a reliable source for cash flow forecasting. Other sources of property financial performance can show different results using similar information. Lenders usually require borrower's property income tax statements to analyze historical performance and verify cash flow. Such data can lead to distorted results because statements often overemphasize expenses to reduce taxable income. Expense items relating to repairs and maintenance may reflect cost items that should be capitalized rather than expensed. In any case, prudent underwriting stresses an extensive review of any extraordinary expenses. In addition, this analysis should focus on any improvements and replacements necessary during the loan term to determine proper annual replacement reserves.

With a complete understanding of income, expenses, historical operating history, and cash flow projections, DICE analysis moves to the next level, Level IV, targeting loan underwriting or leverage analysis.

Level IV. Leverage Analysis

Level IV analysis reaches the core of DICE analysis: the lender's loan underwriting. The previous three analysis levels characterize more broad realty investment underwriting decisions applicable to choosing sponsorship for acquiring or developing realty investment opportunities. Funding strategies must be created to custom-tailor the financing to meet the needs of both lenders and borrowers. This level continues building upon the path of the lender's underwriting taken from Level III, further emphasizing "performance" and using the "pros/cons" of the 5 P's to adjust the loan amount and other terms to facilitate an "accept or reject" decision for the funding.

DICE Level IV uses debt-related ROI indices for static underwriting, including the cap rate, LTV, mortgage constant, DSCR, debt yield, and breakeven point to evaluate the pre-tax cash flows. With the healthier ROI ratios, lenders gain comfort with solid performance margins, while borrowers enjoy profitable returns based on sufficient leverage – a win-win scenario.

Level IV supports underwriting analysis under various interest-rate cycles. Higher values occur if cap rate compression continues in a low-rate environment, forcing borrowers to raise more equity due to LTV restrictions. During high-interest rate cycles, debt service coverage governs loan proceeds.

Regardless of interest-rate cycles, ROI analysis emphasizes generating an income stream above the borrowing cost to ensure profitability. As a rule, the more profit flowing to the leveraged equity, the lower the loan default probability. Such a scenario offers an ideal risk/reward relationship as the lender and sponsorship benefit from the cash flow stream.

Illustration: Using the Back Door analysis shown below, The Wharton Village Lifestyle Shopping Center, containing 401,170 ft.^{2} and located in Philadelphia, Pennsylvania, generates a stabilized net operating income of $6,985,265. Eternal Sequoia Realty Partners, the sponsorship group, requires a 12% cash-on-cash minimum equity investment. The borrower's Back Door value is about $102 million, translating to a 6.85% cap rate. In seeking debt, Sequoia requests a permanent mortgage at a 4.5% interest rate for a ten-year term based on a 30-year amortization schedule (6.08%K), using a DSCR of 1.3X. However, upon reviewing the borrower's funding request, the lender, Ludwig Life Insurance, raises concerns about funding a retail property in a challenging market and views the borrower's cap rate as overly optimistic. Ludwig responds with a more conservative proposal, featuring a higher mortgage rate of 5% and a reducing the amortization schedule to 25 years (7.02%), supporting a minimum DSCR of 1.5X. The loan offer of over $66 million equates to an 8.15% cap rate and requires the borrower to contribute nearly six million dollars of additional equity. The results show different risk perceptions given the dramatic difference between borrower and lender Back Door analyses. Such funding conditions often exist when property types fall out of favor with debt sources.

BACK DOOR ANALYSIS		DICE BACK DOOR ANALYSIS		DIFFERENCE
DEBT - BORROWER REQUEST		**DEBT TERMS REVISED - LEVEL IV**		
NOI	$ 6,985,265	NOI	$ 6,985,265	$ -
÷ DSCR	1.30	÷ DSCR	1.50	
Debt Service	$ 5,373,281	Debt Service	$ 4,656,843	$ 716,437
÷ Constant	6.08%	÷ Constant	7.02%	0.94%
Loan	**$ 88,373,080**	**Loan**	**$66,336,800**	**$ (22,036,280)**
EQUITY		**EQUITY**		**EQUITY**
NOI	$ 6,985,265	NOI	$ 6,985,265	
- Debt Service	$ 5,373,281	- Debt Service	$ 4,656,843	$ (716,437)
Pre-Tax CF	$ 1,611,984	Pre-Tax CF	$ 2,328,422	$ 716,437
÷ C-O-C	12.00%	÷ C-O-C	12.00%	12.00%
Equity	**$ 13,433,200**	**Equity**	**$19,403,512**	**$ 5,970,310**
BACK DOOR PROJECT VALUE		**BACK DOOR PROJECT VALUE**		
Loan	$ 88,373,080	Loan	$66,336,800	**$ (22,036,280)**
Equity	$ 13,433,200	Equity	$19,403,512	$ 5,970,310
Value	$101,806,280	**Value**	$85,740,312	**$ (16,065,970)**

Observation: Lenders often approach underwriting based on conservative assumptions for challenging property types, but the opposite holds for favored property types. In the case of multifamily assets, lenders approach cash flow analysis with more liberal viewpoints due to intense funding competition. For instance, various government-sponsored agencies ("GSE") provide more attractive funding terms based on energy savings, sustainability, rent affordability, etc.

If Level IV analysis justifies the loan underwriting terms, the investor moves to the next level of DICE analysis, reviewing project costs to qualify the debt investment further.

Level V. Project Cost Analysis

Upon reaching sufficient debt service coverage and valuation-based leverage thresholds, DICE Level V focuses on project costs compared to the loan amount. In particular, Level V applies to stabilized projects with cash flow streams that meet the underwriting tests of the previous DICE levels by touching upon all of the 5 P's, particularly "sponsorship," project," and "performance."

Level V analysis examines how the sponsorship project cost basis measures up to project economics. Lenders use this metric to determine how close the loan amount flirts with replacement cost, especially in debt fundings based on higher LTVs. Also, project costs remain relevant for reinforcing [or rejecting] any replacement or renovation plans for generating additional funding.

Illustration: The Super Chief Badger Investment Fund acquires older student housing apartment properties in Madison, Wisconsin. The firm targets a maximum price of $200,000 per unit based on a value-add risk/reward investment thesis. Such units rent for, say, $3,000 per month. New construction, however, for similar properties costs over $400,000 per unit, meaning rents need to double to use the same yield profile – an unlikely scenario. Therefore, substantial rental and financing subsidies exist to fill such profitability gaps, emphasizing the affordable housing shortage crisis in the workforce.[83] As is often the case with existing projects suffering functional obsolescence, replacement costs seldom justify investment economics.

Observation: Lenders gain comfort with larger margins between cost and loan proceeds due to a lower probability of default risk based on more sponsorship equity. Level V determines the financial strength of the debt yield compared to cap rate values and cost. Also, project cost analysis is another determining factor for the funding proposal if other underwriting variables appear too aggressive.

Assuming the loan review process successfully passes Level V analysis, lenders apply the last DICE underwriting test, DICE Level VI, covering the sponsorship's existing cost basis in the venture.

Level VI. Existing Basis Analysis

DICE Level VI Existing Basis Analysis serves as the final test. Lenders use this level as another optional benchmark to measure sponsorship motivation for staying in the venture through the loan term. Numerous 5 P's elements apply to Level IV, as the previous levels of analysis cleared most hurdles.

The central theme of the existing basis revolves around understanding the sponsorship's adjusted equity position in the venture. Borrowers argue for adjusting the basis to include the equity position's market value [appreciation]. On the other hand, Lenders prefer to focus on the actual equity dollars invested. In either case, the equity position remains illiquid until a sale occurs. Otherwise, if the lender agrees to use the market value of the equity and funds additional loan proceeds, the borrower benefits from "cashing out" some portion of the equity via a debt disbursement. Lenders find such cashouts acceptable, especially if the borrower owns the property over a more extended period and creates more significant cash flow streams.

In particular, a longer length of ownership fortifies the sponsorship position in funding discussions. Over expanded time horizons, borrowers usually make additional capital contributions to keep the project competitive. Furthermore, the ownership depreciation of the taxable basis calculated for federal income tax purposes creates a more considerable income tax liability. In the event of foreclosure, any forgiven debt is taxable income above the [larger] depreciated basis. In other words, the income tax recapture risks to the borrower potentially outweigh loan default risks to the lender.

Illustration: Oregon Duck Apartment Partners purchased the Boilermaker Arms, a smaller, six-flat apartment property, thirty-two years ago for $275,000 in West Lafayette, Indiana. The property value dramatically appreciated due to a gentrifying neighborhood, and today's worth over $1.2 million. The property featured a self-amortizing loan that was fully paid off two years ago. Sam expects to retire soon and wants to keep this asset as part of his retirement. Spartan Community Bank of East Lansing, Michigan, agrees to lend Oregon Duck $600,000, well above the original purchase price. Although fully cashing out the borrower, the bank retains a comfortable loan margin of 50% LTV. Lastly, the risk of default remains low due to the borrower's tax recapture trigger upon sale or foreclosure.

Observation: The definition of sponsorship equity ranks as one of the most debated figures in the capital stack. The discussion emphasizes developer fees and any costs related to completing the project requiring ownership control for development deals. Lenders often restrict such fees if the analysis demonstrates these costs appear excessive because of the perception of "disguised" profits. And some lenders, such as the Federal Housing Authority ("FHA"), impose strict guidelines on cost segregation for new development. Otherwise, equity basis calculations are often negotiable, depending on how sponsorship demonstrates total project value vs. cost.

In conclusion, Level VI is the finishing touch for completing DICE analysis from nearly all angles of static investment analysis, as discussed below via a decision path.

DICE DECISION PATH

Given the number of underwriting decisions leading to this final level, The DICE Decision Path chart illustrates how the analysis process works, including examples.

By deploying the DICE Level I-VI loan underwriting sequence, the lender decides funding feasibility using the 5 P's based on a decision path starting with sponsorship, followed by collateral, cash flow, leverage, project cost, and existing basis, illustrated as follows:

DEBT INCOME CALCULATION ECONOMICS "DICE" DECISION PATH

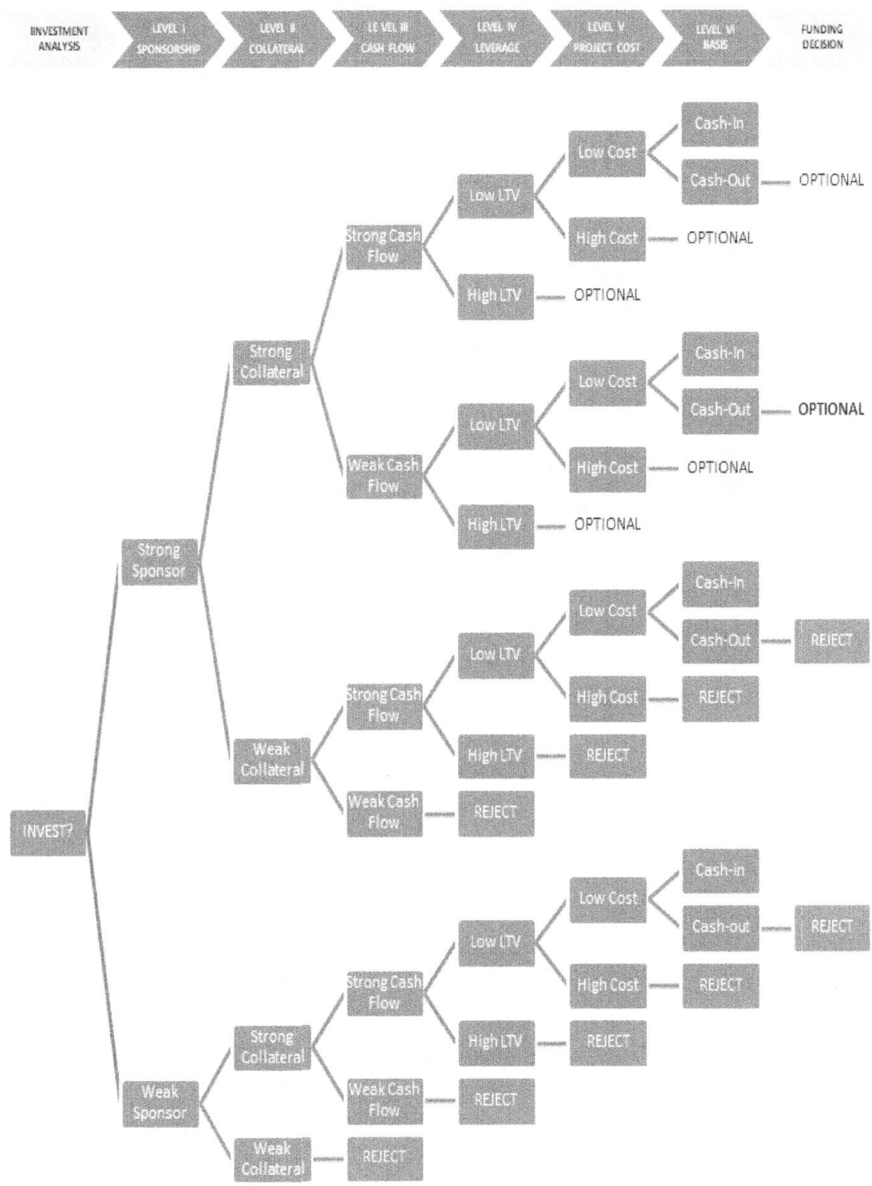

The DICE Decision Path chart outlines the investment analysis thought process, progressing in order of the importance of each analysis. The decision-making prioritizes sponsorship, followed by collateral and cash flow. After that, financing structure details prioritize debt [leverage] underwriting. Lastly, project cost and basis information round out the funding decision where applicable. Depending on the decision path, the lender chooses to accept, conditionally, or reject the funding request.

The lender accepts the loan opportunity if the project analysis demonstrates a smooth progression of achieving favorable underwriting benchmarks. If certain levels prove challenging, such as concerns of the debt amount being too close to project cost vs. value, the lender has the option to decide whether the financing appears an acceptable risk. If the initial levels (e.g., sponsorship and collateral) demonstrate concern, the lender is likely to reject the loan request during the early stages of review. Depending on each project, the lender may offer an alternative funding structure that fits the DICE process more closely than the sponsorship's loan request. The following examples show the DICE decision path:

Weak sponsorship with substantial collateral: The project's strength outweighs borrower weaknesses. The lender accepts a loan opportunity backed by unproven sponsorship if considerable collateral with proven cash flow exists. The additional collateral acts as a credit enhancement of the venture. The loan funding remains conservatively low leverage and structured well below project replacement cost with no cash-out of equity from the venture. However, if the borrower requests higher leverage or the cash flow demonstrates any concerns, the lender rejects the offer.

Strong sponsorship featuring substantial collateral at high LTV: The lender conditionally decides to fund a project at a higher leverage level. Assuming acceptable sponsorship, collateral, and cash flow quality, the lender accepts more risk because of additional collateral, as in the previous scenario. That said, the lender would be stricter on judging project costs and borrower basis for demonstrating that ample cash remains in the project.

The "Ideal" loan: The lender captures a nearly perfect funding opportunity. The loan underwriting includes strong sponsorship with the desirable collateral, supporting substantial cash flow based on a low leverage loan request. Furthermore, the mortgage represents a deep discount relative to project cost, and the borrower retains a high investment basis in the venture for income tax purposes. Such financing profiles attract the most competitive loan terms, as minimum default risk exists.

Low default risk can exist for projects lacking income streams, as more DICE examples are demonstrated below.

DICE CASE STUDIES

Real estate investment analysis classically emphasizes underwriting assets that generate durable cash flows. However, non-cash-flowing ventures occasionally represent some of the most profitable and often conservative funding opportunities. Such underwriting scenarios filter through the first two levels of DICE analysis, sponsorship, and collateral, as cash flow fails to exist. The following example illustrates such an opportunity.

Illustration: Harvard Tufts Capital Partners owns a laboratory research facility building within the MIT Intellectual Research Park in Cambridge, Massachusetts. The firm plans to acquire an adjacent vacant land parcel for five million dollars. However, many issues negatively impact the site, including abandoned right-of-way passage rights owned by a railroad company, Brownfield contamination, and disallowed zoning for additional development. As a result, the project requires an extra seven million dollars to cover site remediation and correct the zoning and ROW (right-of-way) legal issues within three years. After that, Harvard Tufts plans to improve the site with an $80 million state-of-the-art cold storage warehouse facility.

Harvard Tufts requests a $5 million loan for five years plus a seven-million-dollar line of credit to cover the land development costs. BC Eagle Union Savings Bank, a local labor union-owned financial institution, wants to fund the construction loan. The sponsorship has maintained a successful 15-year relationship with the bank, with average deposits above $50 million. Harvard Tufts also boasts a net worth of nearly $300 million. Nevertheless, the bank's challenge rests on providing a fully-leveraged land loan backed by a contaminated parcel lacking definitive zoning rights. Further complications include the possibility that the railroad company may not agree to sell its ROW rights.

To help mitigate the risks discussed, Harvard Tufts proposes obtaining insurance to cover unforeseen environmental cleanup costs. Harvard Tufts also offers full recourse, providing a 100% repayment guarantee. The sponsorship promises to repay the land loan in five years or less, irrespective of the collateral value. Last but not least, Harvard Tufts agrees to use the bank for the eventual construction loan and build the project, using labor sourced from local union trades on an exclusive basis.

According to the DICE underwriting model, sponsorship is the main reason for the loan funding, passing the Level I test. The collateral, cash flow, and leverage tests never achieve a passing grade, so further analysis stops at Level II. The sponsorship relationship and recourse guarantee backed by solid financial strength drive the funding economics. Lastly, the bank is motivated to fund this loan as more jobs will be created by constructing this project using union labor.

A more typical DICE underwriting example includes progressing through higher levels of analysis along the decision path, as shown below.

Jayhawk Shopping Center Capital Corporation of Kansas City owns The Mall of DePaul, a 177,535 $ft.^2$ shopping center located in Lincoln Park, Illinois. The center features the tenant anchor, a regional grocer built over twenty years ago. The grocer occupies approximately 50% of the center and accounts for about one-third of the total rent. The remaining tenants include local, non-credit tenants with an occupancy history of nearly 100%. The grocer's lease expires within two years but includes multiple five-year extension options at below-market rents. However, grocery sales declined due to increased local market competition. That said, the rent represents less than half of a percent of gross sales, indicating a comfortable profit margin for the grocer, even at lower sales levels. The leases for the remainder of the tenants also feature leases of various terms with staggered expirations.

The net operating income equates to $1,800,000. Based on a 7.5% capitalization rate, the project value is about $24 million ($135/ft.^{2}). The estimated replacement cost represents approximately $300/ft.^{2}, translating to $53.3 million.

A $17 million first mortgage loan, maturing within twelve months, encumbers the property, representing a 71% loan to value. Jayhawk seeks to refinance the project, including closing costs, with a fresh 10-year, non-recourse loan. The primary loan terms include a $17.25 million permanent debt request at a rate of 4.25% using a 30-year amortization schedule.

Jayhawk claims a net worth of about $10 million with approximately $2 million liquidity. Also, the firm actively owns and operates other shopping centers in the Falls area.

Upon discussing this funding opportunity with a variety of permanent debt sources, the borrower discovers the loan is ineligible for refinancing for the following reasons using the DICE decision path:

Level I (Sponsorship): While the ownership net worth appears sufficient to operate the property, a common rule of thumb for sizing such properties equates to a net worth of nearly one times the loan amount with about 25% liquidity. Thus, regardless of recourse, permanent lenders find the sponsorship financially challenged, possibly lacking sufficient funds to provide an additional cash infusion to re-lease the grocer space or any other larger tenant spaces in the event of non-renewals.

Level II (Collateral): An excellent infill location helps this funding opportunity initially appear favorable. However, concern about other grocers' competition in the area poses a threat, suggesting possible weaker future performance for this center.

Level III (Cash Flow): The anchor tenant's rollover "event" risk during the loan term overshadows the good operating history and occupancy levels. Most lenders expect steady, predictable cash flows during the loan term, especially anchor tenancy. Even with a rapidly amortizing loan, the grocer rollover risk exists. The loan underwriting demonstrates the importance of analyzing tenant sales history, especially for understanding the overage rent structure and strength for drawing shoppers to the center.

Level IV (Leverage): The loan request appears too aggressive. Adjustment is necessary for the grocery space potential vacancy (or going "dark.") Prudent underwriting suggests that funding amounts reflect the cash flow streams under the worst-case scenario, leading to lower loan proceeds. Even then, as occupancy levels drop to 70% or less, permanent funding sources shy away from such properties until at least 85% occupancy.

Level V (Cost): The analysis looks favorable since the current value is about a 70% discount from new construction.

Level VI (Existing Basis): The borrower's equity basis bears minimum relevance to the underwriting process, as the other levels' decision path results in a failing grade.

DICE analysis at four levels concludes that the requested funding structure for refinancing the existing loan proceeds fails to offer an acceptable solution given the tenant rollover risk (Level III). Furthermore, the sponsorship lacks sufficient net worth to subsidize the project adequately in case of anchor tenant departure (Level I). Despite the low-cost basis of the center (Level V), rising competition in the area seeds doubts about the strength of the location (Level II), as well as the grocer's intention to extend the lease after the initial term (Level III). Revisiting the loan underwriting based on a lower loan amount in line with expected income readjustments to meet debt service tests (Level IV) offers a potentially justifiable solution.

The borrower's most crucial concern rests on renegotiating the grocer lease as soon as possible, even at a discount. Alternatively, another temporary financing solution suggests funding the center with an interim/bridge loan at lower proceeds supported by the cash flow readjusted net of the grocer tenant income. Upon renewal [or re-leasing] of such space, the borrower may resubmit the loan request for permanent debt based upon a more stabilized income stream.

In both cases, a workable funding solution requires the borrower to post more cash as a loan risk mitigation strategy unless the cash flow structure improves with more lease-term certainty.

DICE CONCLUSION

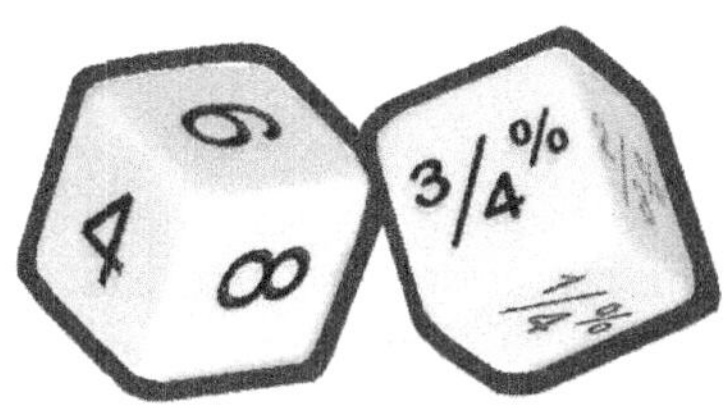

Metaphorically speaking, rolling the Mortgage Dice, as shown above, with whole numbers and fractions, helps illustrate the static real estate investment analysis process. Each dice roll represents random changes in ratios such as interest rates, mortgage constant, debt yields, and cap rates, demonstrating market volatility.[84]

The various DICE indices and decision paths represent lending underwriting benchmarks at fixed points in time, delivering static results. However, static analysis and results plotted over time, accompanied by performance tolerances, or risk ranges, create dynamic analysis. The concept of dynamic underwriting follows below.

DYNAMIC UNDERWRITING

Dynamic analysis forms the next logical step in the investment underwriting process. Such financial models cover the entire investment holding period rather than focusing on a fixed (static) or single point in time.

Dynamic analysis fits projects demonstrating cash flow volatility, namely value-add and opportunity deals. Such ventures include development deals, repositioning/repurposing projects, and assets with more mercurial income characteristics (e.g., lodging). As a result, investment underwriting, whether debt or equity, requires forecasting and measuring cash flow streams, matching the planned investment ownership horizon while applying various assumptions about future conditions.

Upon calculating annual cash flow streams spanning the projected holding period (including reversions), the dynamic analysis draws comparisons between the total income streams and the capital outlays discussed.

Dynamic underwriting represents an investment "movie," filmed with multiple cash flow "scenes" to compose the entire profit "picture." This format assigns a set of assumptions about future cash flows over the holding period. Like a movie, specific scenes (income of any given year) may not reflect the overall movie theme or conclusions. This view over time contrasts with the static format, which focuses on one specific moment in time analogous to a snapshot.

Such analysis emphasizes cash flow projections expected to fluctuate during the planned holding period. These fluctuations include income growth, changes in expenses, reversionary events, additional capital contributions, and other measurable financial events expected to generate profits or losses during the projected holding period.

Dynamic analysis carries underwriting to another level. Sophisticated investors use dynamic analysis to model possible financial outcomes over a longer time horizon. These investors typically include partnerships, syndicates, institutional owners (pension funds, life companies), private equity sources, and public companies needing to compare real estate ROI to alternative investments with similar cash flow and yield characteristics.

Dynamic analysis, capital budgeting, and financial modeling drives real estate investment discussions. The time value of money takes precedence, with discounted cash flow analysis serving as the benchmark calculation.

Projects relying on forward-looking projections heavily depend on dynamic underwriting. These projects include new construction, rehab, and projects with substantial cash flow upside due to above or below-market rents and foreseeable tenant turnover that creates circumstances for income increases/decreases. Also, recurring income and expense increases require factoring substantial growth into the cash flow assumptions under inflationary market conditions, focusing on "global" cash flow behavior vs. measuring "spot" situations.

A significant feature of dynamic analysis focuses on calculating the equity reversion as a distinct component of the process, often an outright sale. Usually, the reversionary proceeds represent a sizeable portion of the profits, particularly with various types of value-add and development ventures. As a result, the capital improvement programs factor into yield calculations. More extended holding periods necessitate continued maintenance and additional improvements to sustain the existing cash flows and increase overall project competitiveness.

Timing the reversion creates additional challenges. The investor seeks an optimum time to sell or refinance, reflecting the best conditions within the investment cycle when cash flow streams appear optimized and fully stabilized. Upon discovering such a point, reversion computations are typically done using the following year's growth for measuring project values based on cap rates. Such reversionary, or "going out" cap rates, are based on 50 to 100 basis points or more risk-adjusted premiums to cover future uncertainty relative to the current valuation.

Also, the dynamic analysis addresses the balance of the income stream and the reversion. The size of the reversion relative to the cumulative cash flow poses unique risk profiles. By definition, a reversion is a future uncertain event—the further into the future the forecast, the greater the margin of error. If a venture is justified based on substantial weight given to the reversion (sale), a higher risk exists than a project with a steadier cash flow stream.

Carrying vacant land represents the ultimate example of unbalanced cash flow. Investors seek profits upon the sale of the land. In the meantime, the investors incur ordinary operating expenses, including property taxes, insurance, and grounds maintenance during the holding period. Additional capital expenditures include entitlement costs, environmental remediation, and special assessments. Compared to stock and bonds, such an investment represents a zero-coupon bond or non-dividend stock with growth providing the return.

The two most popular dynamic underwriting techniques include, the Net Present Value ("NPV") and the Internal Rate of Return ("IRR"), are discussed as follows:

NET PRESENT VALUE

Over a century ago, the finance industry discovered a solution for estimating the value of cash flows projected into the future; a technique known as discounting is the foundation of NPV.[85] The basic definition of NPV states, "Net present value is the present value of the cash flows at the required rate of return of your project compared to your initial investment."[86] In other words, NPV reflects the value in today's dollars of the sum of all cash flows discounted at a stated rate of return during the holding period. A positive number indicates a profitable venture, and a negative number indicates a shortfall. The project meets the targeted return if the PV of cash inflows equals the investment outlay. Raising [lowering] the rate of return forces a higher [lower] threshold of reaching profitability.

The mathematical formula for calculating NPV is as follows:

$$Net\ Present\ Value = \sum_{t=1}^{n} \frac{Total\ Cash\ Flow_t}{(1 + Discount\ Rate)^t}$$

Where "t" is the year of the cash flow discounting

Calculating the discounted value of the annual cash flow streams over the holding period, the formula expresses the total present dollar value of the investment. The longhand formula for projecting each year's cash flow value at a given discount rate helps illustrate the theory of the exercise and is displayed as follows:

$$\frac{FV_1}{(1 + \text{Discount Rate})^n}$$

Where "FV" is the projected cash flow for each year and "n" is the number of periods out the cash flow is from the present.

Manually computing the NPV of the cash flow stream remains a time-consuming, cumbersome task. Spreadsheet software and financial calculators feature NPV functions.

NPV analysis relies on choosing an appropriate discount rate. This critical yield reflects the investor's risk quantification based on stated goals and objectives. Thus, the higher the discount rate, the greater the perceived risk, resulting in a lower present value for a given set of cash flows and vice versa.

The risk profile of income, expenses, debt service, and reversionary measures must be considered in selecting the discount rates. Multiple models can be created with different assumptions for such variables. A common theme, however, relates to uncertainty since larger margins of error exist for cashflows extending further into the future.

Illustration: The Yale Bulldog Realty Growth Fund offers an initial cash flow of $25,000, a 5.5% discount rate, a 3% annual growth rate, an original purchase price of $100,000 per share, and at the end of the holding period, sells for

$120,000. Also, the fifth-year cash flow is added to the sale price for a total cash inflow of $148,138 in that year, as shown below.

Discount Rate	5.5%			
Growth Rate	3%			
Time (t)	Cash Invested (Outflow)	Cash Inflow	PV Factor (1+r)^t	Present Value of Cash Flow
0	-$100,000		1	-$100,000
1		$25,000	0.94787	$23,697
2		$25,750	0.89845	$23,135
3		$26,523	0.85161	$22,587
4		$27,318	0.80722	$22,052
5		$148,138	0.76513	$113,345
			NPV	$104,816

Notice that each year generates a different present value of cash flow. When all these present-value-adjusted cash flows are added from Period 1 through Period 5, the present value (PV) of the benefits generated, including the investment's sale are calculated as follows:

PV of Benefits = $23,697 + $23,135 + $22,587 + $22,052 + $113,345
= $204,816

When subtracting the initial investment amount from these net benefits, the results show the [positive] net present value

NPV = PV of Benefits – Initial Investment = $204,816 - $100,000
= $104,816

The NPV emphasizes that the larger the positive number, the greater the benefit [from the real estate project].[87]

Observation: Inherently complex, the NPV method requires assumptions for each variable, such as the discount rate on income or expense amount or the likelihood of receiving the cash payment. The advantage of using the NPV method over IRR and other discounted cash flow methods lies in quickly testing multiple discount rates for establishing risk sensitivity ranges. Each annual cash flow stream allows for separate adjustments within the holding period for optimizing financial outcomes.

NPV answers an essential question about profitability projected over a holding period based on a targeted yield. However, investors seeking to use project yields as a primary consideration look to the Internal Rate of Return ("IRR").

INTERNAL RATE OF RETURN

IRR is defined as, "For [existing] income properties, it is the interest or discount rate needed to discount the sum of future net cash flows, including amortization and payments of loans and depreciation of the real property, to an amount equal to the initial equity of the property. For development projects, it is the interest or discount rate needed to convert (or discount or reduce) the sum of the development expenditures and incomes to equal zero."[88] Alternatively, IRR represents the project discount rate or yield at breakeven – the rate at which the capital invested equals the projected profits.

As with the case of the NPV, most financial calculators and software instantly compute the IRR (yield) required for the project benefits to equal the initial investment. Otherwise, manually determining the IRR involves calculating multiple iterations of NPV discount rates until zero – a tedious trial-and-error task.

Since the IRR solves for that discount rate that makes the NPV = 0, the Net Present Value Meets IRR chart illustrates the direct relationship between these two calculation methods.

NET PRESENT VALUE MEETS IRR

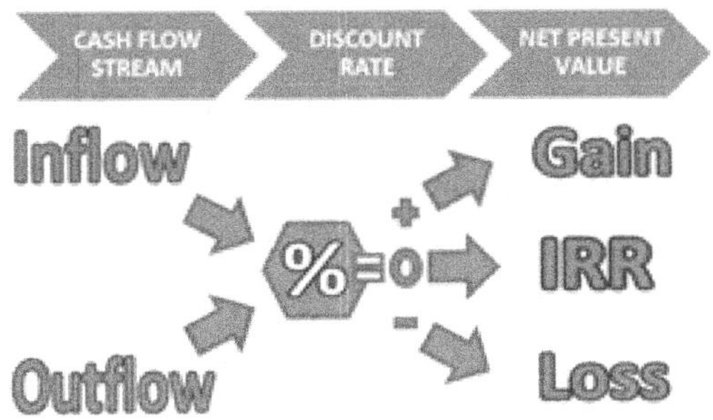

The chart demonstrates that an acceptable IRR needs to meet or exceed the NPV discount rate. Otherwise, if the IRR dips below NPV, the project appears unprofitable, i.e., the yield is below the threshold or required yield that the investor deems necessary for funding the venture. This financial modeling methodology uses a targeted yield up-front, but the actual yield is unknown until the investment is liquidated. Otherwise, an IRR is of limited value other than allowing someone to understand its absolute level, i.e., a high or low number.

Though the two indices share common roots, IRR compares less favorably to NPV as a preferred underwriting method for various reasons. First, IRR results prove most reliable when comparing similar projects sharing the common risk profiles, income streams, and discount rates – a rare occurrence. Second, discount rates fluctuate (e.g., mortgage and cap rates); IRR ignores these rate changes. With NPV, investors define preferred discount rates, bypassing fluctuations. Lastly, various cash flow streams with positive and negative values produce multiple breakeven results, resulting in numerous IRRs for the same project. On the other hand, NPV handles such situations since numerous discount rates generate different comparison results.

Illustration: The Income Property Advisors of Crimson Tide, LLC., compares two different projects based on the exact IRR requirement. The $50,000 up-front investment and holding period requirements are the same. The same IRR or target yield of 20% is used for discounting. Still, the underwriting produces different financial results based on the different levels of cash flows and growth rates, as illustrated in the example below:

Growth Rate: Project A	0.03					
Growth Rate: Project B	0.05					
Year	**0**	**1**	**2**	**3**	**4**	**5**
Project A						
Equity Investment	-$50,000					
Before-Tax Cash Flow from Operations		$10,000	$10,300	$10,609	$10,927	$11,255
+ Before-Tax Equity Reversion						$46,237
Total Cash Flows	-$50,000	$10,000	$10,300	$10,609	$10,927	$57,492
Internal Rate of Return (IRR)	20%					
Project B						
Equity Investment	-$50,000					
Before-Tax Cash Flow from Operations		$7,500	$7,875	$8,269	$8,682	$9,116
+ Before-Tax Equity Reversion						$63,814
Total Cash Flows	-$50,000	$7,500	$7,875	$8,269	$8,682	$72,930
Internal Rate of Return (IRR)	20%					

The present values of the cash flows can be converted to NPV as follows:

Year	**0**	**1**	**2**	**3**	**4**	**5**
Project A						
Before-Tax Cash Flow from Operations		$10,000	$10,300	$10,609	$10,927	$11,255
* Present Value Factor @ 20%		0.8333332	0.6944442	0.5787034	0.4822527	0.4018772
Discounted BTCF from Operations		$8,333	$7,153	$6,139	$5,270	$4,523
PV of Cash Flow from Operations	$31,418					
Before-Tax Equity Reversion						$46,237
* Present Value Factor @ 20%						0.4018772
Discounted BTER						$18,582
PV of Before Tax Equity Reversion	$18,582					
Year	**0**	**1**	**2**	**3**	**4**	**5**
Project B						
Before-Tax Cash Flow from Operations		$7,500	$7,875	$8,269	$8,682	$9,116
* Present Value Factor @ 20%		0.8333332	0.6944442	0.5787034	0.4822527	0.4018772
Discounted BTCF from Operations		$6,250	$5,469	$4,785	$4,187	$3,664
PV of Cash Flow from Operations	$24,355					
Before-Tax Equity Reversion						$63,814
* Present Value Factor @ 20%						0.4018772
Discounted BTER						$25,645
PV of Before Tax Equity Reversion	$25,645					

	Project A	Partition IRR	Project B	Partition IRR
PV of Cash Flow from Operations	$31,418	62.8%	$24,355	48.7%
+ PV of Before Tax Equity Reversion	$18,582	37.2%	$25,645	51.3%
Total PV	$50,000		$50,000	

This example highlights the potential difference in risk. Using the same discount rates suggests similar risk, but 63% of the overall yield of the first investment (Project A) is associated with the annual cash flow, reflecting more certainty and hence less risk. The remaining 37% derives from the equity reversion upon property sale in the fifth year. Conversely, in the alternative investment (Project B), about half (49%) of the yield is from annual cash flow, with the other half from the sale. Project A has more returns from cash flows received earlier, which are therefore viewed as having more certainty. Project

B has most of its return coming from the reversion, which is farther in the future, which creates more risk. This type of analysis, known as partitioning of the IRR, helps with a risk evaluation.

Theoretically, these two investments share similar risk profiles since both would produce the same yields. As shown, however, the risk profiles differ. The two opportunities are likely to appeal to different investor clienteles, e.g., those that prefer less risk, such as older investors who prefer immediate cash flows versus those who are able and willing to wait to receive tax benefits through capital gains (since capital gains taxes are lower than income taxes). More specifically, Project A, perceived as a core investment, appeals to retiree investors valuing more cash flow certainty to match predicted spending needs. Alternatively, Project B, labeled as core-plus, suits a younger investor seeking moderate income growth opportunities. This investor waits for higher profits tied to reversion upside. Neither strategy appears “right” or “wrong.” Assessing risk allows the analyst to account for various viewpoints and conclusions using dynamic underwriting.

Observation: With IRR, securing the highest yield is often a primary goal. However, this reasoning ignores when dollar amounts are collected over time and ignores holding periods. For example, an extremely favorable IRR results from a smaller project based on a short time duration, skewing the results, as with a quick property “flip.” For many owners, longer holding periods remain a vital investment objective. Thus, IRR yields provide reliable results only when comparing similar investment strategies. Otherwise, the NPV analysis offers more consistent results. IRR still appeals to investors since expressing a single yield catches more attention than mentioning an absolute number computation based on a discount rate per NPV. Internal Rate of Return (“IRR”) narrows the investment return to a single yield for determining project profitability.

IRR occasionally overstates profitability since it inherently assumes reinvestment of cash flows at the resulting IRR rate. As a result, investors turn to the modified internal rate of return for additional guidance. The NPV also includes a reinvestment assumption, namely reinvesting the cash flows at the discount rate used to calculate the NPV.

MODIFIED INTERNAL-RATE-OF-RETURN

The Modified Internal Rate of Return ("MIRR") represents an advanced form of IRR. Instead of generating a single rate of return, MIRR applies multiple discount rates to cash flow streams within the holding period. The MIRR is shown as follows:

$$MIRR = (FV_{CI}/PV_{CO})^{(1/n)} - 1$$

Where MIRR indicates the modified internal rate of return, $\mathbf{FV_{CI}}$ shows the sum of future values of all net cash flows at the end of the project, $\mathbf{PV_{CO}}$ presents the initial investment, and $\mathbf{n}$ accounts for the number of periods.[89]

MIRR applies variable discount rates to income streams. Cash inflows from operations or sales use a different discount rate from cash outflows, including staged equity contributions and negative cash flows. Such complicated methods gain acceptance for ventures featuring varying cost-of-capital structures, indicating lower or higher risk premiums. Furthermore, staged equity tends to increase the IRR yield since the initial equity basis is lower, while negative results generate multiple IRR yields.

In contrast, IRR analysis assumes that all equity is an outflow at Period 0. In practice, this means that staged equity contributions need to be discounted back to the present time, including any negative cash flows, to readjust the entire contribution to the "upfront" Period 0.

Illustration: Champaign Illini Flex-Office Ventures contributes $50,000 as an initial equity investment for a vintage, single-story office building in Urbana, Illinois. The cash flow stream provides $7,500 as the first year of cash flow, expected to grow at 1.5% annually. The office building is forecasted to sell at a 5.5% exit cap rate in five years. Champaign can fund all the equity upfront or stage the contributions over time. With IRR, the yield increases under the staged-equity scenario, as shown below, due to the smaller initial equity invested (-$50,000 vs. -$35,000).

Invested Equity	$100,000
Annual Growth Rate	1.5%
Going-out Cap Rate	5.5%

	All Equity Invested Up Front				Staged in Equity		
Time	Equity Invested	Cash Inflow	Total Cash Flow	Time	Equity Invested	Cash Inflow	Total Cash Flow
0	-$50,000		-$50,000	0	-$35,000		-$35,000
1		$7,500	$7,500	1	-$5,000	$7,500	$2,500
2		$7,613	$7,613	2	-$5,000	$7,613	$2,613
3		$7,727	$7,727	3	-$5,000	$7,727	$2,727
4		$7,843	$7,843	4		$7,843	$7,843
5		$154,863	$154,863	5		$154,863	$154,863
		IRR	34.8%			IRR	40.0%

The standard IRR calculation assumes a single equity contribution at the beginning of the investment. Equity demands discounting future contributions to present values for consistent yield results if staged. The present value of the staged equity payments can thus be equivalent to a one-time initial equity contribution.

In this example, the investors assume the next best opportunity [cost of capital] represents a similarly priced stock portfolio yielding 15% per year. The MIRR, using this rate as the opportunity cost of capital, results in a 37.3% yield, shown as follows:

Invested Equity	$100,000
Annual Growth Rate	1.5%
Going-out Cap Rate	5.5%
Opportunity Cost of Capital	15%

Staged in Equity					
Time	Equity Invested	PV Factor (15%)	PV of Equity	Cash Inflow	Total Cash Flow
0	-$35,000	1.0000	-$35,000		**-$46,416**
1	-$5,000	0.8696	-$4,348	$7,500	$7,500
2	-$5,000	0.7561	-$3,781	$7,613	$7,613
3	-$5,000	0.6575	-$3,288	$7,727	$7,727
4				$7,843	$7,843
5				$154,863	$154,863
		PV Equity	**-$46,416**	MIRR	**37.3%**

Observation: Future equity contribution yield thresholds seldom reflect consistent yields unless capital market conditions remain unchanged. MIRR introduces additional levels of discounting by allowing the discount rate to vary over time to address market yield fluidity. That said, MIRR requires forecasting multiple discount rates. Numerous discount rates lead to confusing results without providing net results in actual dollars – an advantage of NPV.

Other more sophisticated dynamic underwriting formats deserve mention, including the Financial Management Rate of Return ("FMRR"), Pooled Internal Rate of Return ("PIRR"), and Monte Carlo Simulation. These methods offer broader yield calculations by introducing concepts such as safe and risk rates, combined IRR yields, and statistical probabilities of income streams. As a result, such investment tools target a very narrow audience of users.

In summary, static and dynamic analyses work in tandem. Investors gain more confidence in understanding venture analytics from different timeline perspectives. On the other hand, investors need to know why the analytics vary substantially. Furthermore, dynamic underwriting methodology applies to static underwriting, as measuring ratios often occur annually. In effect, a series of yearly static underwritings collectively constitute a dynamic analysis, absent of any time-value-of-money discounting (e.g., NPV, IRR).

Ultimately, the best strategies for investment analysis require understanding the 5 P's of each real estate opportunity combined with appropriately using static and dynamic underwriting tools for reaching financial decisions. Beyond project analysis, however, determining the timing of investment decisions tied to market cycles plays an essential role in successful investing, discussed in the next chapter.

CHAPTER 4: CYCLES – TIMING RISK/REWARD DECISIONS

"Don't stay in bed, unless you can make money in bed." - George Burns

The previous two chapters of *Four Pillars* covered definitions (first pillar) and analyses (second pillar) of risk/reward for real estate investments. The chapter discusses the timing of investment decisions by focusing on market cycles (third pillar).

DEFINITION

Market cycles are rooted in greed and fear. However, the timing of real estate investing in matching market cycles proves to remain elusive. The following graph shows cycles are not necessarily synchronized.[90]

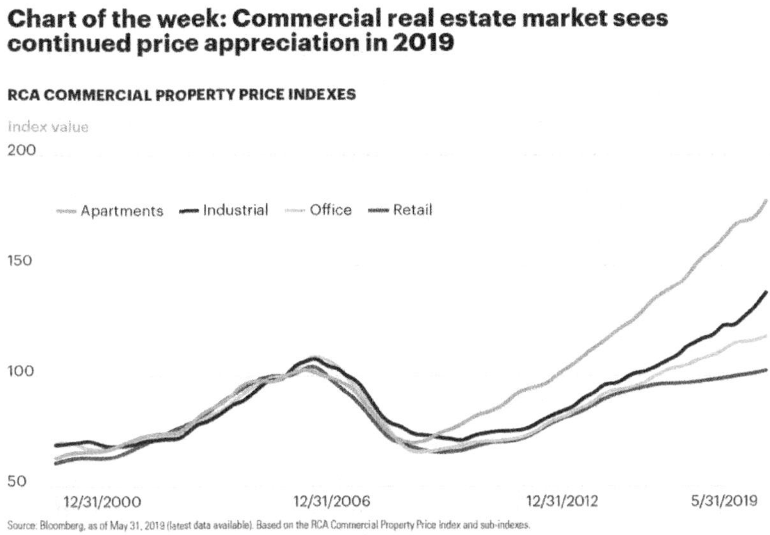

The chart illustrates how popular property types appreciated during various cycles in the first two decades before the pandemic. During the earlier years, prices rose symmetrically and appeared synchronized. In the latter years, apartments and industrial properties increased at much higher rates, leaving retail and office properties with modest increases. Furthermore, the following chart covers how price growth reached new highs in the most recent cycle.

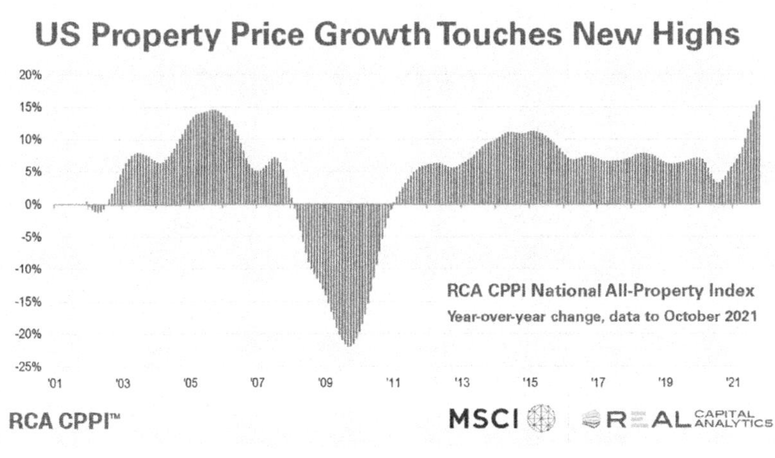

As the chart shows, market cycles exist that few investors predicted. Reaction to COVID, other factors, and industry trends caught most investors off guard. The pandemic proved that shifts from one cycle to another are unpredictable. For instance, the headline rate of U.S. property price growth climbed to the fastest annual rate in the RCA CPPI in October amid intense investor demand for commercial real estate. The RCA CPPI National All-Property Index rose 15.9% from a year earlier and 1.7% from September, an RCA CPPI: US report shows.[91]

These charts demonstrate that the Cycles Pillar influences nearly all real estate types. Unlike analyzing individual investment opportunities, forecasting market cycles rests with scholars and economists. Wall Street analysts, researchers, consulting firms, and government officials guide investors through predicting future cycle behavior. However, such expert opinions also suffer from faulty predictions.

Experts often agree on market cycle momentum. However, few concur about the granular details. For investors, these details matter. Many fortunes exist [or vanish] based on correctly [or incorrectly] timing the cycles. Investors need to know when to buy or sell. Stated differently, when to "surf" the market entails selling as prices rise (waves are reaching tsunami heights) and buying after havoc occurs, e.g., return to shore when the investment waters flood with waves of uncertainty.

"The key is to wait. Sometimes the hardest thing to do is do nothing." - David Tepper

Formulating investment timing requires broadly understanding how cycles behave. Real estate capital market cycles carry various labels: recovery, recessionary, inflationary, hyper-inflationary, and stable. Markets seldom, if ever, reach "ideal" conditions or equilibrium. Steady interest rates, competitive prices, and balanced supply and demand define equilibrium. Instead of waiting for the "perfect" time to invest, savvy entrepreneurs discover values by tracking down mispriced deals, developing new projects and rehabs (opportunity, value-add), or optimizing existing properties (core, core-plus). For instance, when mortgage rates decline, and values correspondingly climb, investors are likely best served by not overbidding on new acquisitions. Instead, such investors should refocus on adding value to existing ventures by fine-tuning net operating income and refinancing using favorable debt.

INCONSISTENT CYCLES

Although no two market cycles share identical characteristics, each cycle shares common elements, namely a consistent set of behaviors over an extended time. When grouped over longer timeframes, these sets of behaviors, or patterns, form overall trends. History repeats itself as the trends show, illustrated by the following graph using the REIT total return index.

The graph demonstrates the 5-year real estate cycle from January 1998 to December 2002 resembles but doesn't precisely mirror the subsequent 5-year process from February 2007 to January 2012. Ultimately, each cycle ties to the supply-demand dynamics of real property and capital.[92]

This cycle inconsistency also transcends property types. The values associated with different kinds of property rise and fall to varying amplitudes within the market cycles, as the following Green Street CPPI by Property Sector chart illustrates.

Chart 1: Green Street CPPI by Property Sector

Price appreciation for self storage, industrial and manufactured homes sectors has greatly outpaced other property types since 2010.

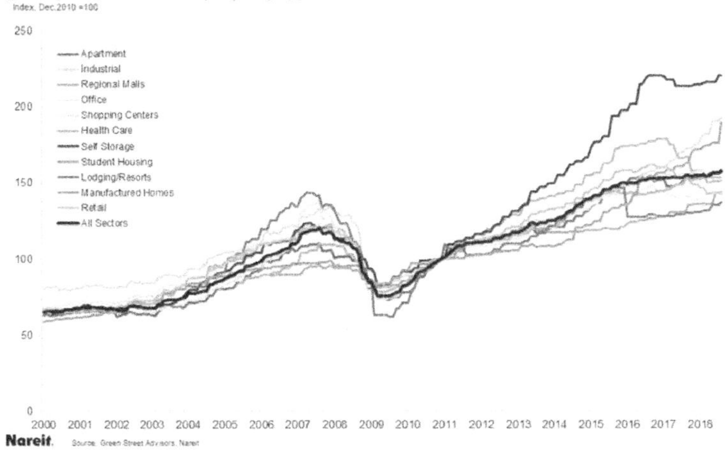

The chart shows how less-popular investment property types (e.g., self-storage) enjoyed the highest appreciation during most of the second decade of this century. This sector grew by over 120%, even as industrial and manufactured homes sectors posted impressive gains of approximately ninety percent. These sections outperformed the composite price index of all property sectors, which rose by nearly sixty percent.[93]

Understanding market cycles become even more challenging, especially during times of incredibly rapid change and instability (e.g., COVID), making turning points harder to identify. In such cases, advanced statistical modeling proves invaluable for measuring extreme market behavior for signaling caution. More specifically, researchers use such analysis for "normalizing" real estate data series to uncover any mathematical milestones. For example, the Z-score generates a "normalized" data series,

$$Z = (\text{Actual Number} - \text{Average})/\text{Standard Deviation}$$

This calculation determines the appropriate series and the time interval needed to calculate the mean or average and the corresponding standard deviation. If one standard deviation (-1.645 lower bound and +1.645 upper bound), then a statistical milestone occurs when the z-statistic climbs above or below the defined bounds. For illustration purposes, the REIT Total Return Index provided by the National Association of Real Estate Investment Trusts (NAREIT) features the following data set from the early 1970s. The REIT index deserves attention since academic studies have shown that securitized real estate is a leading indicator of the performance of the underlying real estate.

Date	REIT Index			
Dec-71	100.00			
Jan-72	100.00			
Feb-72	101.74			
Mar-72	101.42			
Apr-72	105.31			
May-72	95.44			
Jun-72	104.96			
Jul-72	111.05			
Aug-72	109.56			
Sep-72	113.78			
Oct-72	111.15			
Nov-72	109.70	**Average**	**StDev**	**Z-Score**
Dec-72	108.01	105.55	5.51	0.45
Jan-73	109.64	106.29	5.35	0.63
Feb-73	103.59	106.57	5.08	-0.59
Mar-73	106.05	106.90	4.88	-0.17
Apr-73	101.07	106.87	4.91	-1.18
May-73	98.21	106.32	5.46	-1.48
Jun-73	100.30	106.70	4.78	-1.34
Jul-73	103.82	106.61	4.83	-0.58
Aug-73	98.97	105.68	5.06	-1.33
Sep-73	105.39	105.36	4.92	0.01
Oct-73	106.35	104.79	4.25	0.37
Nov-73	91.46	103.27	5.19	**-2.27**
Dec-73	91.25	101.85	5.78	-1.84

In this example, the 12-month rolling window calculation generates the Mean (average), Standard Deviation (StDev), and the Z-score. Also, notice a statistically significant breakout in November of 1973 since the Z-score of -2.27 was more important than the lower statistical bound of -1.645. A three-year timeline presents the Mean (average), standard deviation (StDev), and Z-score of the REIT Index in the following chart.

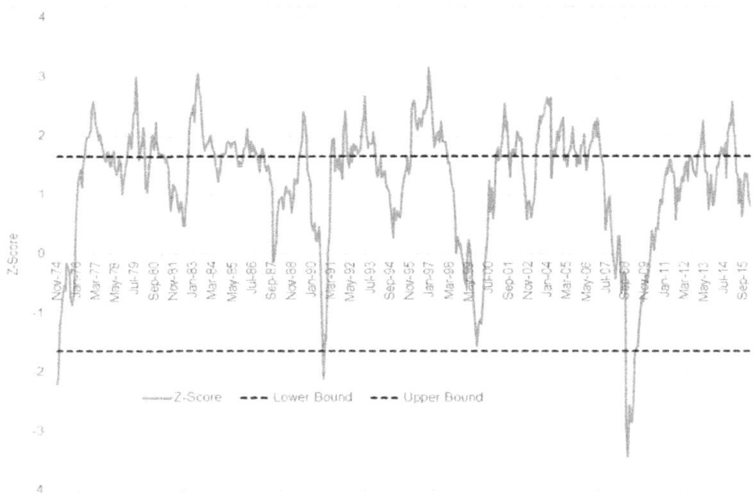

Upon closer inspection, the graph illustrates that in April 2007, the Z-score dropped below the upper band (confidence interval), signaling a sell. Another statistical milestone occurred in May 2009 when the score rose above the lower bound, signaling the beginning of a recovery, e.g., a buy signal. Beginning in April 2015, the graph suggests that investors should exercise caution.

The following chart represents a two-line axis graph confirming cautionary positions per the two warning signs mentioned above.

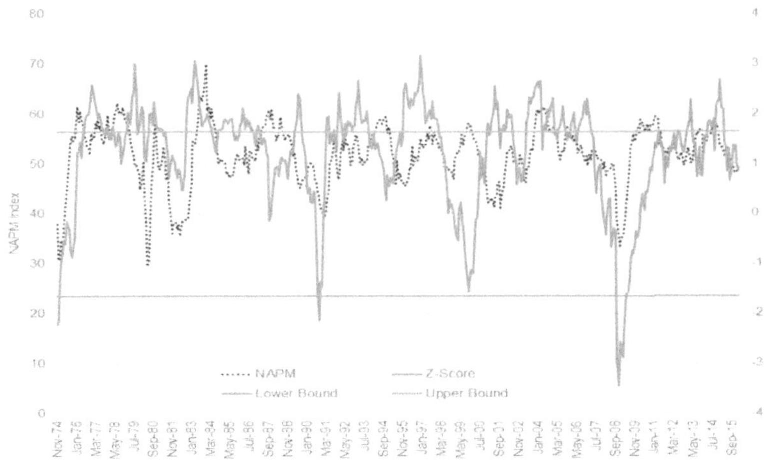

Both charts show that securitized real estate indices are readily observable and provide an early warning signal of performance behavior in the real estate market. Using statistical techniques such as z-scores acts as a "canary in the coal mine."

The "funding pendulum" explains market volatility as an additional perspective that complements using statistical analysis of cycles.

THE FUNDING PENDULUM

The Funding Pendulum concept demonstrates how markets swing in opposite directions, eventually moving towards the middle. In finance jargon, investors identify such behavior as mean reversion. This tenet assumes that asset prices, returns, and other capital market indices will eventually revert to their mean or average level, e.g., moving average. Swings to the left [liberal] represent very favorable capital market conditions; to the right [conservative], cautious; and balanced [neutral] -- the state of equilibrium -- in the middle, as illustrated below.

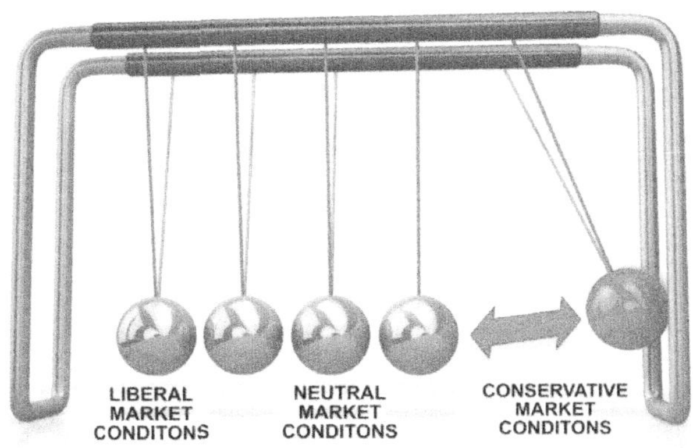

In the following section, real estate capital market cycles categorize these "swing" conditions.

REAL ESTATE CAPITAL MARKET CYCLES

Investors use various labels for identifying the extreme characteristics of cycle behavior, including positive-negative-neutral, high-low-middle, or good-bad-okay. Within *Four Pillars,* as mentioned earlier, these cycles are categorized as (1) Liberal, (2) Conservative, and (3) Neutral. Cycle behaviors overlap; nevertheless, each category displays the most common patterns of the respective cycle. Lastly, each cycle's ebbs and flows, including specific underlying factors, are shown in the following graph:

REAL ESTATE CAPITAL MARKET CYCLES

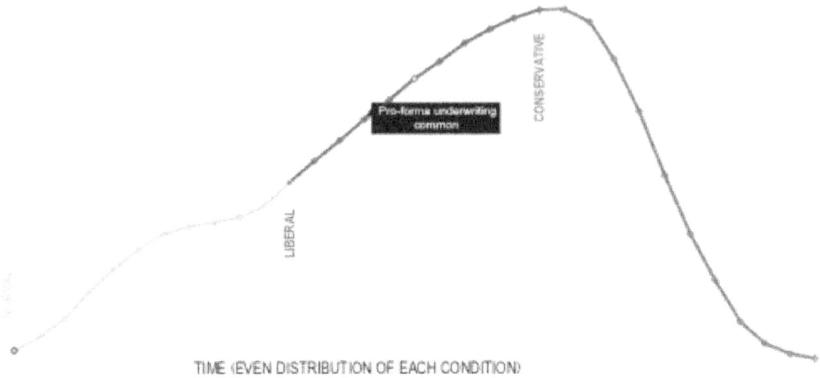

NORMAL	LIBERAL	CONSERVATIVE
Lenders cautious, recourse loans prevale	Abundance of lenders; no dominant sources	Layoffs begin in construction and development
Repriced assets start performing at a prof	Transactions close in 60 days or less	Private, "all cash" players emerge
Transactions mark steady pricing behavic	Pro-forma underwriting common	New construction projects halt
Tighter spreads creating predictable fund	Forward-delivery mortgages offered	Capital sources closing less deals
Owners and developers increase	Less differentiation of property types/locations	Mortgage pricing widening as volume slows
Occupancy levels approach breakeven	Merchant builders active w/ spec construction	Extreme price uncertainty, seller denial
Institutional players return via low levera	New class of lenders/buyers very popular	Vacancies rise below breakeven
Lenders more comfortable trending	Record transaction volume	Owners fight to keep existing tenants
Public markets raising funds, limited dea	Market euphoria, long-term holders sell	Seller financing popular to close transactions
More new funding sources launch prograr	Highest leverage or lowest cap rates	Bankruptcies, foreclosures rampant

The Real Estate Capital Markets Cycle ("RECMC") graph shows the three distinct cycles (Normal, Liberal, and Conservative). Each cycle's ten most unique market conditions are plotted at equal time intervals for illustration purposes. For example, the Liberal Cycle presents "Proforma underwriting common" as a popular cycle characteristic; however, proforma underwriting also exists in other cycles but remains less prevalent. Each cycle is discussed in greater detail as follows:

LIBERAL CYCLE

Liberal cycles signal euphoria. These conditions include "loose money," typified by favorable timing for obtaining attractive debt and leverage, higher prices, and continued optimism backed by a flood of investors. Various indices show minimum yield differentiation between different types of investment risks.

More specifically, cap rate compression occurs between core, core-plus, and value-add properties and favorable debt terms for properties of different categories. Furthermore, pricing in first, second, and third-tier market geographics flattens; the risk differential between these locations is often overlooked. Also, such market conditions encourage income projections to justify yields instead of relying on actual cash flows for stabilized assets. Lastly, prices start to exceed construction costs, fueling overbuilding. All in all, "the future looks good!"

Numerous examples exist demonstrating liberal cycles. The Roaring Twenties, the 1987-90 era of intense foreign speculation in US real estate – predominantly by the Japanese, and the securitized mortgage ("CMBS") craze gained in the early part of this century.

Liberal cycle conditions move towards a crescendo with heightened market euphoria, highlighted as follows:

- Unbridled optimism prevails about realty fundamentals;
- Investors traditionally classified as long-term holders of properties transform to active sellers, as opportunistic pricing encourages dispositions;
- Proforma assumptions painted optimistically as dynamic underwriting readily accepted (e.g., high-income growth rates, lowered vacancy factors, overlooking the impact of frothy pricing on real estate taxes, minimizing or eliminating reserves);
- Rising prices accompany higher leverage financings – typically exceeding 75% for senior debt during inflationary conditions;
- Non-real-estate items drive investment decisions, such as tax avoidance and other special incentives;
- Fee- vs. performance-driven transactions dominate, as promoters take advantage of strong investor appetite;
- Existing properties frequently sell near or above replacement cost;
- New construction volume peaks, including speculative developments with limited preleasing;
- More speculative new construction without ample preleasing to cover permanent financing scenarios;

- Overabundant liquidity lures in many "fresh" investors with little [or no] market experience;
- Offering memorandums exclude asking prices, as sellers expect bidding wars [often above the recommended sales price];
- Transactions close quicker as buyers fear losing deals to competitive bidders;
- "Appraisal lag" created as rapidly rising prices based on faster closing timelines render the Sales Comparison Approach more challenging to use for gauging value;
- Buyers remove more closing contingencies, including financing and detailed property inspections;
- "New" creative financing methods surface, often misunderstood by investors (e.g., Collateralized Debt Obligations "CDO" of 2008);
- Narrowing price differentials between various property types and markets indicating flattening property investment yield curves;
- Straight or inverted treasury yield curves, showing long-term investments appear less risky than shorter-term opportunities;
- Personal guarantees requirements reduced or eliminated on construction ventures and projects with deficit cash flow (e.g., rehabs);
- Loan amortization eliminated, or payment schedules extended for justifying higher leverage loans; and
- Acceptance of more liberal definitions of "equity" beyond actual cash contributions into a venture (e.g., "earned," "imputed," "soft").

Market cycles eventually change, and the euphoria stops, creating a backlash by moving to the other extreme – the conservative cycle. In other words, " the music stops, and not everybody finds a chair."

CONSERVATIVE CYCLE

Often dreaded, conservative market cycles represent some of the best opportunities in real estate, especially for contrarian investors. Many buyers and lenders retreat from real estate due to declining financial performance caused by softening economic conditions. As a result, investors capture some of these failed ventures at deep discounts. The most common reasons for poor performance during such cycles include overleverage, improper management, rising vacancy/collection losses, and other woes exacerbated by tightening credit and reduced user demand. The keyword describing this cycle is "uncertainty."

Conservative cycles develop as dramatic reactions to liberal conditions. The best examples include the two "Greats" – the Depression of 1929 and the Recession of 2008. Uncertainty punishes the markets. Investor expectations remain flat or decline, depending on economic chaos.

During conservative market cycles, the real estate industry mainly focuses on defensive risk reduction strategies featuring the following conditions:

- Emphasis shifts from transactional underwriting to property management with a focus on solving existing portfolio issues, namely insufficient leasing, tenant default, and debt restructuring;
- The sales market is dominated by financial institutions disposing of defaulted debt with properties priced well below replacement costs and favoring "all-cash" buyers due to overall illiquidity;
- For solvent non-distress assets, wide gaps exist between seller and buyer expectations, with few transactions closing as a result of overall market pessimism characterized by "wait and see" attitudes;
- Scarcity of funding options attract higher yield investor based on lower leverage and generous spread premiums at all levels of the real estate capital ratestack;
- Static underwriting, popular as analysis, focuses on immediate performance benchmarks, namely the lower of (1) historically proven or (2) actual income streams;
- Dynamic cash flow proformas limited to rare cases such as longer-term, credit-tenant income;
- Less reliance on variable income generated from overage rents or other cash flows stressing performance above minimum provable thresholds;
- Local and federal government-subsidized financing or grants, high-yield debt funds, and "hard-money" [expensive] lenders gain popularity based on capital availability vs. pricing importance;
- Except for projects under construction, new development activities cease, limited to only to preleased projects;

- Very stringent documentation is required, including extensive financial statement reviews (e.g., workouts, bankruptcies), appraisal and feasibility reports; and
- The strict adherence to personal guarantees, supplemental collateral, and additional credit enhancements for funding any transactions lacking sufficient income streams.

As economic conditions stabilize, markets return to a more normal state, transitioning into a neutral cycle, discussed further below.

NEUTRAL CYCLE

Neutral cycles reflect "normality." While normality suggests different meanings for various investors, steady market behavior prevails. Property values climb [or drop] paced to inflation. Sellers and buyers share similar expectations about overall economic conditions. Under such circumstances, risk/reward analysis appears consistent.

The 1950s served as an example of a neutral real estate cycle.[94] During this era, real estate markets - retail, office, industrial, and hotel - were all entering a period of sustained growth kindled by the pent-up demand and the surging economy.[95] By the decade's end, inflation moderated, indicating a stable economy.

Neutral cycles feature more predictable supply-and-demand fundamentals, with only minor signs of market disruptions, based on the following underwriting conditions:

- No undue external market influences exist, such as major global economic concerns, financial crisis, or rampant inflation;
- Income stream expectations reflect historical data for stabilized properties characterized by stable vacancy rates and minimum rent concessions;
- Cash flow projections are limited to value-creation and new construction ventures;

- Traditional leverage ranges of 65% to 75% LTV prevail using 1.2X-1.40X DSCRs based on underwriting actual cash flows adjusted for growth at the inflation rate;
- Amortizing loans dominate (e.g., 25-30 year schedules), while interest-only payments are reserved for low-leverage debt or construction loans;
- Existing properties typically trade based on cash flow performance metrics (e.g., Sale Comparison and Income Approach) rather than replacement costs;
- Replacement costs justify new construction as land, labor, and material pricing remain under control;
- Cash flow projections are limited to value-creation and new construction ventures;
- Scarcity of newfangled funding programs as ample funding sources dominate, including banks, life companies, securitization sources, government agencies, overseas investors, and pension funds;
- Non-traditional property types and assets located in tertiary markets are priced accordingly, namely higher risk premiums accompanied by lower leverage;
- Forward-delivery fundings selectively surface for presale and new construction projects with adequate pre-leasing;
- Transactions close based on usual timelines of 30 to 90 days since sellers and buyers work under normal due diligence conditions;
- Property valuations reflect close relationships to recent sales and operating data based on the Sales Comparison Approach since minimal pricing differentials exist;
- Short and long-term treasury yields maintain wider spread ratios (e.g., 50-60 basis points), reflecting appropriate extended risk premiums;
- Partial or full personal guarantees are required for construction ventures and projects with deficit cash flow (e.g., rehabs);
- Equity contributions are credited based on actual cash infusions and proven appreciation as measured over longer terms, typically two years or more; and
- Professional investors thrive in traditional roles as mainstream buyers and sellers, with few surprises lurking, such as a flood of inexperienced buyers flooding sellers with countless offers.

Understanding the characteristics of the three cycles leads to a discussion about predicting what future cycles might look like, as discussed below.

THE NEXT CYCLE?

The Funding Pendulum illustrates how the three real estate capital market cycles move based on historical factors. During the past half-century, steady growth characterized the 1960s [neutral], followed by rampant inflation during the 1970s [liberal]. During the 1980s, dramatic interest rate hikes combined with the savings and loan debacle set the stage for a market crash in the early 1990s [conservative]. Later that decade, investors enjoyed a return to profitability by re-entering the markets [neutral]. The new millennium fundamentals improved, but an oversupply of capital flooded the industry [liberal], leading to the Great Recession [conservative]. Since 2012, higher yields have generated a steady return to the sector [normal], led by more institutional and international capital sources. COVID, inflation, and the Ukraine invasion create uncertainty during the 2020 era, leaning towards more cautionary investing [conservative].

While the Funding Pendulum applies to the cyclical behavior of realty capital markets, other non-sector indices also prove helpful. For example, the Institute of Purchasing Managers Index (also known as the National Association of Purchasing Managers Index (NAPM)) tracks domestic industrial buying behavior in 21 industries covering all 50 states, serving as a leading indicator of economic activity. The NAPM index often represents a business confidence barometer. The manufacturing sector is excessively volatile if this index shows three successive months above or below the 50-mark. If the index rises above 50, the manufacturing industry continues expanding; a drop below 50 indicates a contraction.

Looking ahead, investors expect longer-term cycles to be more prevalent. Historically, cycles usually lasted three to five years before losing momentum. For example, the pre-COVID era, known as the "Great Recovery," spans over a decade.[96] Market momentum persists even through the uncertainty of recent pandemics. For example, the RCLCO Current Real Estate Market Sentiment Index (RMI), which measures sentiment on a 100-point scale, has increased

57.5 points over the six months, from 31.6 at YE 2020 to 89.1 at Mid-2021, returning to a high not seen since Mid-2015.[97]

Longer growth streaks are possible due to significantly more governmental intervention. Legislatures target the real estate industry to create better social conditions. Qualified investments attract subsidized funding structures for serving public needs while helping reduce market risk and increasing liquidity. The following section discusses that the net result leads to longer and smoother cycles.

SMOOTHING THE CYCLES

"Events tend to recur in cycles" - W. Clement Stone.

When necessary, the Funding Pendulum "gets a push" from governmental authorities with special funding programs designed to "smooth" real estate market cycle volatility. Policymakers believe in maintaining credit flow into the $7-trillion-plus real-estate industry due to the massive amount of outstanding commercial real estate debt circulating in the credit markets.[98] Moreover, the commercial real estate development industry supports nearly eight million jobs, contributing about ten billion dollars to the economy.[99]

Economic realities offer tremendous upside for real estate capital markets to tap into the public sector. In particular, real estate professionals serve communities as premisists, acting as stewards of the premises focusing on socially responsible ownership and investments.[100] With various agencies and private foundations, investors fulfill many environmental, social, and governance ("ESG") objectives for improving disadvantaged communities.

The public sector offers many tools to encourage real estate investors to own and operate mission-driven asset classes, namely affordable housing, and commercial development, for supporting underserved areas. More specifically, the Department of Housing and Urban Development ("HUD"), FreddieMac, and Fannie Mae ["Government Sponsored Enterprises, or GSEs") competitively fund affordable housing within the multifamily, senior, and student sectors. For commercial properties, tax incremental financing ("TIF"), New Market Tax Credits, historic tax credits, Opportunity Zones, Enterprise Zones, and other subsidized capital vehicles encourage developers to create projects in these communities. Some of these more popular loan programs and grants are highlighted as follows:

GSE Loan Programs: Freddie and FNMA offer below-market mortgage rates, targeting affordable and workforce housing, including tertiary markets. For example, according to the Federal Housing Finance Agency, recent multifamily loan purchase caps for both agencies reached $78 billion each. The combined $156 billion shows the multifamily market's strong support for this sector, typically irrespective of market cycles.[101]

HUD Loan Programs: FHA offers attractive loans for new construction using higher leverage of 80% LTV or more with longer amortization schedules (35-40 years), as well as refinancing existing apartments via Section 221(d) and 223(f) programs, respectively. Also, the Section 8 program provides rental assistance vouchers.

Community Development Block and Real Estate Grants: These real estate grants are available to recipients undertaking neighborhood revitalization and economic development initiatives.

The Lead Hazard Reduction Demonstration Real Estate Grants Program: Over forty-nine million dollars has been allocated to this federal real estate grant program to assist with temporary relocations and interim control of lead-based hazards in eligible privately-owned homes and multifamily units occupied by low-income families.

Supportive Housing for the Elderly Real Estate Grants: This federal money is awarded for acquiring structures to provide supportive housing for the elderly, including the cost of real property acquisition, site improvement, conversion, demolition, relocation, and other expenses of supportive housing for the elderly. Project rental assistance is also available for elderly individuals who qualify;[102]

Miscellaneous: Selective funds surface that private foundations sponsor via real estate grants. An example of a more prolific awarding organization is the Sobrato Family Foundation. This foundation provides unrestricted general operating support, in-kind office and meeting space real estate grants, and affordable housing loans.

Other government initiatives supporting the real estate industry include energy-saving [green] initiatives and various forms of property tax abatement.

Undoubtedly, public-private real estate partnerships will expand as society works to solve basic shelter needs for housing and commercial space.

The discussion of primary realty capital market conditions, including government assistance, helps provide an understanding for quantifying different cycles to formulate investment timing decisions.

QUANTIFYING CYCLES

Profit is the leading benchmark for quantifying market cycles. From a pure business perspective, the only relevant market conditions relate to revenue, expenses, and investment capital, leading to the ROI. The profit motive leads to the concept of economic value added (EVA) to evaluate market performance. EVA equals revenue minus costs, including operational and financing expenses (the cost of capital). The formula for economic profit is as follows:

$$\text{Economic Profit} = (\text{ROIC} - \text{WACC}) * \text{Invested Capital}$$

The ROIC is the return on invested capital, WACC is the weighted average cost of capital, and invested capital is the capital stack (debt + equity). Rearranging the equation results in

$$\text{ROIC} - \text{WACC} = \text{Economic Profit}/\text{Invested Capital}$$

Intuitively, firms profitably perform when generating returns above borrowing costs. If the investor's borrowing cost (mortgage constant and cost of equity combined) is 8%, for economic profit to occur, the deal must support a cap rate (which is the equivalent of ROIC) greater than 8%.

For example, a property generates a cap rate of 6.75%. The buyer obtains a 4% mortgage based on a 60% LTV. The 10-year constant maturity Treasury bond currently yields 1.5%. The necessary risk premium required for the equity is 4.5%, and the beta on REIT stocks relative to the S&P500 shows .83, generating the following results.

ROIC = Cap Rate = 6.75%

Cost of Debt = Mortgage constant = 5.7%

Cost of Equity = Capital Asset Pricing Model = 1.5% + .83*4.5% = 5.2%

WACC = LTVR*Cost of Debt + (1-LTVR)*Cost of Equity = 60%*5.7% + 40%*5.2% = 5.5%

Economic Profit Ratio = Cap Rate – WACC = 6.75% - 5.5% = 1.25%

Various national real estate organizations publish mortgage and valuation data using these formulas, including the following sample graphs.[103]

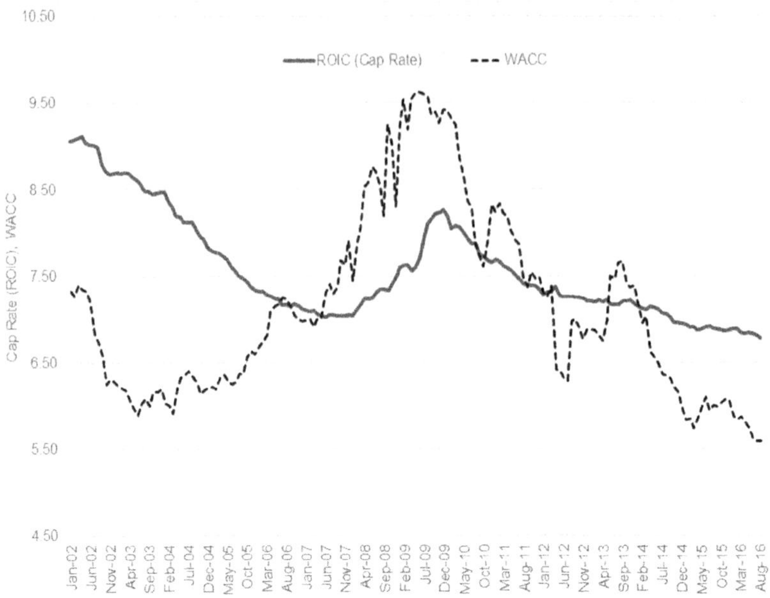

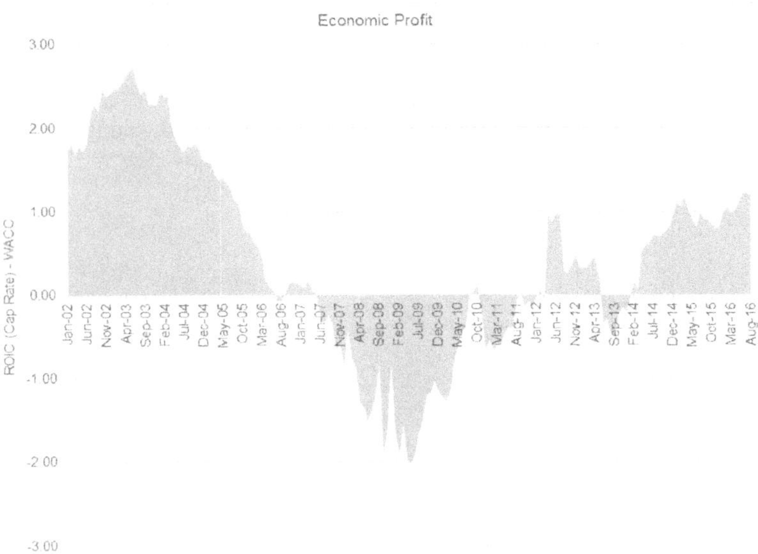

The graphs compare 2002 to 2016, for example. More specifically, the charts show that from June 2002 to May 2005, liberal market conditions existed, resulting from low borrowing costs, compressed cap rates, and values exceeding borrowing costs. From March 2006 until January 2012, conservative market conditions prevailed, with cap rates rising and borrowing costs exceeding cap rates, with most returns generated from reversions (sales) compared to operations. Neutral market conditions appeared in January 2012 and have generally continued steadily improving through August 2016.

The various market data illustrate the importance of tracking cycles for correctly optimizing investment timing, including the acquisition, operations, and final disposition. While the transaction-centric real estate investment analysis, underwriting, and research prove essential, a market cycle potentially wipes out profits based on an incorrectly timed holding period. A famous Warren Buffet quote says, "Never count on making a good sale. Have the purchase price be so attractive that even a mediocre sale gives good results."[104] Or, put more simply: "You make your money when you buy, not when you sell."

Regardless of the numerous tools used for evaluating investments, multiple change agents plotted over time leave the fundamental variables of return on investment (cash flow and principal recovery) intact. Many of these changes improve reaching ROI goals but keep true to the profit motive.

Mathematical modeling and other cycle analysis tools prove academically rewarding. However, investors must stay focused on risk/reward strategies for surviving [and thriving] by maintaining solvency through each cycle.

CYCLE SOLVENCY

History teaches investors that maintaining solvency is one of the most important lessons about market cycles. John Maynard Keynes, the most famous British economist of the 20th Century, commented, "the markets can remain irrational longer than you can remain solvent."[105]

Sufficient solvency will override market cycles, helping the investment weather hard times. Therefore, providing adequate liquidity must be part of every investor's risk/reward strategy. Investors can never be *too* liquid, as the most incredible opportunities emerge during illiquid cycles.

Solvency remains the investor's responsibility. However, prudent funding sources mandate liquidity. For instance, permanent lenders require at least six months of debt service as a minimum cash flow reserve. On a macroeconomic level relating to the most current cycle, the Fed forced liquidity into the financial system during the start of the COVID, thereby avoiding an epic catastrophe.

More fresh learning experiences await in the future. Upcoming cycles will introduce new issues and require creative solutions as real estate investors navigate unknown capital markets.

In conclusion, based on the *Four Pillars*, investors formulate risk/reward strategies [First Pillar]. The appropriate underwriting tools determine how specific investment opportunities translate to the risk/reward yields [Second Pillar]. After that, investors study cycles, determining the investment's timing and the solvency needs [Third Pillar]. Lastly, through funding, the opportunity converts to an actual investment. *Investing – Risk/Reward Capital*, the final pillar of the *Four Pillars*, is discussed in the next chapter.

CHAPTER 5: INVESTING - RISK/REWARD CAPITAL

"Real estate investing, even on a very small scale, remains a tried and true means of building an individual's cash flow and wealth." - Robert Kiyosaki

The Fourth Pillar, Investing, converts land, labor, and capital from the conceptual stage to an actual investment. Real estate investing occurs continuously through all market cycles and liquidity crises. "Money never sleeps,"[106] but rather gravitates to the best risk/reward opportunities. For example, "smart" money flees from this sector when more profitable opportunities exist elsewhere. Under such conditions, the real estate attracts capital but at extremely high yields to compensate for greater risk and illiquidity. Therefore, the wise investor commits substantial time and energy to find the optimum funding structure best suited for the targeted investment at the given time.

This chapter explores various capital options for funding realty investments, including equity, debt, and combinations of both. The Real Estate Capital RateStack format serves as the basis for organizing these funding options according to risk/reward tolerances, progressing from equity [higher risk] to debt [lower risk], followed by hybrid options [mixed risk]. After that, each capital option links to the 5 P's, illustrations, and observations. More specifically, the 5 P's classifies the significant elements of each funding structure, including investors and lenders [people], targeted locations [place], preferred property types [project], underwriting/investing parameters [performance], and issues (pros/cons).

Ultimately, the various funding structures discussed lead investors to choose the best capital options based on ownership objectives. For example, debt sources closely match income streams to funding structures. Permanent debt lenders (e.g., life companies) prefer long-term investments (e.g., annuities), while other lenders (e.g., commercial banks) target shorter-term maturities (e.g., deposits).

Regardless, every real estate investment decision starts with finding equity to launch the venture.

EQUITY

"If companies are able to raise equity from the market, then their problems for financing incomplete projects will come to end. Investment cycle in the capital market can kick-start with the money of savers and investors." - Uday Kotak

Real estate remains one of the most prized investments in America. Over several decades income property ownership evolved from casual investing to highly technical money management, especially for more significant transactions of ten million dollars or more. In fact, since the second half of the twentieth century, realty investment has emerged as an integral portfolio component for larger investors (e.g., public companies, pension funds, and life insurance companies). For example, originating in 1960, REITs now own about one-third of the entire multifamily market[107], valued at more than three trillion dollars.[108]

Before funding equity into real estate ventures, investors need to determine the most suitable ownership format given the sponsorship and investment team composition.

Structuring equity ownership of income properties depends upon various factors, including project size, ownership expertise, capital needs, risk preferences, holding strategies, and income tax consequences. That said, property ownership for most ventures includes three basic formats: sole proprietorships, partnerships, and corporations. Each of these structures offers different advantages and disadvantages.

Sole ownership best suits small-scale projects matched with a single investor. Total property control and risk/rewards flow to the individual, including cash flow and income tax savings[losses]. However, all liabilities flow to the individual as well. For example, any legal or other unfavorable actions against the owner can place all the individual's assets at risk, including personal and real property.

For larger projects, better risk-sharing occurs with partnerships, which provides additional options to expand ownership capacity. Such arrangements introduce other owners interested in sharing profits from the project in return for contributing capital and potentially taking on more risk. Numerous partnerships exist, including simple or general partnerships, limited liability companies ("LLC"), and limited partnerships.

Simple partnerships range from informal agreements to more technical profit-sharing arrangements for the project or real estate business. Partnership structuring requires documenting the partners' capital contributions, profits, and responsibilities.

Next, LLCs offer partnership agreements tied explicitly to investment membership. Each LLC partner is a venture member but not necessarily tied to any other holdings of different partners in the specific deal. An LLC acts as a pass-through entity, allowing individual members to accrue tax benefits. This structure also the liability of the member to the investment amount.

Limited partnerships offer yet another partnership format. Such partnerships apply to larger ventures with general partners controlling the project while limited partners contribute investment capital. These partnership arrangements allow for flexible profit and risk-sharing arrangements by allocating certain investment benefits [restrictions} to various partners. For instance, limited partners avoid operational decisions but receive income tax savings. The liability exposure of the limited partner only extends to the capital contribution.

Finally, corporate ownership suits large-scale investments and portfolios. Profits flow to the stockholders as dividends. Such entities benefit owners earning ordinary income from real estate activities rather than investments. For example, mining companies own and operate properties for extracting coal and other natural resources. However, corporate taxation, cost of compliance, transferability of stocks, and numerous other issues prohibit such structures from working effectively. In particular, taxation occurs at the corporate level, voiding depreciation and other deductions for personal income tax benefits. On the other hand, corporate ownership does provide a shield to protect shareholders from personal liability. In addition, some liquidity is available due to the sale of shares.

Otherwise, REITs, family trusts, and other more complex ownership formats exist for investors needing a wider variety of options. Portfolio management, public market access for raising debt and equity (e.g., stock and bond issuance), and unique wealth transfer needs serve as excellent samples of such options. REITs, in particular, effectively cover corporate ownership while offering investor liquidity and tax pass-thru benefits. More notably, REITs distribute at least 90% of taxable income as dividends, presenting a viable alternative to directly owning real estate.

Given the wide variety of equity ownership options, the chart below illustrates the full equity investment highlights based on the 5 P's of real estate.

FULL EQUITY

PEOPLE	
Investor	→ Owners, developers, all forms
User Eligibility	→ Sufficient experience and expertise to own and operate project
PLACE	
Location	→ Metro and immediate areas justifying property types/uses for investment strategy
Site Characteristics	→ Compliant with local laws, appropriate ingress-egress, environmentally secure
PROJECT	
Property Type	→ Multifamily, industrial, office, retail, self storage, mixed-use, student, senior housing
Grade	→ Existing and to-be-built Class A, Class B, and Class C
Project Economics	→ Various, depending upon strategies (core, core-plus, value-add and opportunity)
Other	→ Product knowledge, capital access and local expertise match investment strategies
PERFORMANCE	
Dollar Size	→ Various, $5MM+ (small), $20-50MM institutional (medium), $50MM+ (large)
Funding Format	→ Leveraged, unleveraged (all-cash) with/without partners
Overall Yield	→ 0-400+ bps mortgage yield (core/core-plus), 401-600+ bps (value-add), 601+ bps (opportunity)
Holding Term	→ 10 yrs (avg), < 5 yrs (short), 5-9 yrs (medium), 11-40 yrs (long)
Leverage (optional)	→ 65%-75% LTV (avg), 80%-90% (high, credit only), < 65% LTV (low), all-cash (rare, except land)
Mortgage Rate	→ 100-150 bps + Treasury (low LTV, Class A), 151-200 bps (avg, Class B), 200-250+ bps (Class C)
Payment Format	→ Interest-only or amortization, proforma underwritten to pref yield with reversion
Debt Coverage	→ 1X+ (core), pre-stabilized 1.15-1.25X (core-plus), 1-1.15X+ (value-add), <1X (opportunity)
Funding Timeline	→ Immediate initial disbursement (0-60 days), phased over investment strategy timeline
Prepayment	→ Minimal lockout until strategy termination, flexible buy/sell provisions
PROS/CONS	
Investor	+ Inflation hedge, cash flow streams plus [reversion] appreciation
	+ Higher leverage provides attractive yields
	+ Non recourse format reduces contingent liabilities, assumability protects leverage yield
	- Illiquid, operational expertise and financial capacity required for non-core ventures
	- Capital market conditions, local supply/demand imbalance, functional obsolescence concerns
	- Improper leverage levels and amortization overburden cash flows

KEY: avg = average, bps = basis point spread, LTV = loan-to-value, credit-only = investment-grade tenant or low LTV, TPC = total project cost, yrs = years

The chart focuses on the most important 5 P's elements relating to profit expectations, namely investor types [people], location/site characteristics [place], asset details [project], yield metrics [performance], and concerns [pros/cons].

The first P of the 5 P's, "People," focuses on ownership structure, talent, and resources. Investors range from individuals casually looking for real estate investments to institutional investors routinely buying and selling larger portfolios. Given the broad choice of real estate opportunities, ownership requires the proper mix of experience, capital, and market/property expertise to execute various investment strategies.

The second P, "Place," emphasizes finding communities with social and physical infrastructures that effectively support various local sites for the intended property uses. This equity investment decision mainly relies on understanding the chosen location's demographics and specific site attributes.

The third P, "Project," section covers the most popular investment property types, including apartments, industrial, office, retail, self-storage, mixed-use, student, and senior housing. The overall grading system for physical conditions ranks from Class A to C. The project economics explores existing rent rolls and cash flow characteristics. That said, property preferences and cash flow dynamics change over time. For example, during the 1980s, suburban office buildings reigned; in the 1990s, shopping centers dominated; throughout much of this century, industrial and multifamily assets top the investment charts.

The fourth P, "Performance," delves into the return on investment metrics, the heart of profit expectations. Investments fall into small, medium, and large categories, peaking at $50 million. The dollar size ranks essential for choosing the ownership format, financing, and investment talent. In particular, projects below $5 million typically don't appeal to institutional investors who must put longer blocks of cash to work. On the other hand, substantial projects eliminate most investors due to intensive capital requirements.

Regardless of dollar size, all property types and sizes are judged in the context of the appropriate yield. Generally, investors target risk premiums 600 basis points or more over a safe benchmark rate for overall yields for the highest risk (opportunity investments). For example, if ten-year mortgage rates generate 4% returns, investors expect 10% or more overall yields using ROI, NPV, IRRs, or other applicable underwriting formulas. In the same example, core, core-plus, and value add investment strategies fall between the 4% to 10% overall yield range. Most to-be-built properties require at least 50 to 100 basis points premiums to cover uncertainty, cash flow quality (preleasing), and property-type differences. Pricing exceptions apply for unique "trophy" properties in most categories. Also, except in rare instances (e.g., net-lease properties with "flat" cash flows), annual income and property values are expected to increase at least by the inflation rate during the holding period. Therefore, overall yields (IRR) exceed current estimates (such as cash on cash and ROI).

Profit expectations directly correspond to the length of the investment horizon. Many investors target ten-year holding periods. Five-year- or-less periods fall into the "short" category, while 11 years or more rank as "long" holds. Also, longer-term holding periods tend to reduce overall yields. Value-creation and speculation thresholds typically require the highest returns and the shortest holding periods.

Adding leverage by obtaining mortgages usually amplifies overall returns to the extent that ROI exceeds borrowing costs, creating positive leverage. However, the use of leverage (use of debt) remains optional. Large institutional investors sometimes avoid debt, depending on their cost of capital and investment goals (e.g., core strategies). Otherwise, 65% to 75% LTV stands as a historical norm. That said, debt coverage ratios (1-1.5X+) limit loan proceeds.

Leverage pricing mainly links to LTV levels and asset classes. In general, mortgage rates are based on the yield of comparable maturity treasuries, e.g., a mortgage with a ten-year term is priced off a 10-year Treasury bond, starting as low as 100 basis points spread (100 bps is equal to 1%), climbing above 200 basis points (2%) for riskier assets or higher leverage. For example, if the current ten-year treasury bond yield is 3%, mortgage rates range from four to five percent. However, during a highly low-rate environment, lenders will price mortgages at minimum rates instead of using an index.

Lenders allow flexible payment formats to enhance investor equity yields, including interest-only for shorter-term debt, preferring amortization for loans of ten years or more. Lastly, unleveraged and leveraged yields can overlap substantially due to varying investor expectations.

The fifth and final P, "pros/cons," applies to specific real estate equity investment opportunities. Since no two investments share identical risks and rewards, analysis of pros and cons allows for unique insights and conclusions such as those shown by the example below.

Illustration: The Trojan shopping center consists of a 232,987 square foot building situated on 14.7 acres in University Park, California. The center was purchased for $34,375,000. Even though this older center is 94% occupied, the property represents a value-add opportunity as the rent roll features substantial tenant rollover risk. The buyer, Joe Bruin, plans to upgrade and re-lease the center using additional out-of-pocket equity as needed. As such, Bruin obtained a 10-year loan for $27,500,000 at 5.23% with a 30-year amortization, open to prepayment after five years, when Bruin expects to sell the property. Bruin wants to maintain flexibility with the loan in case a sale is not feasible at that time, hence the longer permanent loan term. Bruin provides full recourse and additional collateral to the lender for funding the loan. Also, Bruin plans to sell the center based on a residual (going-out) cap rate of 7.5%.

Bruin calculates the weighted average lease maturity for the center (WALM) with the results below.

Year Ending Dec 31,	Year	Expiring GLA	%GLA	Yr*%GLA
MTM	0	4,636	1.99%	0
2012	1	1,840	0.79%	0.007897436
2013	2	18,365	7.88%	0.157648281
2014	3	24,120	10.35%	0.310575268
2015	4	27,913	11.98%	0.479219871
2016	5	29,280	12.57%	0.628361239
2017	6	34,156	14.66%	0.879602725
2018	7	0	0.00%	0
2019	8	20,911	8.98%	0.71801431
2020	9	30,718	13.18%	1.186598394
2021	10	0	0.00%	0
2022	11	26,751	11.48%	1.262993214
Vacant	0	14,297	6.14%	0
Total		232,987	100.00%	**5.6**

The WALM shows 5.6 years, yet the lender funds a 10-year loan. Typically, the loan term remains less than the WALM period to reduce risk. In this case, however, additional collateral and full recourse allow the lender to accept the substantial lease rollover risk during the loan term. The forecasted cash flows for the center appear below.

	0	1	2	3	4	5	6
Base Rent		$3,831,628	$3,721,626	$3,778,300	$3,834,975	$3,892,499	$3,950,887
Percentage Rent		-1,408	3,704	4,409	4,794	4,866	4,939
Total Reimbursables		1,308,860	1,187,075	1,072,845	1,265,542	1,284,525	1,303,793
Other Income		21,013	40,774	27,483	27,483	27,483	27,483
Potential Gross Income		5,160,093	4,953,179	4,883,037	5,132,793	5,209,372	5,287,101
Less Vacancy & Credit Loss (6%)		-229,898	-223,298	-226,698	-230,098	-233,550	-237,053
Effective Gross Income		4,930,195	4,729,881	4,656,339	4,902,694	4,975,823	5,050,048
Less: Total Operating Expenses		1,476,040	1,447,186	1,340,071	1,470,808	1,492,747	1,515,014
Net Operating Income		3,454,155	3,282,695	3,316,268	3,431,886	3,483,076	3,535,033
Less: TI/LC		738	3,396	1,227	1,300	1,300	1,300
Less: Capital Expenditures		0	0	0	0	0	0
Net Cash Flow		3,453,417	3,279,299	3,315,041	3,430,586	3,481,776	3,533,733
Net Operating Income		$3,454,155	$3,282,695	$3,316,268	$3,431,886	$3,483,076	3,535,033
Less: Debt Service		$1,818,186	$1,818,186	$1,818,186	$1,818,186	$1,818,186	
Before Tax Cash Flow		$1,635,969	$1,464,509	$1,498,082	$1,613,700	$1,664,889	
Net Operating Income (Year 6)						3,535,033	
÷ Residual (Going Out) Cap Rate						7.50%	
Expected Sale Price						$47,133,778	
Less: Selling Costs @ 6%						$2,828,027	
Net Sale Price						$44,305,751	
Less: Mortgage Balance (EOY5)						$25,334,151	
Before Tax Equity Reversion						$18,971,600	
Initial Equity (Levered)	$6,875,000						
Initial Equity (No Debt)	$34,375,000						
Static Analysis: No Debt Case							
Net Operating Income		$3,454,155					
÷ Initial Equity (No Debt)		$34,375,000					
Cash on Cash Return		10.05%					
Static Analysis: With Debt Case							
Before Tax Cash Flow		$1,635,969					
÷ Initial Equity (Levered)		$6,875,000					
Cash on Cash Return		23.80%					
Cash Flows (No Debt)							
Initial Equity (No Debt)	($34,375,000)						
Net Operating Income		$3,454,155	$3,282,695	$3,316,268	$3,431,886	$3,483,076	
Net Sale Price						$44,305,751	
Total Cash Flows (No Debt)	($34,375,000)	$3,454,155	$3,282,695	$3,316,268	$3,431,886	$47,788,827	
IRR (No Debt)	14.2%						
Cash Flows (With Debt)							
Initial Equity (Levered)	($6,875,000)						
Before Tax Cash Flow		$1,635,969	$1,464,509	$1,498,082	$1,613,700	$1,664,889	
Before Tax Equity Reversion						$18,971,600	
Total Cash Flows (With Debt)	($6,875,000)	$1,635,969	$1,464,509	$1,498,082	$1,613,700	$20,636,490	
IRR (With Debt)	39.1%						

The cash flow projections show the sale reversion at the end of the fifth year. However, the expected sale price uses the net operating income of the following (Year 6) rather than Year 5 – the preferred methodology for computing reversions.

Next, the return on equity ("cash on cash") is magnified with leverage; 10.05% (no debt) vs. 23.8% (with debt) indicates that the project has positive leverage. Additionally, using dynamic analysis, the IRR with debt (39.1%) exceeds the IRR without a mortgage (14.2%), confirming the concept of positive leverage for projects with healthy, increasing cash flows.

The projections show a current yield (cash on cash) of 23.8%. This yield is greater than the mortgage constant (annual debt service ÷ loan amount = $1,818,186 ÷ $27,500,000) at 6.6%. Also, since the current yield exceeds the cap rate of 10% (net operating income in Year 1 ÷ Purchase Price = $3,454,155 ÷ $34,375,000), positive leverage is demonstrated with static (one period) analysis. Intuitively, the return on equity (cash on cash) not only exceeds the borrower's cost of debt (mortgage constant) but also exceeds the return if no debt exists (100% equity), as demonstrated by the cap rate. Combined with the other underwriting indices, this test indicates that the Trojan center ranks as a profitable investment opportunity.

Observation: Equity investing profit benchmarks serve as guidelines rather than rules. Although many approaches stand the test of time, conventional wisdom sometimes fails investors. For example, traditional thinking suggests that investors demand higher yields due to greater risk associated with time exposure when planning extended holding periods. Dynamic cash flow analysis usually proves the opposite, as longer projections erode yields. Also, lower interest rates typically suggest slowing economic conditions and less overall demand for money. However, the second decade offered different results, with the lowering of interest rates translating to lower cap rates and correspondingly higher prices. The most crucial real estate equity investing guidelines require flexible and creative thinking by mixing new ideas with proven past concepts.

After understanding the role of equity capital in real estate projects, the next step involves analyzing debt options. The optimal combination of equity with debt produces some of the most profitable investment opportunities, as positive leverage amplifies yields while reducing equity capital exposures.

DEBT

Encumbering properties with mortgages remains a desirable option for most investors. Most often, debt represents the largest component of the Real Estate Capital RateStack (e.g., 65% LTV). While Investors occasionally purchase projects on an all-cash basis or eventually retire existing debt, over sixty percent of U.S. households carry mortgages.[109] And the total commercial and multifamily debt outstanding climbed to about $3.5 trillion by the decade's end.[110]

In return for assuming debt, investors jeopardize equity which moves down along the Real Estate Capital RateStack. In other words, equity becomes "first in, last out." Since lenders (mortgagees) assume risk by usually funding significant portions of the investment, debt positions get secured to formalize the status of the lender claim on the real estate as collateral, with a public recording of the mortgage interests done to perfect the lien. In return, borrowers (mortgagors) promise to pay principal and interest as specified in the loan documents. In default, lenders become property owners after completing the foreclosure process. At that point, debts are repaid in order of lien priority, with senior lenders paid first, with any additional proceeds disbursed to the remaining subordinate lienholders such as second mortgage lenders, gap, or mezzanine lenders.

Properly structured debt positively impacts real estate transaction sizes, yields, and tax benefits. Due to the sheer size of real estate investments, using debt allows investors to enter the market for unaffordable properties by exclusively using cash. Leverage priced below investor equity costs of funds provides for favorable spreads, primarily based upon appreciating cash flow throughout the life of the investment. In addition, leveraged yields provide total overall returns, often far above all-cash returns. Finally, tax benefits through interest payments and leveraged depreciation offer tax savings, which are otherwise not possible for smaller-scale non-real estate investments based on the same equity contributions.

Along with overall capital supply and demand, leverage pricing and terms influence real estate investment metrics. Depending upon a variety of factors relating to the amount of debt and how that debt is structured, leverage either creates value or wipes out existing equity. Using leverage wisely (positive leverage) is key to successful real estate investing.

Real estate debt exists in various formats, classified by usage, duration, payment formats, and collateral repayment priorities. Sorted by duration and repayment priorities, these categories include temporary, construction, permanent and subordinate debt – each discussed in the remainder of this section.

TEMPORARY DEBT

Temporary financing, also known as bridge, transition, gap, or interim debt, targets funding investments in a transitional phase. This short-term funding vehicle ranges from days, weeks, months, or years needed for completing different real estate investment strategies. Fundings target construction loans, rehabs, dealer warehousing (buy-sell flips), and other short-term strategies used for value-creation or other purposes requiring funding flexibility. Due to the short-term funding horizon of temporary debt, floating-rate payment structures on an interest-only basis are typical.

Floating-Rate Loans

Fluid project conditions require flexible lending terms, namely new construction and redevelopment. As a result, variable-rate loans surface as the preferred financing format under such conditions. Often referred to as floating-rate mortgages, these temporary debt vehicles include bridge loans, indexed, or adjustable-rate mortgages ("ARM"). More exotic variations of floating rate debt include accrual loans and rarely used standby commitments, i.e., loans funded based on contingent terms relating to completion and cash flow performance.

Payments on floating-rate loans are pegged to spreads over popular benchmark indices to calculate debt service payment schedules. The most popular indices include Bank Prime, U.S. Treasuries, the Federal Home Loan Bank, SOFR, and LIBOR (discontinued). Unless agreed otherwise, indices remain transparent and easy to reference. Some lenders use more arbitrary indices (e.g., internal cost of funds) for higher-risk loans carrying costlier pricing. Also, indices tied to the interest rate futures market (e.g., Treasuries) allow borrowers to convert floating-rate to fixed-rate debt by purchasing commonly traded financial hedging instruments.

Highly volatile interest-rate environments pose concerns for lenders and borrowers alike. Floating-rate loans incorporate rate adjustment limits (ceiling and floors) and hedging programs for controlling debt service payments against wildly gyrating rates during volatile rate cycles. Also, interest rate accruals exist for capturing adjustments beyond debt service. By building the extra amounts into principal repayments, lenders typically recapture these accruals upon a liquidity event, such as financing or a sale. Additional charges apply for structuring these rate recapture and protection programs to compensate for the added risk.

Conversely, low volatility in interest rates during low inflation periods creates an opposite lending effect for floating-rate debt. Benchmark indices hardly move, eliminating the need for substantial hedging and other rate movement protection programs. Debt service payments appear predictable, helping to reduce borrowing costs (i.e., no prepayment penalty).

Lenders often customize floating-rate loan payments to match cash flows. For example, floating-rate debt fits income properties with variable cash flows, including multifamily, lodging, and self-storage assets. Under such conditions, cash flows often move in tandem with minimally changing debt service payments. In such circumstances, if cash flow is insufficient to pay debt service, the loan will feature an accrual to cover shortfalls.

Before payment resets, borrowers receive advanced notice of pending adjustments. As such, loan provisions include continuing payments at the readjusted debt service, converting to fixed-rate, or retiring the debt. The rate adjustments usually correspond to the payment periods, sometimes featuring alternative timelines. For instance, rate adjustments might occur quarterly, but debt service payments stay on monthly schedules.

Borrowers prefer floating rate debt for a variety of reasons. Under normal market conditions, floating-rate prices are below fixed-rate debt costs. However, borrowers favoring floating-rate loans seldom use lower pricing as the main reason for choosing such funding structures. Instead, debt flexibility remains tantamount, as projects needing value creation demand funding flexibility for proceeds to match an exit strategy, namely project completion for eventual sale or refinance.

Floating-rate debt programs offer favorable yield opportunities for lenders. Funding sources favor such debt investments for maintaining profitable indexed-based pricing while protecting yields from inflation erosion. Lenders using shorter-term deposits and investment capital dominate this funding arena, including commercial banks, savings banks, credit unions, credit companies, and private/public debt funds. Occasionally, some funding sources assume more significant maturity risk positions by funding long-term loans with short-term deposits. These borrow-short-lend-long strategies capture profitable outcomes when interest rates remain steady. However, rising short-term rates combined with flattened long-term yields (inverted yield curve) can produce unfavorable results. Accrual loans partially solve this dilemma for managing less predictable floating-rate payments.

Accrual loans require adding unpaid interest to the remaining principal by creating negative amortization.[111] For example, although interest rates float, payment schedules remain fixed. Or, lenders recover any accrued interest upon sale or refinancing. These loans provide effective results, assuming cash flows and property values keep pace with rising interest rates. Otherwise, results lead to disaster if interest rates sharply decline and property values suffer as the higher loan balances prove challenging to repay.

Sometimes characterized as "permanent construction loans," accrual loans share construction and permanent loan elements. Like construction loans, interest costs accrue into the development budget. The lender allows the incorporation of interest costs into the development budget, effectively allowing payments to be funded from loan disbursements. When used in construction or value-add situations, these loans feature interest-only payments (with accruals) until a stipulated debt coverage emerges, converting to amortization based on fixed payments -- known as "mini-perm" debt, deferring any surplus interest buildup to the principal.

Floating rate debt offers many features, summarized in the following table based upon the 5Ps:

FLOATING-RATE DEBT	
PEOPLE	
Borrower	→ Short-term income investors, public/private funds
User Eligibility	→ 1-2X net worth of loan amount, 6-12 months liquidity, substituted with more equity
Lender	→ Banks, debt funds, public/private debt funds
Source Eligibility	→ Regulated and unregulated institutions with short-term capital base
PLACE	
Location	→ Metro and immediate areas economically justifying property types/uses
Site Characteristics	→ Compliant with local laws, appropriate ingress-egress, environmentally secure
PROJECT	
Property Type	→ Multifamily, industrial, office, retail, self storage, mixed-use, student, senior housing
Grade	→ Existing Class A (non-recourse), Class B (selective recourse), Class C (full recourse)
Project Economics	→ Cash flowing (fluid), pending stabilization, operating history (optional)
Other	→ Ideal funding for flexible business plan or portfolio assemblage
PERFORMANCE	
Dollar Size	→ Various (recourse), $5MM+ (non-recourse), $20MM+ institutional (full non-recourse)
Funding Format	→ Adjustable-rate mortgage (typical), accrual loan (rare), standby commitments (very rare)
Leverage	→ 65%-75% LTV (avg), 80%-90% (high, credit only), < 65% LTV (low)
Term	→ < 5 yrs (avg), 5-10 yrs (long)
Rate (Yield)	→ Floating-rate indexed to Prime, cost of funds, or other index, +/- 100 bps of fixed-rate
Payment Format	→ Interest-only (typical), amortization (rare)
Debt Coverage	→ 1.25-1.3X (avg), 1.31-1.50X+ (high), <1.25X (rare)
Funding Timeline	→ Immediate (0-60 days), semi-forward (61-120 days), forward (121+ days)
Prepayment	→ Minimal lockout, declining balance (%), flexible pricing with rate premiums
Other	→ Rate [hedging] protection, credit-enhancement fees, recourse apply for structured fundings
PROS/CONS	
Borrower	+ Variable debt service payments matched to fluid cash flows
	+ Recapitalization flexibility for reversion, stabilization, portfolio assemblage
	+ Non recourse format reduces contingent liabilities, assumability protects leverage yield
	- Rate and term risks unsuitable for stable cash flows
	- Improper leverage levels and rate fluctuations overburden cash flows
	- Limited protection against dramatic rate hikes
Lender	+ Different maturities balance loan portfolio term risk
	+ Lower leverage loans attract premium quality sponsors and projects
	+ Popular funding structure for capturing fixed-rate debt upon stabilization
	- Higher leverage increases default risk
	- Mismatched rates and terms suffer value erosion
	- Difficult to retain profitable loans due to payoff flexibility

KEY: avg = average, bps = basis point spread, LTV[C] = loan-to-value[cost], credit-only = investment-grade tenant or low LTV, yrs = years

The Floating-rate debt chart shows nearly all the same investment analysis principles that apply to equity investments and debt based on the 5Ps of real estate. However, more emphasis lies on the sponsorship expertise, background, and talents to bring properties to financial stabilization. Additionally, since many of these funding sources are banks that fall under federal regulations, loan risk rating and compliance issues influence lending decisions. That said, private debt investors offer more flexibility due to less regulation but at higher prices and stricter terms.

Performance (the 4th P of the 5Ps) focuses on loan underwriting variables. Overall pricing on floating-rate deals generally ranges within 100 basis points of fixed-rate debt, starting about 150 basis points over applicable floating rate indices. However, floating-rate loans often cover transitional properties, and mortgage spreads increase dramatically with added risk, sometimes more than 600 basis points or more, using "hard money" funding sources. Additionally, debt service coverage requires careful analysis, with lenders using 125% to 150% or more based on the conservative underwriting to allow for interest rate movements during the term (usually 1 to 5 years). Lastly, leverage levels range between 65% to 75% for typical requests, with more aggressive financing reaching as high as 90%, available to the highest quality sponsors carrying strong cash-flowing ventures.

Focusing on the pros/cons (the 5th P), the ability to sustain rate increases within the given funding strategy takes precedence.

Illustration: Marquette Development Enterprises recently completed Graaskamp Breeze Tower, a 275-unit student apartment complex near the University of Wisconsin in Madison. The total project cost is $45 million and features an appraised value of $50 million. The project generates a net operating income of $3.5 million, resulting in a 7% cap rate and a 7.78% return on cost. Marquette seeks a $37.5 million loan translating to a 75% LTV. Instead, Marquette finds a lender willing to fund the loan but at fewer dollars.

The Federal Hawkeye Mortgage Investment Trust of Iowa City funds a $36 million first mortgage structured as a floating-rate loan. The debt is priced at 250 basis points over 30-day LIBOR, currently at three percent. Thus, the initial all-in rate is 5.5%, with interest-only (IO) payments for five years. An additional option is to extend the loan for five more years, which features a rate reset underwritten with a 25-year amortization schedule if exercised. The interest rate payments feature rate protection, with a three-percent lifetime cap (ceiling), limiting the maximum interest rate paid to 8.5%. In addition, rates readjust every six months, confined to a ten percent increase, regardless of the rate based on the base index and spread. If rate increases surpass the ten-percent debt service limit, the additional payments accrue are added to the original loan balance and repayable upon maturity. Lastly, the loan allows for prepayment in full after the first year without penalty.

Graaskamp Breeze Tower features attractive underwriting metrics for the lender. Hawkeye finances this venture based on the lowest loan amount generated by the following indices: (a) 75% loan-to-value, (b) 125% minimum debt service coverage, or (c) 80% loan-to-cost threshold. In this case, an 80% loan-to-cost limit restricts loan proceeds to $36 million ($45,000,000 x .80), instead of the 75% LTV limit of $37,500,000 ($50,000,000 x .75), or the debt service coverage ceiling of $50,900,000 ($3,500,000 / 1.25 / .055). The loan also offers an ample debt service cushion of 177% based on the current rate. Underwriting tolerates a mortgage ceiling of 8.25% in a worst-case scenario, supporting a 114% coverage ratio.

The loan also appeals to the borrower—the Marquette ownership strategy banks the strong demand for student housing near the university. Marquette believes rents will rise by ten percent annually during the next few years. A very tight housing supply exists near the campus, combined with limited buildable sites, rising construction costs, and a highly restrictive development environment within the community. As a result, Marquette favors a floating-rate funding strategy, hoping to sell the project within the next three years as cash flows peak and before new supply appears.

Observation: Floating-rate loan alternatives often include various funding combinations designed for maximum debt structuring flexibility. Borrowers use hybrid payment loans, namely ARMs, or fixed-period ARMS, combining desirable features of fixed-rate and adjustable-rate mortgages. The loans initially feature interest rates fixed for either 3, 5, 7, or 10 years. After the fixed period, the loans convert ARMs. For example, a loan features seven years of fixed-rate payments, then readjusts to a 23-year floating rate term. In this instance, the interest rate for the seven years would be priced lower than the current 30-year fixed-rate mortgage. This type of loan suits borrowers intending to hold the commercial property for shorter periods but desiring more pre-tax cash flow.

Construction Loans

Another form of temporary debt, construction loans, deserves special attention. Construction loans represent one of the most common forms of temporary debt. This loan type facilitates the purest kind of value creation.

Construction loan terms depend upon numerous variables, including physical aspects of the project, its design, local governmental regulations, the supply of material and labor, builder background and expertise, and budget constraints.

Construction loan draws usually disburse on timelines coinciding with a project's physical completion schedule. Most construction projects require six months or more for completion and up to three years or more to stabilize. Significant mixed-use developments can take even longer to reach stabilization. As a result, the loan customizes to fit the project's construction schedule and lease-up projection.

In most instances, developers provide personal guarantees during the loan term, at least until physical completion, if not breakeven. In addition to recourse, completion bonds and other guarantees ensure successful completion within specified conditions. Loan funding options include floating or fixed-rate payments, depending on the lending source and borrower needs. Debt service payments are typically lumped into the construction budget as part of the cost line items. Lastly, construction lenders earn additional revenue via loan origination and administration fees.

As with any debt instrument, full repayment of loan principal at maturity ranks the top priority for any lender. Funding sources reach a critical decision point at the termination of the construction of improvements, along with a sufficient lease-up period. Lenders may continue to hold the construction loan at the same or revised terms and conditions or request payoff. Similarly, the borrower compares what the construction lender offers as a "mini-perm" or construction loan replacement vs. what competing lenders provide.

Loan payoff strategies determine how funding sources initially underwrite the construction loan. Closed-ended, open-ended, and bridge loans serve as the leading construction lending platforms that lenders prefer, depending upon risk tolerances. These formats are discussed below.

Before considering construction loans, some conservative funding sources require developers to procure permanent loans or presale commitments upfront, assuring a "takeout" of the construction loan at maturity. In such instances, the loans convert to "close-ended" status based on pre-committed fundings. Depending on the financial strength of the "takeout" commitments, the construction loan funding sources offer more attractive pricing, terms, and assurance that the take-out will pay them off, compared to more risky loan funding strategies such as standby commitments.

Commercial banks and debt funds are the primary sources for construction loans. Investment/mortgage bankers and life companies offer construction loans to a lesser extent. These funding sources control project financing throughout the development lifecycle to maintain client relationships while earning additional yields and fees. Such lenders cluster various loan products to offer one-stop funding solutions.

Of course, "takeout" funding sources still assume various risks when agreeing to a closed-end financing transaction. The hazards include changing market conditions within the funding term, project completion, and economic performance issues. "Takeout" funding sources demand significant rate premiums and impose restrictions to earn appropriate yields compared to standard debt. Risk mitigation measures include substantial preleasing, additional developer guarantees, and bank letters of credit ("LOC") to cover performance shortfalls.

On the opposite end of the construction loan risk spectrum, the open-ended loan offers higher yield opportunities for more entrepreneurial lenders. Open-ended construction loans capitalize on speculative projects that lack sufficient preleasing and takeout financing. Such loans rely upon the developer's financial strength and equity contribution. Should the development fail, the construction lender assumes "open-ended" loan exposure, needing to collect funds from the developer based on repayment guaranty obligations and recover any unpaid principal and interest payments via foreclosure or sale. Given such risks, the open-ended construction loans reflect very high pricing, particularly with less equity and weaker-credit borrowers.

The standby commitment surfaces as a rare funding tool offered for construction loans based on credit enhancements. Standby commitments launched many successful developments when funds remained scarce based on the 1980s credit crunch. This financial commitment serves as a take-out loan guarantee allowing borrowers to complete projects without pre-specified permanent financing or sales options. Burdened by prohibitively-high floating rates, these commitments serve as "stand by" fundings in case other takeout financing sources evaporate, so borrowers are discouraged from accepting the takeout commitment offered by the standby lender. Also, commitment issuers [lenders] generally prefer not to fund the transaction, instead focusing on generating profits via standby commitment fees.

Given the generous supply of real estate capital in today's marketplace, most construction loans feature substantial equity, translating to more "vanilla" funding structures, as shown below.

Illustration: Violet Bobcat Industries plans to expand an existing 126,000 ft.^{2} industrial facility situated on a 9.75-acre site in NYU Industrial Park near Villanova Williecat, Pennsylvania. The development plan includes renovating and expanding the existing building to form a new 45,000 ft.^{2} warehouse. The development will proceed in two phases: i) the redevelopment of the existing building (Phase 1) and ii) the new development of the 45,000 ft.^{2} building (Phase 2). Bobcat expects lease stabilization within ten months of construction completion for Phases 1 and 2. Bobcat requests an 80% loan-to-cost construction financing with a one-year term and two one-year extension options. The anticipated development cost totals $14.175 million and includes interest-only payments throughout the loan term and full recourse guarantees until completion. A standby commitment is available to substitute for the takeout if the original lender's underwriting criteria ultimately cannot match the finished project. The Sources and Uses Statement for the property breaks down as follows:

CONSTRUCTION LOAN - SOURCES AND USES STATEMENT			
SOURCES		**USES**	
Constr. Loan	$11,340,000	Land	$ 740,000
Equity	$ 2,835,000	Building	$ 8,415,000
		Other	$ 1,940,000
		TI/Leasing Fees	$ 1,480,000
		Total Interest	$ 1,600,000
Total Sources	**$14,175,000**	**Total Uses**	**$14,175,000**

The draw schedule for the first 12 months of the loan, including the renovation and new construction, is shown as follows:

Month		1	2	3	4	5	6	7	8	9	10	11	12
Phase I													
Development	**Total**												
Land	360,651	360,651											
Building Acquisition	4,833,803	4,833,803											
Infrastructure	11,097	3,699	3,699	3,699									
Acquisition Shell Preparation	1,574,400	524,800	524,800	524,800									
Other Development/Contingency	1,309,360	109,113	109,113	109,113	109,113	109,113	109,113	109,113	109,113	109,113	109,113	109,113	109,113
TI and Leasing Commission	809,033						250,800		210,349		210,349		137,536
Total Development (Phase 1)	**8,898,344**	**5,832,066**	**637,612**	**637,612**	**109,113**	**109,113**	**359,913**	**109,113**	**319,462**	**109,113**	**319,462**	**109,113**	**246,649**
Phase II													
Development	**Total**												
Land	380,546	380,546											
Building	1,997,403			249,675	249,675	249,675	249,675	249,675	249,675	249,675	249,675		
Other Development/Contingency	633,277			79,160	79,160	79,160	79,160	79,160	79,160	79,160	79,160		
TI and Leasing Commission	667,143									166,786			
Total Development (Phase 2)	**3,678,369**	**380,546**	**0**	**328,835**	**328,835**	**328,835**	**328,835**	**328,836**	**328,835**	**495,621**	**328,835**	**0**	**0**
Development Cost	**12,576,713**	**6,212,612**	**637,612**	**966,447**	**437,948**	**437,948**	**688,748**	**437,948**	**648,297**	**604,734**	**648,297**	**109,113**	**246,649**
Construction Interest	1,618,694		21,108	25,225	31,423	34,356	37,308	41,846	44,845	49,071	53,051	57,239	58,038
Dev Cost + Construction Interest	**14,195,407**	**6,212,612**	**658,720**	**991,672**	**469,371**	**472,304**	**726,056**	**479,794**	**693,142**	**653,805**	**701,348**	**166,352**	**304,687**
Equity													
Beginning Balance		0	2,835,342	2,835,342	2,835,342	2,835,342	2,835,342	2,835,342	2,835,342	2,835,342	2,835,342	2,835,342	2,835,342
Equity Draw	**2,835,342**	**2,835,342**											
Ending Balance		2,835,342	2,835,342	2,835,342	2,835,342	2,835,342	2,835,342	2,835,342	2,835,342	2,835,342	2,835,342	2,835,342	2,835,342
Construction Loan													
Beginning Balance			3,377,270	4,035,990	5,027,662	5,497,034	5,969,338	6,695,395	7,175,190	7,851,331	8,488,134	9,158,222	9,286,082
Loan Draw	**10,019,145**	**3,377,270**	**658,720**	**991,672**	**469,371**	**472,305**	**726,057**	**479,795**	**676,141**	**636,804**	**670,088**	**127,859**	**251,935**
Repayment	(10,019,145)												
Ending Balance		**3,377,270**	**4,035,990**	**5,027,662**	**5,497,033**	**5,969,339**	**6,695,395**	**7,176,190**	**7,851,331**	**8,488,135**	**9,158,222**	**9,286,081**	**9,538,017**

The construction draw schedule illustrates that the equity contribution and the land purchase occur upfront. Also, the loan disbursements total just over $10 million. The construction loan schedule closely approximates the Sources and Uses Statement by the end of the year, nearing $14.2 million. The schedule demonstrates how many moving parts comprise a commercial property construction loan.

Observation: Construction loan negotiations frequently rely on the development budget and the draw schedule. Land purchase, hard costs, and other easily documentable line items pass with less scrutiny as such charges disburse to third-party, unrelated ventures. That said, development fees, profits, and overhead bills draw more attention. Lenders shun releasing construction draws on unearned profits. In particular, construction budgets need to reflect market-justified-cost line items.

Upon completing and stabilizing projects via temporary debt, investors choosing to own the project for a longer-term hold explore permanent debt options as discussed in the following section.

PERMANENT DEBT

The permanent loan is usually synonymous with fixed-rate debt, implying "permanency." This funding structure features longer-term debt based on a fixed-rate payment structure. Investors seek more cashflow certainty by locking in debt service payments.

Permanent loans usually feature amortization. The history of amortization dates to the Great Depression. Before that time, loans were typically interest-only with balloon payments. Amortizing loans were created to provide funding terms that approximated the useful economic life of the real property, typically thirty years. As a result, borrowers paid down the principal amount, creating equity buildup, while lenders systematically reduced loan exposure through principal repayment.

Over time, permanent loan holding periods shortened. In the late 1970s, borrowers migrated to 15 years or less, sometimes opting for even shorter-term maturities. Even so, traditional 30-year amortization schedules persisted in taking advantage of rising property values while building more equity. During this era, continued inflation motivated borrowers to refinance frequently to recapture rising equity values. Lenders, however, reduced funding exposure of long-term loans to avoid the risks of below-market investments and illiquidity.

Although inflation persists today, especially after the pandemic, the Fed controls this problem. As a result, bond markets have faith in domestic interest rate policies and continue funding long-term fixed-rate debt within the real estate sector. Furthermore, the formation of the securitized debt market in the 1990s created liquidity for longer-term mortgages. Commercial banks, investment bankers, and other Wall Street funding sources freely originate and distribute such securities, featuring various credit ratings issued by major credit rating agencies such as Standard & Poor and Moody's.

As baby-boomers flood the retirement market, investment demand continues for bond-like mortgage debt instruments, further fueling demand for mortgage securities. Besides domestic capital, overseas investors regard various forms of American securitized real estate investments as "safe havens," especially mortgage notes or bonds.

Traditional balance-sheet lenders also continue to provide permanent debt. Lenders, particularly life companies, prefer investing in longer-term, fixed-rate debt with terms to match cash flow liability structures. In addition to life companies, government-sponsored enterprises ("GSE"), commonly known as "agencies," offer long-term fixed-rate debt and other funding instruments to help maintain liquidity in that area of the capital markets that fund housing. The most popular agencies include the Federal Home Loan Mortgage Corporation ("Freddie Mac") and the Federal National Mortgage Association ("Fannie Mae"). These various lending sources offer a variety of loan maturities, pricing options, and prepayment provisions to assure intense competition and benefit borrowers. And in particular, balance-sheet lenders exert control over the loan terms, offer additional proceeds and extend maturities in addition to marking the loan to market, if justified.

Since public and private mortgage capital markets offer more transparency in pricing and terms, fixed-rate mortgages feature similar underwriting parameters. For example, the ten-year mortgage maturity ranks as the most popular note. Still, lenders balance portfolios with other loan maturities, namely, five, seven, twelve, fifteen, twenty years, or longer terms. Other negotiated features include the length of loan amortization, interest-only payments, leverage levels within acceptable LTVs and DSCR, and prepayment provisions. Most importantly, the loan terms must match the project cash flows using these underwriting criteria.

Longer-term, permanent fixed-rate debt typically suits projects with similar cash flow behavior, namely stable and predictable income streams, for, say, ten years or longer. Since funding sources match the debt to cash flows with longer-term payment characteristics, higher-quality Class A or Class B office, retail, industrial and multifamily properties often fit such profiles. Lower quality Class C properties can also qualify, usually with additional financial enhancements, including personal recourse, letters of credit, and extra cash or collateral. As for the yield protection covering such loans, usually the first half of the term, at a minimum, prohibits any prepayment, followed by yield maintenance, defeasance, or other formulas. The same restrictions apply to due-on-sale clauses. And, if the property sells, loans sometimes feature assumption provisions requiring approval of the new buyer and incurring assumption fees for the process (e.g., one percent of the remaining balance.)

Intermediate-term permanent rate mortgage remains popular with syndicators and property owners. This term usually supports more liberal prepayment provisions. Investors are willing to sell or refinance assets more frequently, regularly taking advantage of changing market conditions. Six to nine-year maturities are the favored holding time horizons. This timeline often allows borrowers to avoid spending on any upcoming significant capital improvements. Lastly, intermediate-term debt allows for the generous use of interest-only payments and partial amortization, as substantial principal paydown rarely occurs at these maturity levels.

Fixed-rate loans with terms of five years or less appeal to borrowers operating transitional assets with quasi-fixed cash flows or properties that will be ready to sell relatively soon. These owners also avoid interest payment volatility.

Banks are the primary funding sources of such short-term debt. Also, short-term fixed-rate loans resurface during inflationary interest rate cycles (e.g., the 1980s "bullet" loans), allowing lenders to minimize longer-term yield exposure, reflecting less uncertainty about the near-term future.

Most permanent fixed-rate loans fund within 30 to 120 days after applying for the financing. Rates locks usually occur at the signing of an application or commitment. Thus, borrowers and lenders commit funds with more certainty of completing an acquisition or financing, subject to due diligence before closing.

Forward-delivery fundings also surface using fixed-rate debt for new construction ventures. Depending upon interest rate volatility, forward loans can reach as far into the future as two years, providing proper project completion and stabilization time. For additional costs and rate premiums, loan extensions and earnouts often supplement project financing.

Lastly, selective forward-delivery programs feature a construction loan tied into the permanent loan. Under such scenarios, the construction and permanent loan rates may feature identical pricing. The construction timeline extends the loan's entire term (e.g., a 10-year deal with a 12-year all-in term). Furthermore, these programs readily exist to construct multifamily projects with even longer periods, as much as 40 years, via the FHA/HUD 221(d)4. The following chart summarizes the significant highlights of using fixed-rate permanent debt based on the 5Ps.

FIXED-RATE PERMANENT DEBT	
PEOPLE	
Borrower	→ Long-term income investors, pension plans, public/private funds, owner-users
User Eligibility	→ 1-2X net worth of loan amount, 6-12 months liquidity, substituted with more equity
Lender	→ Banks, life companies, mortgage conduits, public/private debt funds
Source Eligibility	→ Regulated and unregulated institutions with long-term capital base
PLACE	
Location	→ Metro and immediate areas economically justifying property types/uses
Site Characteristics	→ Compliant with local laws, appropriate ingress-egress, environmentally secure
PROJECT	
Property Type	→ Multifamily, industrial, office, retail, self storage, mixed-use, student, senior housing
Grade	→ Existing Class A (non-recourse), Class B (selective recourse), Class C (full recourse)
Project Economics	→ Cash flowing, stabilized, 3-year operating history (less for new construction)
Other	→ Special-purpose acceptable, depending on cash flow and recourse
PERFORMANCE	
Dollar Size	→ Various (recourse), $5MM+ (non-recourse), $20MM+ institutional (full non-recourse)
Leverage	→ 65%-75% LTV (avg), 80%-90% (high, credit only), < 65% LTV (low)
Term	→ 10 yrs (avg), < 5 yrs (short), 5-9 yrs (medium), 11-40 yrs (long)
Rate (Yield)	→ 100-150 bps + Treasury (low LTV, Class A), 151-200 bps (avg, Class B), 200-250+ bps (Class C)
Payment Format	→ Interest-only (low LTV, Class A), 25-30 yrs (avg, Class B), <25 yrs (Class C)
Debt Coverage	→ 1.25-1.3X (avg), 1.31-1.50X+ (high), <1.25X (low, credit only)
Funding Timeline	→ Immediate (0-60 days), semi-forward (61-120 days), forward (121+ days)
Prepayment	→ Yield-maintenance, declining balance (%), flexible pricing with rate premiums
Other	→ Proceeds restricted to lower of LTV, debt coverage, LTC or cashout (optional)
PROS/CONS	
Borrower	+ Fixed debt service payments matched to predictable cash flows
	+ Higher leverage provides attractive yields
	+ Non recourse format reduces contingent liabilities, assumability protects leverage yield
	- Rate and term risks unsuitable for fluid cash flows
	- Improper leverage levels and amortization overburden cash flows
	- Arduous prepayment and due-on-sale provisions reduce reversion options
Lender	+ Different maturities balance loan portfolio term risk
	+ Lower leverage loans attract premium quality sponsors and projects
	+ Popular funding structure for note liquidity and lender syndications
	- Higher leverage increases default risk
	- Mismatched rates and terms suffer value erosion
	- Shorter terms loans at above-market rates mature too early

KEY: avg = average, bps = basis point spread, LTV[C] = loan-to-value[cost], credit-only = investment-grade tenant or low LTV, yrs = years

Illustration: The Manufacturing & Trading Company "VO" Distribution Center in Rochester, Oklahoma, recently completed a new facility for $40 million. Selfreliance Credit Federation of Hamtramck, Michigan, commits to funding a $30 million first mortgage based on 75% of the project cost. The mortgage carries a 6% interest rate based on a 25-year amortization schedule and a ten-year term with monthly payments of $193,290. The loan balance at maturity will be $22,905,594, representing a 24% principal reduction. The borrower is the owner-occupant, manufacturing and distributing a line of safety products based on fifty years of successful operation, so the predicted cash flow for repaying the debt suits fixed-rate financing. At the same time, the bank has a high comfort level since it understands the owner's financial statements and proven operating history, along with sufficient liquidity and downpayment for constructing the facilities. Lastly, Selfreliance captures VO's other banking needs, including accounts receivable and regular checking services.

Observation: Besides rate and term, prepayment formulas, escrows, and recourse often surface as important negotiating points. Usually, prepayment formulas are arranged for flexibility in return for additional rate premiums to the lender. Also, lower leverage loans (e.g., <50% LTV) often eliminate the need for escrow accounts to cover insurance, real estate taxes, and replacement reserves. Personal guarantees might be fully or partially waived, especially with proven cash flows and adequate debt service coverage. Recourse dismissal is significant when using outside investor capital, as few passive investors will agree to recourse without any control of property operations. Regardless, borrowers take responsibility for "bad-boy" carveouts with recourse liability for fraud, waste, and mismanagement. Essentially, nearly every type of loan features the triggering of springing recourse for borrowers acting in bad faith regarding property operations and preservation of loan collateral.

In addition to exploring temporary and permanent debt programs, investors search for other debt formats to supplement equity contributions, with junior debt as an option discussed in the next section.

SUBORDINATE DEBT

Subordinate or junior debt supplements senior debt, serving as an additional funding tranche to raise more investment capital. Subordinated debt is a loan with a lower priority repayment than other outstanding debt encumbering a property. Multiple loans occasionally encumber the property for higher leverage ventures or larger projects, with legal priority determining collateral security claims. These situations include secured (e.g., first mortgage, second mortgage) and unsecured (e.g., mezzanine) debt. Such loans depend upon the senior debt terms, as subordinate debt often pays off on or before the maturity date of the senior loan slice or tranche.[112]

Since this funding format serves as debt, the costs to the borrower are usually lower than equity. Also, junior debt supplements and does not disturb any below-market-priced senior debt already in place. Lastly, subordinated debt provides additional funds for investors to achieve liquidity without triggering a sale. Reasons include funding further physical improvements, tax-free loan proceeds (e.g., cashing out), increasing leverage yields, and replacing costlier equity.

From the lender's view, junior debt instruments offer higher yields than senior debt, based on assuming the intermediate risk of recovering principal in the event of loan default – ahead of equity but behind senior debt. Funding sources include banks, credit companies, thrifts, Wall Street (loan securitizations), private capital, and, to a lesser extent, life insurance companies and pension funds.

The most popular secured subordinate debt vehicles include second mortgages and mezzanine debt. Wraparound mortgages also surface during high-interest rate cycles.

Secured

A secured subordinated loan carries a publicly recorded lien providing proof of a debt lien position tied to real estate collateral. Such a loan has a lower repayment priority than any recorded senior debt.

A second mortgage is the simplest and most common form of secured subordinated debt. The second mortgage is also a Junior Mortgage; the second mortgage appears as a recorded lien encumbering real property and is subordinated to a senior lien position. Second mortgages use various payment formats, including fixed-rate, variable-rate, participating, convertible, and preferred equity.

Another type of secured junior debt deserves mention, the wraparound or "wrap" or "blanket" mortgage. Popular during the 1980s, when interest rates peaked, the wrap mortgage remains dormant as interest rates hover in lower, more stable ranges. This mortgage format involves adding a layer of subordinated debt by "wrapping around" favorable, lower-rate first debt. The wraparound loan combines the undisturbed loan with freshly generated proceeds. As a result, a "new" loan exists with a higher blended interest rate and proceeds.

Wraparound Mortgages are often similar to other subordinate debt instruments, except for a few distinguishable features. Existing and newly advanced total proceeds emerge as the "face" amount throughout the loan documentation. A special agreement between senior and wrap lenders covers debt service payment responsibilities and discusses cure provisions in default.

Furthermore, a promissory note and liens, where applicable, secure the debt position.

In many instances, senior lenders disallow additional secured debt. Therefore, borrowers turn to unsecured lending sources for tapping additional loan proceeds.

Unsecured

Unsecured subordinated debt instruments appear as mortgages void of any lien rights. As a result, such loans look to ownership equity positions for repayment rights. These loans straddle any recorded property liens and investor equity in repayment risk. Essentially, such lenders convert debt positions into equity in the event of default, taking control of the investment as the "new" owners. Mezzanine financing serves as such an option if permitted by a senior lender.

Another variation of unsecured financing includes preferred equity, often referred to as "Pref" equity. A close cousin of Mezz debt, pref equity features similar payment characteristics but possibly includes equity participation features, sharing profits at reversion, or some other agreed-upon terms. Also, pref equity documents resemble equity ownership provisions rather than mortgage notes. These distinctions surface as many senior lenders demand very restrictive control rights in covering defaults, often prohibiting rights to cure loan defaults sought by Mezz lenders.

Based on the 5 P's of real estate, the Subordinated Debt chart below highlights major subordinate debt discussion points.

SUBORDINATED DEBT	
PEOPLE	
Borrower	→ Various-term income investors, public/private funds
User Eligibility	→ 1-2X net worth of loan amount, 6-12 months liquidity, substituted with more equity
Lender	→ Banks, debt funds, life companies, public/private debt funds
Source Eligibility	→ Regulated and unregulated institutions with short/long-term capital base
PLACE	
Location	→ Metro and immediate areas economically justifying property types/uses
Site Characteristics	→ Compliant with local laws, appropriate ingress-egress, environmentally secure
PROJECT	
Property Type	→ Multifamily, industrial, office, retail, self storage, mixed-use, student, senior housing
Grade	→ Existing Class A (non-recourse), Class B (selective recourse), Class C (full recourse)
Project Economics	→ Cash flowing to meet combined [senior and junior] debt service payments
Other	→ Driven by senior debt terms and economics
PERFORMANCE	
Dollar Size	→ Various (recourse), $5MM+ (non-recourse), $20MM+ institutional (full non-recourse)
Leverage	→ 65%-75% LTV (avg), 80%-90% (high, credit only), < 65% LTV (low)
Term	→ Senior loan dependent (</= coterminous), < 5 yrs (avg), 5-10 yrs (long)
Rate (Yield)	→ Fixed or floating-rate, 100-400+ bps above senior rate
Payment Format	→ Interest-only, senior loan coterminous
Debt Coverage	→ 1.25-1.3X combined (avg), 1.31-1.50X+ combined (high), <1.25X combined (rare)
Funding Timeline	→ Immediate (0-60 days), semi-forward (61-120 days), forward (121+ days)
Prepayment	→ Minimal lockout, declining balance (%), flexible pricing with rate premiums
Other	→ Secured or unsecured driven by senior loan restrictions
PROS/CONS	
Borrower	+ Favorable existing senior debt undisturbed + Less costly alternative to raising equity, tax-free capital without triggering reversion + Additional leverage increases yields - Frequently disallowed by senior lenders - Improper leverage levels and rates overburden cash flows - Non coterminous refinance, prepayment issues
Lender	+ Offers additional yields + Lower leverage loans attract premium quality sponsors and projects + Effective loan portfolio retention tool for existing funding source - Additional leverage increases default risk - Mismatched rates and terms suffer value erosion - Subordinate position sacrifices direct control

KEY: avg = average, bps = basis point spread, LTV[C] = loan-to-value[cost], credit-only = investment-grade tenant or low LTV, yrs = years

The chart illustrates the importance of finding the optimum loan underwriting elements for combined debt. Since senior debt exists, much of the analysis already accounts for the people, place, and project variables. The [cash flow] performance focuses on determining how the inclusion of subordinated debt influences various aggregated ratios, including LTV, DSC, term, and prepayment provisions. Subordinated debt is compatible with the investment profile if enough cushion exists to carry full debt service based on the combined loan amounts.

Illustration: Renegade Realty Development Company seeks to develop an $80 million mixed-use apartment complex with retail and office space in

Tallahassee, Florida. Since the developer has owned the site for more than ten years, the project underwrites very favorably, featuring a high return-on-cost of 7%, while similar properties sell for 5.5% cap rates or lower upon completion. Since the project offers no preleasing on the commercial [non-multifamily] space, Renegade negotiates a $40 million construction loan with Nittany Lion National Mortgage Bank of University Park, Pennsylvania, representing a 50% LTC based on a three-year term with a 4% interest rate. However, the developer still needs an additional $20 million of capital upfront. In addition, Nittany Lion prohibits any type of secondary debt financing, including Mezz debt. As a result, Renegade taps into Mustang Money Managers of Dallas for a pref equity investment to supplement the capital stack. The pref equity loan features a 6% interest rate paid by the developer out of pocket (not funded by any of the construction loan disbursements) during the construction loan. Mustang recaptures the $20 million loan investment only after fully Nittany Lion Bank's construction loan is fully repaid upon sale or refinancing. After that, Renegade enjoys any surplus profits.

Observation: Unsecured debt ranks as a cost-effective option if equity yields remain substantially higher. However, many senior lenders restrict using unsecured debt, regardless of format, given concerns about additional "partners" [pref equity capital] sharing project control and cash flow distribution. Furthermore, the project costs, yield pricing differences, and the legal/financing fees need to justify involving another funding source. This logic also applies to any subordinated debt, secured or unsecured.

Other funding options exist beyond traditional debt and equity capital. Hybrid funding offers additional choices for creative financing, as described in the next section.

HYBRID

Other alternatives to either equity or debt include blending these capital formats into hybrid funding options. Depending on the funding sources, such forms include hybrid debt and hybrid equity.

Investors continuously seek partners to expand profits and capture more opportunities while sharing risks. As a result, funding sources often customize hybrid structures to fit a given venture. This funding structure is identified by many names, including joint ventures ("JV"), debt joint ventures, participating mortgages, and convertible loans. Irrespective of titles, hybrid funding involves sharing risk and rewards, including minimum payments to debt or preferred equity (if available) and distributions of reversionary profits/losses.

Hybrid funding structures cover the range of capitalization options falling between pure debt and equity. Since both debt- and equity-like features exist, legal and financial variations blur the distinction between them. In some cases, such as debt JVs, lenders act as equity partners, creating potential conflicts of interest. Partners generally share equal or nearly equal profits with other joint ventures, with the capital contributions reflecting debt-priced yield preferences. Also, even as partners proportionally share profits, tax benefits and other factors might be allocated differently to suit a given partner's goals or depend on each partner's organizational structure.

Hybrid funding structures use varying terminology to describe the sharing of cash flow and reversionary profits, including "participation," "promote," "sale-leaseback," "kicker," "supplemental," "add-on," and "bonus," to name a few. The cash flow sharing differences relate to financing and legal implications – debt or equity – and how the parties classify cash flow and reversionary profits. For practical purposes, all hybrid structures include provisions for sharing additional profits relating to project performance.

Legal structuring and financial analysis require more expertise and accountability with hybrid funds. Smaller ventures of $20 million or less hardly justify this funding format unless the real estate strategies involve formula-based (" programmatic") investing covering multiple properties using similar financing structures. Given the complex sharing arrangements targeting higher overall yields, hybrid fundings work best for value-add and opportunity ventures.

Hybrid funds maintain popularity with more sophisticated financial institutions teaming up with renowned borrowers based on different characteristics linked to the funding source and the ownership group. New development or significant renovation ventures in larger metro areas attract institutional partners, namely life companies, debt funds, pension funds, and public/private wealth managers. Ventures funded by non-taxable entities (e.g., pension funds) negotiate tax savings to benefit developers in exchange for more attractive yields.

With hybrid structures, ownership splits and net cash flow profit and loss distribution ratios are not necessarily equal. "Sweat equity" is considered depending upon equity contribution and project control. Higher equity ownership ratios compensate for lower preferred returns, while lower equity participation and cash flow percentages translate to higher coupon rates. Also, cash flow participation formulas are typically linked to effective gross income, net operating income, or cash flow after regular debt service payments. The closer the participation reflects gross income, the lower the participation percentage, as the risk avoids more operational factors (e.g., management expenses).

In general, NOI participations offer higher profit percentages for lenders, typically 25 to 50 percent or more. Participations below 50% are reserved for lower leverage, premium cash flow (substantial preleasing), developer guarantees, and other financial enhancements (letters of credit), allowing borrower/developer more control. Blended cash flow participation, including preferred pay rate, generally translated to 50% to 85 percent of cash flow or conversion, depending upon yield requirements and leverage. Last, annual cash flow profit shortfalls are recaptured using preferred return formulas (e.g., "waterfalls") to repay debt-oriented partners first, followed by the developer's profits using staged performance levels.

Reversion profit formulas include minimum yield thresholds ("waterfalls"), premiums, predetermined figures, fixed percentage of net profits, and custom formulas linked to various market indexes. Reversion sale and refinancing profits often blend with cash flow profit sharing for calculating overall yields, equating to unpaid preferred funding amount (e.g., loan balance) plus the appraised value (if not sold) of the developer's equity.

The Hybrid Debt Equity chart below describes the main underwriting elements based on the 5Ps.

HYBRID DEBT EQUITY	
PEOPLE	
Investor	→ Owners, developers
User Eligibility	→ 1-2X net worth of loan amount, 6-12 months liquidity
Venture Partner	→ Private/public opportunity funds, pension funds, life insurance companies
Partner Eligibility	→ Passive investment funds with multiple strategies (core-plus, value-add, opportunity)
PLACE	
Location	→ Metro and immediate areas justifying property types/uses for investment strategy
Site Characteristics	→ Compliant with local laws, appropriate ingress-egress, environmentally secure
PROJECT	
Property Type	→ Multifamily, industrial, office, retail, self storage, mixed-use, student, senior housing
Grade	→ Existing and to-be-built Class A, Class B, and Class C
Project Economics	→ Various, depending upon strategies, proforma, existing cash flows, value-add, opportunity
Other	→ More investor equity and preleasing reduce venture partner participation role and yields
PERFORMANCE	
Dollar Size	→ Various, $5MM+ (small), $20-50MM institutional (medium), $50MM+ (large)
Funding Format	→ Joint venture, participating loan, preferred equity, any hybrid format with profit participation
Overall Yield	→ 200-400+ bps mortgage yield (core-plus), 401-600+ bps (value-add), 601+ bps (opportunity)
Term	→ Tailored to core-plus, value-add, opportunity hold strategy
Leverage	→ JV 50/50 +/-, Participating loan 80%-95%+ TPC with pref yield and sharing 50/50 +/- reversion
Pref Rate (Yield)	→ Fixed or floating-rate tied to overall return on investment (IRR, NPV, payback, return on cost)
Payment Format	→ Interest-only (typical), proforma underwritten to pref yield with reversion
Debt Coverage	→ Pre-stabilized 1.15-1.25X (core-plus), 1-1.15X+ (value-add), <1X (opportunity)
Funding Timeline	→ Immediate initial disbursement (0-60 days), phased over investment strategy timeline
Prepayment	→ Minimal lockout until strategy termination, flexible buy/sell provisions
PROS/CONS	
Investor	+ Existing project repositioned or new construction completed for creating value
	+ Maximum leveraged return based on minimum equity contributions, along with risk sharing
	+ Successful partnership arrangement leads to additional projects
	- Construction, completion and stabilization risk exposure until reversion
	- Improper budgeting, cost overruns affect profitability
	- Incompatible venture partner leads to conflicts
Venture Partner	+ Attractive yields compared to stabilized assets
	+ Higher proceeds attract premium quality developers and projects
	+ Popular funding structure for larger institutional projects with long stabilization timelines
	- Construction, completion and stabilization, repositioning risk exposure until reversion
	- Higher proceeds increase default risk
	- Incompatible owner/developer partner leads to conflicts

KEY: avg = average, bps = basis point spread, LTV[C] = loan-to-value[cost], TPC = total project cost, yrs = years

The logic of hybrid investment analysis follows the same principles regardless of the number of partners/investors.

The most noticeable underwriting differences apply to the 4th P, Performance. The various funding formats such as joint ventures, participating loans, preferred equity, and other hybrid formats dominate, emphasizing how the partners share capital contributions, partner responsibilities, and profit distributions. Negotiations start with equity contributions, with seasoned developers supplying expertise, effort, and resources (known as “sweat equity”) instead of cash equity. In such situations, contributions of 95% equity by the venture partner and 5% with developers remain popular. Shares often do not reflect actual cash contributed, with developer expertise somehow priced and positioned in the continuum of "who gets what when." Cash flow splits factor into the overall internal rate of return calculations, which are generally 200 to 400 basis points over mortgage yields [or about 350 basis points or more over comparable term treasuries]

Illustration: Sebastian Ibis, a prominent developer, recently renovated the Hurricane Professional Office Plaza office building in Miami, Florida. Ibis seeks a long-term participating loan to maximize his yield and minimize equity while the property reaches cash flow stabilization. The Big Red Realty Mortgage Fund, Ltd. of Ithaca, New York, structured an $11,250,000 loan for this property based upon a $15 million value. The debt features a 4.5% interest rate based on a 25-year amortization schedule, plus additional profit participation calculated as 25% of any net operating income increases above the base-year net operating income of $1,500,000 during the ten-year loan term. That said, the NOI expectations included two percent growth per year. Also, the debt fund charged a two percent origination fee. As a result, the net loan amount funded by lender equates to $11,025,000 ($11,250,000 x .98).

At the end of ten years, the participating loan was retired based on a property sale that generated net sales proceeds of $18,284,916. Furthermore, the NOI increased by the projected annual growth rate throughout the loan term. The IRR yield calculations appear as follows.

Year	1	2	3	4	5
Net Operating Income	$1,500,000	$1,530,000	$1,560,600	$1,591,812	$1,623,648
Less: Annual Debt Service	$750,374	$750,374	$750,374	$750,374	$750,374
Less: Participation Payment	$0	$7,500	$15,150	$22,953	$30,912
Before Tax Cash Flow	$749,626	$772,126	$795,076	$818,485	$842,362

Year	6	7	8	9	10
Net Operating Income	$1,656,121	$1,689,244	$1,723,029	$1,757,489	$1,792,639
Less: Annual Debt Service	$750,374	$750,374	$750,374	$750,374	$750,374
Less: Participation Payment	$39,030	$47,311	$55,757	$64,372	$73,160
Before Tax Cash Flow	$866,717	$891,559	$916,898	$942,743	$969,105

Resale Price	$18,284,916
Less: Resale Costs	0
Less: Loan Balance	$8,174,079
Before Tax Equity Reversion	$10,110,838

	Yield (APR) to Lender Calculations				Yield (IRR) to Investor (Borrower)		
Year	Annual Debt Svc	Participation	Loan Balance	Total Pmt	BTCF	BTER	Total CF
0				-$11,025,000			-$3,975,000
1	$750,374	$0		$750,374	$749,626		$749,626
2	$750,374	$7,500		$757,874	$772,126		$772,126
3	$750,374	$15,150		$765,524	$795,076		$795,076
4	$750,374	$22,953		$773,327	$818,485		$818,485
5	$750,374	$30,912		$781,286	$842,362		$842,362
6	$750,374	$39,030		$789,404	$866,717		$866,717
7	$750,374	$47,311		$797,685	$891,559		$891,559
8	$750,374	$55,757		$806,131	$916,898		$916,898
9	$750,374	$64,372		$814,746	$942,743		$942,743
10	$750,374	$73,160	$10,110,838	$10,934,371	$969,105	$10,110,838	$11,079,943
			APR	6.48%		IRR	25.1%

Although Big Red's coupon rate appears as 4.5%, the actual yield translates to 6.48%, incorporating the fees (2 points) and the 25% "kicker" income based on all pre-tax cash flow increases over the base year NOI ($1,500,000) during the loan term. The lender's yield is 6.19% instead of 6.48% without considering any loan fees. At the same time, the borrower's yield is 25.1% IRR, a favorable margin exceeding the 6.48% borrowing cost, indicating positive leverage.

Observation: As with most investments, cash flow and reversion profits seldom provide guaranteed returns using hybrid funds. For instance, the borrower forfeits cash flow overages if distribution levels dip below minimum profit thresholds. Other examples include gross income formulas burdened by unanticipated expense increases, eroding market conditions, and numerous factors beyond the direct control of sponsorship. The identity of interest between partners demands special attention to solve problems or issues. Due to the financial complexities of such ventures, partners with similar investment goals and philosophies typically work together best.

In summary, this chapter demonstrates the depth and scope of the real estate capital markets. The wide variety of funding options based on equity, debt, and hybrid formats allow investors to pursue numerous profitability [risk/reward] strategies. However, the ultimate success of any real estate venture rests with an adequately qualified investor's ability to manage the property through various cycles based on ample liquidity— a challenging but rewarding responsibility.

Given the complexities of real estate investing, the final chapter offers some closing thoughts on effectively navigating through this process based on the *Four Pillars.*

CHAPTER 6: CLOSING THOUGHTS

"With the new day comes new strength and new thoughts." - Eleanor Roosevelt.

This chapter presents closing thoughts to wrap up the *Four Pillars* real estate investment concept, including glimpses into this industry's future, followed by closing remarks.

A PICTURE IS WORTH A THOUSAND WORDS

The above illustration summarizes the Four Pillars' concept for real estate investing. First, the four pillars represent the main principles of earning profits based on defining, measuring, timing, and risking [investing] capital with the expectation of rewards [profits] for an investment. The pillars themselves epitomize classical Greek and Roman architecture. Each pillar shows strength [Risk Pillar], knowledge [Evaluation Pillar], durability [Cycle Pillar], and proven design [Investment Pillar]. Also, based on a sound foundation [liquidity], the four pillars can weather shocks by equally bearing heavy loads. No one pillar carries all the weight; all pillars rely on the strength of the weakest pillar -- as with any real estate investment.

Second, the arrow positioned in front of the pillars shows the flow of capital into an investment. As symbolized by the upward direction of an income stream, the investor sets expectations for generating yields to provide for the return *of* and *on* capital contributions. The arrow also crosses each pillar in order of the investment creation flow. The flow identifies the business plan [**R**isk/Reward Pillar], followed by reviewing specific project feasibility parameters as applied to the plan [**E**valuation Pillar], then setting transaction timing [**C**ycle Pillar], and finally funding the venture [**I**nvesting Pillar] to create the investment.

Third, the dollar signs on both ends of the pillars show financial growth during the investment timeline. The smaller dollar symbol represents the invested capital. At the same time, the larger sign indicates capital appreciation at the end of the investment cycle—furthermore, the percent sign at the top of the arrow illustrates yield growth.

Fourth, a skyline rests firmly on top of the four pillars, demonstrating that the pillars "support" real estate investing. The skyline shows different real estate investment opportunities, including office, retail, warehouse, multifamily, and single-family properties.

The fifth element, the planet earth, floats in the background, symbolizing the global realty investment opportunities for real estate investing.

While this illustration focuses on the investment discussion of the *Four Pillars,* the following image covers most of the process, the people involved in the venture, and the investors.

The above illustration shows the investor as a homeowner, hotelier, retailer, warehouse operator, distributor, developer, apartment manager, office user, premisist (a socially responsible steward of the premises), capital funding source (debt, equity), or others with a financial interest in real estate. Regardless of the type of realty investment, brainpower ranks as the most crucial element of any investment. In other words, unified brainpower fueled by sufficient capital forms the basis of all investment decisions, now and into the future.

FUTURE THOUGHTS

The future bodes well, with some exciting changes on the horizon for the industry. Real estate remains a permanent fixture among investment choices through all market cycles, technological changes, and dynamic property and location trends. Key trends are outlined below.

INFLATIONARY THOUGHTS

Since the beginning of this decade, investors have enjoyed the longest-running streak of lowest rates in modern times. In comparison, interest rates plummeted to -10% during the 1930s and reached nearly 18% during World War I. Furthermore, during the 1970s, inflation ran out of control at an annual rate of over 7%. And by the end of 2021, inflation re-appeared to levels not witnessed since the early 1980s.[113]

Today, investors struggle with rising labor and material costs. Restrictive immigration, more retirees, and reduced workforce participation has created a nominal unemployment rate within the three-percent range. Yet the future looks bright, as the public and private sectors offer more corrective solutions than in the past. Policymakers have better decision-making tools for monitoring trends. The Fed Reserve quickly intervenes when necessary, including taming the severity of the Great Recession and Covid crises. The Fed targets a 2%/year goal as an acceptable target growth rate. Also, for example, real estate investors macroeconomically control rising operating costs. Key measures include productivity gains and improved income performance (e.g., more tenant services and amenities). Most importantly, the real estate sector offers outstanding inflation protection as tenants eventually absorb rising costs.[114]

THOUGHTS ACROSS THE BORDER

Despite a respite in investing resulting from Covid travel restrictions, foreign investors, mainly off-shore, continue "shoring up" the U.S. realty markets. For all of 2019 and the first quarter of 2020, cross-border capital represented about eight percent of all commercial real estate investment activity in the U.S. Compared to 2015 to 2018, the average figure stood at 15 percent.[115] Regardless, the U.S. realty market remains a haven for domestic and foreign investors based on the favorable tax treatment and perceived territorial safety.

HOUSING SHORTAGE THOUGHTS

Innovative thinking suggests the real estate sector's most attractive future investment opportunities hide within the nation's supply and demand imbalances. Insatiable investor demand continues flooding core and core-plus ventures, targeting multifamily and industrial assets. Conversely, the vast oversupply of underutilized commercial properties presents a large redevelopment inventory, especially office and retail sectors, as the chart below illustrates.

Estimates of Commercial Property Value: 2018Q4

Sector	Square Footage (Millions)	Price per Square Foot ($)	Value ($ Trillions)
Multifamily	17,541	$165	$2.9
Office	11,266	$218	$2.5
Retail	13,646	$179	$2.4
Health Care	2,705	$864	$2.3
Specialty, Sports and Other	N/A	N/A	$2.2
Hospitality	2,625	$617	$1.6
Industrial	20,749	$73	$1.5
Flex	2,402	$145	$0.3
Self-Storage	N/A	N/A	$0.2
Towers	N/A	N/A	$0.1
Total	**70,933**		**$16.0**
High Estimate			**$17.0**
Low Estimate			**$14.4**

Source: Nareit calculations using the CoStar All Properties database 2018:Q4 and CoStar's Commercial Real Estate Market Size Estimates 2018Q4.

The domestic and commercial real estate market stands at about 16 trillion dollars.[116] The chart shows the most sought investment sectors, multifamily, and industrial assets, representing about $4.5 trillion in combined value. However, the disinvested sectors, namely office and retail boast about $5 trillion. National vacancy rates for multifamily and industrials enjoy record-low levels in the single digits. In contrast, office and retail properties suffer record-high levels of about 20% and 12%, respectively.[117]

Theoretically, the nation's housing shortage vanishes if investors reallocate sizable portions of unoccupied office/retail space to apartments. The vacant space translates to nearly four million new units by converting four billion ft.^{2}.[118] And, slightly more than half of this inventory fulfills the national housing shortfall of 2.5 million units.[119]

Alternatively, the reallocation of space also applies to other sectors, including healthcare, senior housing, self-storage, and data centers. In summary, "Repurpose with a purpose" is a rallying cry for the industry.

DOWN-TO-EARTH THOUGHTS

Realty investing is literally "down to earth." Meaningful thought about investing focuses on making the world a better place to live, one property at a time. More specifically, socially-conscious investors embrace Environmental, Sustainable Governance ("ESG") as part of a comprehensive ownership strategy that responsibly serves users, the community, and of course, the earth. ESG is *for, about,* and *with* the earth.

ESG is *for* the earth by advocating for the environment based on "green" buildings and other design improvements enhancing rather than harming the community. These initiatives include LEED certification, World Green Council Net Zero Carbon Buildings Commitments, and "Green leases" – targeted towards reduced pollution and better living quality. In return, investors enjoy varying levels of reduced operating costs, translating to more desirable assets at the time of sale.

ESG is *about* the earth by helping society through sustainability. In return for forming a productive, engaged workforce, investors reap the benefits of employee loyalty and retention. Workforce equality and diversity are crucial social impact considerations for improving the investor's organization. More recently, the concept of Diversity, Equity, Inclusion, and Belonging ("DEIB") reinforces sustainability. Diversity focuses on broadening the investor's organization to include social and cultural identity groups more reflective of the community. Equity understands how individuals face societal challenges based on their social identity groups at the cultural and industry levels Inclusion is a choice to include and welcome others. Belonging is rooted in feelings—individuals need to feel leveraged, valued, and celebrated for who they are and what they bring to a given situation.[120]

Lastly, ESG is *with* the earth by showing responsible governance. The investment organization needs to demonstrate constructive societal change: compensation, diverse management, thoughtful and inclusive leadership, and investor relations are essential governance topics.

Independent ratings provide the best gauge for reaching ESG investment goals for achieving environmental performance, social impact, and governance issues. For example, the Global Real Estate Sustainability Benchmark (GRESB) is an excellent ESG gauge.[121] Furthermore, policymakers will eventually issue more legislative actions supporting ESG, creating concise compliance regulations for the industry to follow.

FOOD FOR THOUGHT

Data is food for thought as the real estate industry voraciously feeds information to artificial intelligence ("AI"). Artificial intelligence propels risk/reward analysis far beyond traditional investment thought. AI uses machine learning to reach learning, planning, and problem-solving levels far beyond human intelligence.[122] The future portends fully automated analysis, due diligence, appraisals, capital placement, and transaction management.

Illustration: In 2057, real estate investing has heavy regulation, requiring properties to comply with strict ESG standards and affordability tests applying to the multifamily sector. Owners and properties need full licensing, first at the federal level, followed by local authorities. George Jetstone carries a Class C200 realty owner's license (Class C denotes a multifamily permit of 200 units or less). Jetstone identifies a qualified fifty-unit apartment building in Chicago's East Humboldt Park community available for sale by Flash Gordone. On-site and document inspection is unnecessary since the property license remains valid. All due diligence materials, including financial statements and physical condition reports, are verified as true and correct, backed by title insurance. Both parties use the "Meeting of the Minds" virtual negotiation process for the transaction -- thought-processing technology based on brain scans that reduces all negotiations to stored thoughts converted to form. After that, Jetstone uses a global cryptocurrency clearinghouse to complete the transaction with Gordone.

Observation: AI will significantly impact ownership operations over the next few decades. AI will drive most mundane ownership management functions, including coordinating repairs and maintenance, processing financial records, and tracking federally-mandated building health and welfare standards. Under such conditions, all [common area] property activities will be monitored to ensure social interaction and health/safety compliance by owners, tenants, and others on the premises. Furthermore, AI will assume increased responsibility for planning and managing income and expense flows. The investor's primary responsibility will focus on strategic planning and maintaining sufficient liquidity (solvency) beyond operating accounts to perform capital improvements and fulfill other funding requirements as recommended by AI for complying with stringent property licensing compliance of the future.

Many powerful technologies aid real estate investing. Also, new technologies will soon emerge, leading to a bright and exciting future. As investors adapt to these changes, fierce competition will continue, so investors will need to use instinct, something AI lacks.

Honing the investor's instincts by "outsmarting" AI creates new opportunities for successful investing. Such instincts depend on developing thought leadership for determining what users and the community *want* compared to what they currently *have*. The *wants* create newer and better space usage compared to competing inventory. More importantly, technology is never a substitute for ownership's ability to communicate directly and personally with users and others who want better quality space.

FINAL THOUGHTS

Real estate never loses favor, as shelter remains a basic human need. This investment sector represents far more than profits. Unlike stocks and bonds, owning this asset satisfies the basic urge to help people, mainly users and the community. Such investors are socially responsible stewards of the premises.[123]

In conclusion, the principles outlined in the Four Pillars guide investors to earn profits while at the same time "doing the right thing." Dr. James Graaskamp, one of the industry's most outstanding thought leaders, stated, "Real estate is a process of dynamic interactions rather than functional and historical facts. The entrepreneur should have the creativity of Leonardo da Vinci, the sensitivity for the natural world of John Muir, and the political humanity with cash management skills of [the renowned developer] James Rouse." Sir Winston Churchill noted, echoing similar thinking, "We shape our buildings; thereafter, they shape us."

These words of wisdom serve as guideposts to help investors maintain balanced perspectives on real estate design/development, profitability, user needs, society, and the environment. The same concept applies to investors shaping the future. Fear of change paves a path to mediocrity and eventual failure in their working environments. On the other hand, investors embracing change to shape the future with "good" real estate benefit from personally rewarding and profitable outcomes.

ABOUT THE AUTHORS

The *Four Pillars* authors, Dr. Crocker H. Liu, John Oharenko, Jeanne Peck, and Dean Larkin, are respected industry experts sharing over a century of combined knowledge of income-property, academic research, finance, mortgage banking, asset management, and development.

Jeanne Darrow Peck boasts a multifaceted commercial real estate background spanning over two decades of development, institutional investment, and mortgage banking. Ms. Peck's transaction volume spans over two billion dollars, including new development joint ventures, acquisitions, permanent debt, and other structured debt/equity deals. Also. She serves as the Director of the Real Estate Capital Institute®, publishing numerous commercial real estate finance articles. Ms. Peck is a graduate of the University of Illinois in Finance and DePaul University with an MBA in Real Estate.

Dean Larkin, MAI, offers "hands-on" experience in several real estate disciplines, including appraisal, consulting, mortgage banking, development, property management, and acting as a principal in real estate investments both as a sponsor and a private investor. In addition, he was active as an educator, having taught Valuation of Real Estate at the University of Wisconsin-Milwaukee for ten years. Mr. Larkin holds the MAI designation (now a non-practicing, retired Member) from the Appraisal Institute. Dean has a Master's Degree in Real Estate Appraisal and Investment Analysis from the University of Wisconsin-Madison.

Dr. Crocker H. Liu is a chaired professor of real estate at Cornell. He taught at New York University's Stern School of Business (1988-2006) and Arizona State University's W.P. Carey School of Business (2006-2009). His research interest focuses on issues in real estate finance. He formerly served as the co-editor of *Real Estate Economics*, the leading real estate academic journal. For many years, Dr. Liu worked as a professional realtor in Hawaii and vice president with the Prudential Real Estate Investment Group. He consulted with RREEF (now part of Deutsche Bank's Asset Management division), Milliman and Robertson, and Standard and Poor's. Crocker holds a BBA in real estate and finance from the University of Hawaii-Manoa, a Master's Degree in Real Estate Appraisal and

Investment Analysis from the University of Wisconsin-Madison under Dr. James Graaskamp, and a Ph.D. in finance and real estate from the University of Texas.

John Oharenko is an active real estate investment banking veteran of numerous market cycles and actively operates workforce housing properties in the Chicagoland area. Mr. Oharenko shares hidden insights about successfully investing and leveraging commercial real estate, regardless of overall market conditions – recession, depression, or a high-flying economy. He has published *The Real Estate Capital Scoreboard®*, a monthly newsletter covering finance market trends and pricing indices, since 1983. Mr. Oharenko authored numerous real estate investment books, including *The Premise for Premises, The Evicted Landlord,* and *Combat Investor: Real Estate Investment Warfare Guide*. John also co-authored *The Guide to Realty Capital Markets,* used by major universities as a definitive real estate finance handbook. Furthermore, he wrote over a hundred articles and regularly lectured on real estate finance, capital market trends, and realty investment banking. John holds a Master's Degree in Real Estate Appraisal and Investment Analysis from the University of Wisconsin – Madison.

ACKNOWLEDGMENTS

"Be thankful for what you have; you'll end up having more. If you concentrate on what you don't have, you will never, ever have enough." - Oprah Winfrey

Thank you to all those operating premises to the best of their abilities and talents: all who consciously create a better living, working, and recreational conditions, as well as the environment in their communities.

We're very grateful to our families, friends, and colleagues who've supported us —spiritually, socially, academically, and professionally.

—Dean, Dr. Crocker, Jeanne, and John

REFERENCES

[1] "Land." Merriam-Webster. Merriam-Webster. Accessed June 23, 2019. https://www.merriam-webster.com/dictionary/land.

[2] Answers. "What Percentage of the Earth Does the US Take Up." Answers. Answers Corporation. Accessed April 25, 2019https://www.answers.com/Q/What_percentage_of_the_earth_does_the_US_take_up.Cornish, Cheryl, Stephen Cooper, Salima Jenkins, and US Census Bureau. "Characteristics of New Housing." > Highlights, August 23, 2011.; https://www.census.gov/construction/chars/highlights.html.FRED. "Housing Inventory Estimate: Total Housing Units for the United States." FRED, October 29, 2019. https://fred.stlouisfed.org/series/ETOTALUSQ176N.; Moura, Maria Cecilia P., Steven J. Smith, and David B. Belzer. "120 Years of U.S. Residential Housing Stock and Floor Space." PLOS ONE. Public Library of Science. Accessed November 25, 2019. https://journals.plos.org/plosone/article?id=10.1371/journal.pone.0134135.; Nareit. "Estimating the Size of the Commercial Real Estate Market in the U.S." Nareit. Accessed December 25, 2019. https://www.reit.com/data-research/research/nareit-research/estimating-size-commercial-real-estate-market-us; Otet, Ama, and Ama OtetAma Otet. "How Big Is a Rental Home in the US? Average Apartment Size by State." RENTCafé rental blog, December 12, 2017. https://www.rentcafe.com/blog/rental-market/average-apartment-size-in-the-us-by-state/; US Census Bureau. "U.S. Cities Home to 62.7% of Population but Comprise 3.5% of Land Area." The United States Census Bureau, January 9, 2017. https://www.census.gov/newsroom/press-releases/2015/cb15-33.html.

[3]"Labor." Merriam-Webster. Merriam-Webster. Accessed October 13, 2019. https://www.merriam-webster.com/dictionary/labor.

[4] "About the Real Estate and Rental and Leasing Sector." U.S. Bureau of Labor Statistics. U.S. Bureau of Labor Statistics. Accessed September 24, 2019. https://www.bls.gov/iag/tgs/iag53.htm.

[5] "Employment by Major Occupational Group." U.S. Bureau of Labor Statistics. U.S. Bureau of Labor Statistics, September 4, 2019. https://www.bls.gov/emp/tables/emp-by-major-occupational-

group.htm.

[6] Inc. "70% Of Americans Prefer Do-It-Yourself Home Improvements." PR Newswire: press release distribution, targeting, monitoring and marketing, June 29, 2018. https://www.prnewswire.com/news-releases/70-of-americans-prefer-do-it-yourself-home-improvements-209184081.html.

[7] "Capital." Merriam-Webster. Merriam-Webster. Accessed December 23, 2019. https://www.merriam-webster.com/dictionary/capital.

[8] "Global wealth report". www.credit-suisse.com. Credit Suisse. Retrieved 25 October 2019

[9] Hackett, Robert. "Just How Much the World Is Worth." Fortune. Fortune, January 26, 2016. https://fortune.com/2016/01/26/rea-estate-global-economy/.

[10] "Distributional National Accounts". federalreserve.gov. February 16, 2020. Retrieved February 20, 2020

[11] "Entrepreneurship." Merriam-Webster. Merriam-Webster. Accessed December 23, 2019. https://www.merriam-webster.com/dictionary/entrepreneurship.

[12] Sobel, Russell S., Michael Munger, Rob Norton, Al Ehrbar, and Garrett Hardin. "Entrepreneurship." Econlib. Accessed December 24, 2019. https://www.econlib.org/library/Enc/Entrepreneurship.html.

[13] "U.S. Income-Property Capital Market Research." The Real Estate Capital Institute®. Accessed December 24, 2019. https://reci.com/wordmfg-com/wordlist/.

[14] "U.S. Commercial Real Estate Transactions 2007-2020." Statista, June 24, 2020. https://www.statista.com/statistics/245103/real-estate-capital-flows/.

[15] "Risk." Merriam-Webster. Merriam-Webster. Accessed December 26, 2019. https://www.merriam-webster.com/dictionary/risk; "Reward."

Merriam-Webster. Merriam-Webster. Accessed December 26, 2019. https://www.merriam-webster.com/dictionary/reward.

[16] Graaskamp, James A. "Fundamentals of Real Estate Development." Journal of Property Valuation and Investment, vol. 10, no. 3, 1 Mar. 1992, pp. 619–639, 10.1108/14635789210031253. Accessed 28 Feb. 2022

[17] Curtis III, James J. Managing Director and Founder of Bristol Group, Inc., San Francisco, Ca. https://bristolgroupinc.com/about-us/leadership/

[18] Talia Lakritz. "These 11 Sinking Cities Could Disappear by 2100." World Economic Forum. Accessed January 24, 2022. https://www.weforum.org/agenda/2019/09/11-sinking-cities-that-could-soon-be-underwater/.

[19] Ludgin, Mary. "Rising Sea Levels Pose Risk to Institutional Real Estate Investment." Urban Land Magazine, January 7, 2019. https://urbanland.uli.org/sustainability/rising-sea-levels-pose-risk-to-institutional-real-estate-investment/.

[20] Putzier, Will Parker and Konrad. "Commercial Property Sales Slow as Rising Interest Rates Sink Deals." Wall Street Journal, 7 June 2022, www.wsj.com/articles/commercial-property-sales-slow-as-rising-interest-rates-sink-deals-11654594380.

[21] US Census Bureau. "Older People Projected to Outnumber Children." The United States Census Bureau, October 10, 2019. https://www.census.gov/newsroom/press-releases/2018/cb18-41-population-projections.html.

[22] "Sun Belt States Benefit from Migration Trends in Pandemic." REIM, January 7, 2021. https://reintelligent.com/sun-belt-states-benefit-from-migration-trends-in-pandemic/.

[23] Robinson, Dana. "The Worst Outbreaks in U.S. History." Healthline.

Healthline Media, March 24, 2020. https://www.healthline.com/health/worst-disease-outbreaks-history.

[24] Zhu, Linna, and Sheryl Pardo. "Understanding the Impact of Property Taxes Is Critical for Effective Local Policymaking." Urban Institute, November 5, 2020. https://www.urban.org/urban-wire/understanding-impact-property-taxes-critical-effective-local-policymaking.

[25] "These States Save the Most on Property Taxes." U.S. News & World Report. U.S. News & World Report. Accessed September 3, 2021. https://www.usnews.com/news/best-states/articles/2021-02-23/these-states-have-the-highest-property-taxes.

[26] "Quarterly Returns Up for All Property Types Except Retail." Accessed November 28, 2019. https://www.ncreif.org/globalassets/public-site/research/ncreif-insights/2q2019-highlight.pdf; "U.S. Cap Rate Survey H1 2019 Advance Review." CBRE US. Accessed October 29, 2019. https://www.cbre.us/research-and-reports/U-S--Cap-Rate-Survey-H1-2019-Advance-Review.

[27] Parker, Will. "Built-to-Rent Suburbs Are Poised to Spread across the U.S." The Wall Street Journal. Dow Jones & Company, June 7, 2021. https://www.wsj.com/articles/built-to-rent-suburbs-are-poised-to-spread-across-the-u-s-11623075610?mod=article_inline.

[28] PricewaterhouseCoopers. "Future of Work: What Boards Should Be Thinking About." PwC. Accessed September 3, 2021. https://www.pwc.com/us/en/services/governance-insights-center/library/covid-19-returning-workplace-boards.html.

[29] "Airbnb Is Now Bigger than the World's Top Five Hotel Brands Put Together." The Spaces, August 15, 2017. https://thespaces.com/airbnb-now-bigger-worlds-top-five-hotel-brands-put-together/.

[30] Perkel, Barry. "Hospitality Trends." November 18, 2022.

[31] "America's Infrastructure Grades Remain Near Failing." American

Society of Civil Engineers (ASCE). Accessed December 29, 2019. https://www.asce.org/templates/press-release-detail.aspx?id=24013.

[32] "Synonyms for Liquidity." Synonyms for liquidity | EnglishThesaurus.com. Accessed December 28, 2019. https://englishthesaurus.net/synonym/liquidity.

[33] "Illiquidity and Real Estate: Capturing the Upside." RealtyShares.com. Accessed December 28, 2019. https://www.realtyshares.com/learn/article/illiquidity-real-estate-investing-capturing-upside; Marketing, Thirty. "Understanding the Illiquidity Premium in Real Estate." Trion Properties, November 26, 2019. https://trion-properties.com/education/articles/understanding-the-illiquidity-premium-in-real-estate/;

[34] Jaleesa, and Bustamante. "Property Management Industry Statistics & Trends [2020]." iPropertyManagement.com, December 23, 2019. https://ipropertymanagement.com/research/property-management-industry-statistics.

[35] Cannon, E., Susanne. "How Accurate Are Commercial Real Estate Appraisals? Evidence from 25 Years of NCREIF Sales Data." SSRN, April 27, 2011. https://papers.ssrn.com/sol3/papers.cfm?abstract_id=1824807; Fisher, Jeffrey, "US commercial real estate indices: the NCREIF property index - BIS Papers No 21, part 29", April 2005

[36] Mantovani, Andrea. "Known Knowns, Known Unknowns, Unknown Unknowns & Leadership." Medium. Medium, April 28, 2020. https://medium.com/@andreamantovani/known-knowns-known-unknowns-unknown-unknowns-leadership-367f346b0953.

[37] Marshall, Alasdair, Udechukwu Ojiako, Victoria Wang, Fenfang Lin, and Maxwell Chipulu. "Forecasting Unknown-Unknowns by Boosting the Risk Radar within the Risk Intelligent Organisation." International Journal of Forecasting. Elsevier, October 23, 2018.

https://www.sciencedirect.com/science/article/abs/pii/S0169207018301420.

[38] "Definitions for Hard Assethard as·Set." What does hard asset mean? Accessed January 7, 2022. https://www.definitions.net/definition/hard%20asset.

[39] Securities Industry and Financial Markets Association, as of the first quarter, 2017.

[40] Jones, Jeffrey M. "In U.S., Real Estate Still Leads Stocks as Best Investment." Gallup.com. Gallup, August 13, 2021. https://news.gallup.com/poll/251696/real-estate-leads-stocks-best-investment.aspx.

[41] "Stocks, Bonds, or Commercial Real Estate: Which Is the Better Investment?" First National Realty Partners, June 28, 2021. https://fnrpusa.com/blog/stocks-bonds-or-commercial-real-estate-which-is-the-better-investment/.

[42] "S&P/Case-Shiller U.S. National Home Price Index." FRED, August 31, 2021. https://fred.stlouisfed.org/series/CSUSHPISA.

[43] Hanlon, Seth. "The Mortgage Interest Deduction." Center for American Progress, February 7, 2013. https://www.americanprogress.org/issues/general/news/2011/01/26/8866/tax-expenditure-of-the-week-the-mortgage-interest-deduction/.

[44] "IRS Provides TAX Inflation Adjustments for Tax YEAR 2021." Internal Revenue Service. Accessed September 3, 2021. https://www.irs.gov/newsroom/irs-provides-tax-inflation-adjustments-for-tax-year-2021.

[45] Brumer-Smith, Liz. "Top 5 Tax Advantages of Real Estate Investing." Millionacres. Millionacres, February 4, 2021. https://www.millionacres.com/taxes/real-estate-tax-deductions/top-5-

tax-advantages-real-estate-investing/.

[46] Kalsi, Sonny. "Council Post: What It Means to Be a Socially Responsible Real Estate Investment Manager." Forbes Magazine, February 5, 2021. https://www.forbes.com/sites/forbesrealestatecouncil/2021/02/08/what-it-means-to-be-a-socially-responsible-real-estate-investment-manager/.

[47] "U.S. Income-Property Capital Market Research." The Real Estate Capital Institute®. Accessed December 30, 2019. https://reci.com/research/capitalization-rates/real-estate-capital-ratestack/.

[48] "English and US Private Equity Real Estate Funds: Key Features: Insights: DLA Piper Global Law Firm." DLA Piper. Accessed December 31, 2019; Schilling, James, and Wurtzebach. , Charles. "Is Value-Added and Opportunistic Real Estate Investing Beneficial? If So, Why ?" SSRN, January 22, 2013. https://papers.ssrn.com/sol3/papers.cfm?abstract_id=2205191.

https://www.dlapiper.com/en/us/insights/publications/2018/11/english-and-us-private-equity-funds-real-estate-key-features/;https://activerain.com/blogsview/2068191/core--core-plus--value-add--and-opportunistic---4-commercial-real-estate-strategies; Cacciapaglia, Joseph. "Core, Core Plus, Value Add, and Opportunistic - 4 Commercial Real Estate Strategies." ActiveRain, November 14, 2011. https://activerain.com/blogsview/2068191/core--core-plus--value-add--and-opportunistic---4-commercial-real-estate-strategies.; Episcope, Michael. "What Are Core, Core Plus, Value Add and Opportunistic Investments?" Origin Investments, December 6, 2019. https://origininvestments.com/2018/02/21/what-are-core-core-plus-value-added-and-opportunistic-investments/; Kwek, Ju-Hon. "A Turning Point for Real Estate Investment Management." McKinsey & Company. November, 2019. https://www.mckinsey.com/industries/private-equity-and-principal-investors/our-insights/a-turning-point-for-real-estate-investment-management; "Know Your Asset Class: Core, Value-Add and Opportunistic Commercial Real Estate Investing." ArborCrowd, December 13, 2018. https://www.arborcrowd.com/education/know-your-asset-class-core-value-add-and-opportunistic-commercial-real-estate-investing/.

[49] Baxter, Amy. "Seeing Green: Why Ventas Is Going Big on Sustainability." Senior Housing News. Senior Housing News, October 20, 2015. http://seniorhousingnews.com/2015/10/20/seeing-green-why-senior-housing-reits-are-going-big-for-sustainability/.

[50] Royal, James. "Americans' Favorite Long-Term Investment Is..." Bankrate. Bankrate.com, August 19, 2019. https://www.bankrate.com/investing/financial-security-july-2019/.

[51] "Publication 925 (2018), Passive Activity and At-Risk Rules ..." Accessed January 3, 2020. https://www.irs.gov/publications/p925.

[52] "TOPIC: Number of Office Employees Per Apartment Community." Number of Office Employees Per Apartment Community :: Apartment Ideas. Accessed January 3, 2020. https://www.multifamilyinsiders.com/apartment-ideas/apartment-jobs/3020-number-of-office-employees-per-apartment-community.

[53] Oharenko, John. *Infinite Personalities: Searching for the Stars*. Chicago, Illinois, RECI, 2020.

[54] 75 Sources of Economic Data, Statistics, Reports, and Commentary." Lillian Goldman Law Library, November 26, 2012. https://library.law.yale.edu/news/75-sources-economic-data-statistics-reports-and-commentary.;Walker, Rick. "The 20 Top Commercial Real Estate Research Tools – Revised for 2019." CXRE Commercial Real Estate, January 3, 2020. https://cxre.co/real-estate-investment/top-commercial-real-estate-tools-and-books-2020/. ; "U.S. Income-Property Capital Market Research." The Real Estate Capital Institute®. Accessed January 3, 2020. https://reci.com/resources/.

[55] Bloomberg.com. Bloomberg. Accessed January 4, 2020. http://www.bloomberg.com/quote. The index can either be accessed online (http://www.bloomberg.com/quote/BNYCM:IND) or on the Bloomberg Terminal55. Notice that the index peaked in May 2007, hit a trough at the end of February 2009, and then gradually increased until May 2015 when it once

again reached a peak. Since the stock market is regarded as a leading indicator of economic activity, it can be used as an advanced warning indicator of what happens to commercial real estate e.g., tenants downsizing, rising vacancies, etc.

[56] "Property Condition Assessments." Partner Engineering and Science, Inc. Accessed January 5, 2020. https://www.partneresi.com/services/building-assessments/property-condition-assessments.

[57] Riquier, Andrea. "Here's Why America's Houses Are Getting Older." MarketWatch, August 17, 2018. https://www.marketwatch.com/story/heres-why-americas-houses-are-getting-older-2018-08-14; "Research Commentary." Research: Score Distribution; Commercial Building Age, Use, Value - Commercial Property Data. Accessed December 28, 2019. http://www.commbuildings.com/ResearchComm.html; Yale, Aly J. "The Average Lifespan of a House: How Long Will It Last?" The Balance. The Balance, March 14, 2019. https://www.thebalance.com/the-average-lifespan-of-a-house-and-its-features-4584868; "Average Life Span of Homes, Appliances, and Mechanicals." ATD Home Inspection. Accessed December 28, 2019. https://www.atdhomeinspection.com/advice/average-product-life/ ; "Adding Value in the Age of Amenities Wars." National Apartment Association, April 27, 2017. https://www.naahq.org/news-publications/units/may-2017/article/adding-value-age-amenities-wars.

[58] "Turner Building Cost Index: Construction Activity Continues at High Level." News | Turner Building Cost Index: Construction Activity Continues at High Level | Turner Construction Company. Accessed January 29, 2020. https://www.turnerconstruction.com/news/item/9f84/Turner-Building-Cost-Index-Construction-Activity-Continues-at-High-Level.

[59] "4 Energy Efficiency." National Academy of Sciences, National Academy of Engineering, and National Research Council. 2009.

America's Energy Future: Technology and Transformation. Washington, DC: The National Academies Press. doi: 10.17226/12091; "Technological Advances in the Construction Sector." National Research Council. 1988. Globalization of Technology: International Perspectives. Washington, DC: The National Academies Press. doi: 10.17226/1101.

[60] "Bond Ratings." Fidelity. Accessed January 5, 2020. https://www.fidelity.com/learning-center/investment-products/fixed-income-bonds/bond-ratings.

[61] CoStar Glossary. Accessed January 6, 2020. https://www.costar.com/about/costar-glossary#go_n; "Industry Terms and Definitions." NAIOP Commercial Real Estate Development Association. Accessed January 6, 2020.https://www.naiop.org/en/Education-and-Career/Industry-Terms-and-Definitions?letter=N.

[62] "United States Inflation Rate in 1980." The United States of America Inflation Rate in 1980. Accessed January 6, 2020. https://www.statbureau.org/en/united-states/inflation/1980.

[63] RUBS Billing - Infomation About RUBS - Allocation Method for Apartment Water Billing. Accessed January 28, 2020. http://www.aabs1.com/RUBS.html.

[64] "2018 NAA Survey of Operating Income & Expenses in Rental Apartment Communities." National Apartment Association, September 16, 2019. https://www.naahq.org/news-publications/units/september-2018/article/survey-operating-income-expenses-rental-apartment.;

[65] "Self Storage Valuation." CBRE. Accessed January 28, 2020. https://www.cbre.com/united states/real-estate-services/real-estate-industries/self-storage/self-storage-valuation.

[66] Chance, Gary. "Downtown Office vs. Suburban Office National Income / Expense Review (Chart of the Week)." Bisnow, March 9, 2017. https://www.bisnow.com/national/news/office/downtown-office-vs-suburban-office-national-income-expense-review-chart-of-the-week-50534.

[67] Unger, Walter. "Glossary of Commercial Real Estate Terms ." Walter Unger CCIM, July 15, 2016. http://walter-unger.com/glossary-of-commercial-real-estate-terms-2/. Fisher, Jeffery, Maritn, Robert, "Income Property Appraisal", 1991.

[68] Oharenko, John. "Combat Investor: Guide to Real Estate Investment Warfare." Authorhouse, 2013. https://www.combatinvestor.com

[69] CoStar Glossary. Accessed January 9, 2020. https://www.costar.com/about/costar-glossary.

[70] Banton, Caroline. "Return on Investment (ROI) Versus Internal Rate of Return (IRR)." Investopedia. Investopedia, November 18, 2019. https://www.investopedia.com/articles/investing/111715/return-investment-roi-vs-internal-rate-return-irr.asp. "70 Return on Investment Synonyms in Return on Investment ..." Accessed January 20, 2020. https://www.powerthesaurus.org/return_on_investment.

[71] CoStar Glossary. Accessed January 9, 2020. https://www.costar.com/about/costar-glossary.

[72] "Life Insurers Fact Book." . Accessed January 21, 2020. https://www.acli.com/Industry-Facts/Life-Insurers-Fact-Book.

[73] "Single-Family." FreddieMac. Accessed January 22, 2020. https://sf.freddiemac.com/working-with-us/origination-underwriting/mortgage-products/home-possible.

[74] "Amortization Calculation Formula." Vertex42.com. Accessed January 11, 2020. https://www.vertex42.com/ExcelArticles/amortization-calculation.html.

[75] Carnahan, Ira. "Mortgage Tricks." Forbes. Forbes Magazine, June 6, 2013.
https://www.forbes.com/forbes/2003/0609/126.html#21ff8e3e474a.

[76] Liu, Catherine. "Nearly $100 Billion of CMBS Matures Through 2020." January 11, 2019. https://info.trepp.com/trepptalk/nearly-100-billion-of-cmbs-matures-through-2020.

[77] Unger, Walter. "Glossary of Commercial Real Estate Terms ." Walter Unger CCIM, July 15, 2016. http://walter-unger.com/glossary-of-commercial-real-estate-terms-2/.

[78] "Symbols and Formulas - Appraisal Institute." Accessed January 19, 2020. https://www.appraisalinstitute.org/assets/1/7/PCSYMBOL-E_.pdf.

[79] Garfield, Eric B., Mai, and Matthew T. VanEck. "Cap Rate Calculations." Cap Rate Calculations | CCIM Institute. Accessed January 23, 2020. https://www.ccim.com/cire-magazine/articles/cap-rate-calculations/?gmSsoPc=1.

[80] Oharenko, John. "Infinite Personalities: Searching for the Stars." Kindle Edition, January, 2020.

[81] "Glossary." American Bar Association. Accessed January 23, 2020. https://www.americanbar.org/groups/real_property_trust_estate/resources/real_estate_index/glossary/#R.

[82] Word List, "Premisist", "U.S. Income-Property Capital Market Research." The Real Estate Capital Institute®. Accessed January 23, 2020. https://reci.com/wordmfg-com/wordlist/.

[83] NMHC. Accessed January 25, 2020. https://www.nmhc.org/advocacy/issue-fact-sheet/affordable-housing-fact-sheet/.

[84] "US20060192337A1 - Method of Advertising Financial Services and Interest Rate Dice." Google Patents. Google. Accessed January 28, 2020. https://patents.google.com/patent/US20060192337.

[85] Fisher, and Irving. "The Rate of Interest, by Fisher, Irving." History of Economic Thought Books. McMaster University Archive for the History of Economic Thought, January 1, 1970. https://ideas.repec.org/b/hay/hetboo/fisher1907.html.

[86] Harvard Business Review, Joe Knight, and Joe Knight. "Financial Intelligence, Revised Edition: A Manager's Guide to Knowing What the

Numbers Really Mean ^ 10833." HBR Store. Accessed January 18, 2020. https://store.hbr.org/product/financial-intelligence-revised-edition-a-manager-s-guide-to-knowing-what-the-numbers-really-mean/10833?sku=10833-HBK-ENG.

[87] Gallo, Amy, and Maxwell Wessel. "A Refresher on Net Present Value." Harvard Business Review, December 6, 2017. https://hbr.org/2014/11/a-refresher-on-net-present-value.

[88] "Industry Terms and Definitions." NAIOP Commercial Real Estate Development Association. Accessed January 6, 2020.

[89] "Modified Internal Rate of Return." (MIRR). Accessed January 27, 2020. https://xplaind.com/882858/modified-internal-rate-of-return.

[90] "Chart of the Week: Commercial Real Estate Market Sees Continued Price Appreciation in 2019." Chart of the week: Commercial real estate market sees continued price appreciation in 2019 | FS Investments, July 19, 2019. https://www.fsinvestments.com/perspectives/articles/chart-of-the-week-2019-07-19-cre-price-growth.

[91] "US Property Price Growth Breaks Records as Demand Swells." Real Capital Analytics, Inc., December 8, 2021. https://www.rcanalytics.com/us-prices-oct-2021-rcacppi/.

[92] Nareit. "REITs & Real Estate Investing: Real Estate Working For You: Accessed August 13, 2019. https://www.reit.com/.

[93] Nareit. "Tracking Property Prices and REIT Total Return Beyond the Core Sectors." Nareit. Accessed January 30, 2020. https://www.reit.com/news/blog/market-commentary/tracking-property-prices-and-reit-total-return-beyond-core-sectors.

[94] Goldschein, Eric. "The Complete History of US Real Estate Bubbles since 1800." Business Insider. Business Insider, January 10, 2012. https://www.businessinsider.com/the-economic-crash-repeated-every-generation-1800-2012-1?op=1.

[95] Tyson Freeman, "The 1950s: POST-WAR America Hitches up and Heads for the 'Burbs." Wealth Management, March 11, 2021. https://www.wealthmanagement.com/news/1950s-post-war-america-hitches-and-heads-burbs.

[96] "Great Recession, Great Recovery? Trends from the Current Population Survey : Monthly Labor Review." U.S. Bureau of Labor Statistics. U.S. Bureau of Labor Statistics, April 1, 2018. https://www.bls.gov/opub/mlr/2018/article/great-recession-great-recovery.htm.

[97] "As the Nation Reopens: Mid-Year Sentiment Soars in the Real Estate Industry." RCLCO Real Estate Consulting, July 15, 2021. https://www.rclco.com/publication/as-the-nation-reopens-mid-year-sentiment-soars-in-the-real-estate-industry/.

[98] "Professionally Managed Global Real Estate Hits $7 Trillion in 2014." MSCI. Accessed January 30, 2020. https://www.msci.com/www/blog-posts/professionally-managed-global/0239625714.

[99] "News ." NAIOP Commercial Real Estate Development Association. Accessed January 31, 2020. https://www.naiop.org/en/Research-and-Publications/News/NAIOP-News/2018/Contributions-of-CRE-2018.

[100] Real Estate Capital Investors. "Real Estate CAPITAL Investors." Real Estate Capital Investors. Accessed January 31, 2020. https://realestatecapital.com/.

[101] T, David, By, David T, January 8, October 10, January 1, January 3, et al. "Is Fannie Mae a Government Agency." KnowYourGovernment.net, December 18, 2021. https://www.knowyourgovernment.net/is-fannie-mae-a-government-agency/.

[102] "Grants for Real Estate." Government Grants, October 16, 2018. http://government-grants.us/grants-for-real-estate/.

[103] Cushman and Wakefield. 2016,

/www.cushmanwakefield.com/en/services/equity-debt-structured-finance/, 2016 ;Real Capital Analytics, https://www.rcanalytics.com/, 2016

[104] "Warren Buffett: 10 Investment Insights from the Master." The Christian Science Monitor. The Christian Science Monitor, August 30, 2013. https://www.csmonitor.com/Business/2013/0830/Warren-Buffett-10-pieces-of-investment-advice-from-America-s-greatest-investor/Never-count-on-making-a-good-sale.-Have-the-purchase-price-be-so-attractive-that-even-a-mediocre-sale-gives-good-results.

[105] O'Brien, Matthew. "John Maynard Keynes Was the Warren Buffett of His Day." The Atlantic. Atlantic Media Company, April 3, 2012. https://www.theatlantic.com/business/archive/2012/04/john-maynard-keynes-was-the-warren-buffett-of-his-day/255356/.

[106] Business Insider. "The 10 Best Quotes From Wall Street 2: Money Never Sleeps." Business Insider. Business Insider, January 29, 2010. https://www.businessinsider.com/the-best-quotes-from-wall-street-2-money-never-sleeps-2010-1.

[107] Published by Statista Research Department, and Oct 4. "Largest Apartment Owners in U.S. by Units Owned 2021." Statista, October 4, 2021. https://www.statista.com/statistics/603416/leading-apartment-owners-in-the-us-by-units-owned/.

[108] "U.S. Multifamily Housing: A Primer for Offshore Investors." CBREUS. Accessed January 16, 2022. https://www.cbre.us/real-estate-services/real-estate-industries/multifamily/us-multifamily-housing-primer.

[109] "Almost 40% of US Homes Are Mortgage Free" Bloomberg. July 17, 2019. https://www.bloomberg.com/news/articles/2019-07-17/close-to-40-of-u-s-homes-are-free-and-clear-of-a-mortgage.

[110] "Commercial/Multifamily Mortgage Debt Reaches Nearly $3.5 Trillion

in the First Quarter of 2019: Mortgage Bankers Association." MBA. Accessed February 4, 2020. https://www.mba.org/2019-press-releases/june/commercial/multifamily-mortgage-debt-reaches-nearly-35-trillion-in-the-first-quarter-of-2019.

[111] Arnold, Alvin and Oharenko, John. "Guide to Real Estate Capital Markets." Warren, Gorham & Lamont. 1988. Accrual debt carries several names including, negative amortization, reverse payment, step-up and Bow Tie loans (circa 1985).

[112] "Glossary and Definitions." Institutional Real Estate, Inc. Accessed January 31, 2020. https://irei.com/glossary/.

[113] Federal Reserve Bank of Minneapolis. "Consumer Price Index, 1913-." Accessed January, 12, 2022.

[114] Eppli, Dr. Mark, "What's on the Horizon for the Commercial Real Estate Industry in 2022?", Graaskamp Center Virtual Leadership Series Webcast, James A. Graaskamp Center for Real Estate, University of Wisconsin, Madison, Wisconsin, January 19, 2022.

[115] Egan, John. "Foreign Investors Have Stayed Away from U.S. Real Estate in Recent Months. That Trend Is Not Expected to Hold." Wealth Management, June 17, 2020. https://www.wealthmanagement.com/real-estate/foreign-investors-have-stayed-away-us-real-estate-recent-months-trend-not-expected-hold.

[116] Estimating the Size of the Commercial Real Estate Market in the U.S." *Nareit. Accessed January 20, 2022. https://www.reit.com/data-research/research/nareit-research/estimating-size-commercial-real-estate-market-us.* Nareit estimates that the 2018 total dollar value of commercial real estate was between $14 and $17 trillion, with a mid-point of $16 trillion. This study was conducted primarily using data from CoStar and other sources. We used a bottom up approach identifying and estimating the number of units and total square footage by property sector and property quality type for the largest 200 markets in the U.S.